Law Made Simple

Powers of Attorney Simplified

DANIEL SITARZ, ATTORNEY-AT-LAW

Nova Publishing Company
Small Business and Consumer Legal Books
Carbondale Illinois

ISBN 978-1-892949-56-1
Book w/CD-Rom   price: $29.95

Cataloging-in-Publication

Sitarz, Dan, 1948-
Powers of attorney simplified / by Daniel Sitarz. -- 2nd ed. --
    Carbondale, Ill. : Nova Pub. Co., 2010.
      p. ; cm. + 1 CD-ROM.
      (Law made simple)
      ISBN-13: 978-1-892949-56-1
      ISBN-10: 1-892949-56-3
      Includes index.
      1. Power of attorney--United States. 2. Power
    of attorney--United States--Forms. 3. Agency (Law)
    --United States. 4. Agency (Law)--United States--Forms. I. Title.
        KF1347.Z9 S58 2010   346.73/029--dc22 0712

Nova Publishing Company is dedicated to providing up-to-date and accurate legal information to the public. All Nova publications are periodically revised to contain the latest available legal information.

2nd Edition; 1st Printing /September 2010
1st Edition; 2nd Printing /November 2008
1st Edition; 1st Printing /December 2007

This publication is designed to provide accurate and authoritative information in regard to the subject matter covered. It is sold with the understanding that the publisher and author are not engaged in rendering legal, accounting, or other professional services. If legal advice or other expert assistance is required, the services of a competent professional person should be sought.
—From a Declaration of Principles jointly adopted by a Committee of
the American Bar Association and a Committee of Publishers

DISCLAIMER

Nova Publishing Green Business Policies

Nova Publishing Company takes seriously the impact of book publishing on the Earth and its resources. Nova Publishing Company is committed to protecting the environment and to the responsible use of natural resources. As a book publisher, with paper as a core part of our business, we are very concerned about the future of the world's remaining endangered forests and the environmental impacts of paper production. We are committed to implementing policies that will support the preservation of endangered forests globally and to advancing 'best practices' within the book and paper industries. Nova Publishing Company is committed to preserving ancient forests and natural resources. Our company's policy is to print all of our books on 100% recycled paper, with 100% post-consumer waste content, de-inked in a chlorine-free process. In addition, all Nova Publishing Company books are printed using soy-based inks. As a result of these environmental policies, Nova Publishing Company has saved hundreds of thousands of gallons of water, hundreds of thousands of kilowatts of electricity, thousand of pounds of pollution and carbon dioxide, and thousands of trees that would otherwise have been used in the traditional manner of publishing its books. Nova Publishing Company is very proud to be one of the first members of the Green Press Initiative, a nonprofit program dedicated to supporting publishers in their efforts to reduce their use of fiber obtained from endangered forests. (see www.greenpressinitiative.org). Nova Publishing Company is also proud to be an initial signatory on the Book Industry Treatise on Responsible Paper Use. In addition, Nova Publishing Company uses all compact fluorescent lighting; recycles all office paper products, aluminum and plastic beverage containers, and printer cartridges; uses 100% post-consumer fiber, process-chlorine-free, acid-free paper for 95% of in-house paper use; and, when possible, uses electronic equipment that is EPA Energy Star-certified. Nova's freight shipments are coordinated to minimize energy use whenever possible. Finally, all carbon emissions from Nova Publishing Company office energy use are offset by the purchase of wind-energy credits that are used to subsidize the building of wind turbines on the Rosebud Sioux Reservation in South Dakota (see www.nativeenergy.com). We strongly encourage other publishers and all partners in publishing supply chains to adopt similar policies.

Nova Publishing Company
Small Business and Consumer Legal Books and Software
1103 West College St.
Carbondale, IL 62901
Technical support: (800) 748-1175
www.novapublishing.com

Distributed by:
National Book Network
4501 Forbes Blvd., Suite 200
Lanham, MD 20706
Orders: (800) 462-6420

Table of Contents

List of Forms-on-CD

All forms are provided in text and PDF format unless noted otherwise.

Additional Information for Power of Attorney
Agent's Certification of the Validity of Power of Attorney and Agent's Authority
General Power of Attorney
Unlimited Power of Attorney
Limited Power of Attorney
Limited Power of Attorney for Real Estate
Limited Power of Attorney for Child Care
Durable Unlimited Power of Attorney (effective immediately)
Durable Unlimited Power of Attorney (effective on disability)
Durable General Power of Attorney (effective immediately)
Durable General Power of Attorney (effective on disability)
Durable Health Care Power of Attorney
Revocation of Durable Health Care Power of Attorney
Witness Affidavit of Revocation of Durable Health Care Power of Attorney
Revocation of Power of Attorney
State-Specific Durable Powers of Attorney for Financial Affairs (PDF only)
      Alaska, Arkansas, California, Colorado, Connecticut, District of Columbia, Georgia,
      Illinois, Minnesota, Montana, Nebraska, New Hampshire, New Mexico, New York,
      North Carolina, Oklahoma, Pennsylvania, Rhode Island, Texas, Wisconsin
Revocation of Advance Health Care Directive
Witness Affidavit of Revocation of Advance Health Care Directive
Additional Information for Advance Health Care Directive
Living Will Declaration and Directive to Physicians
Revocation of Living Will
Designation of Primary Physician
Organ Donation

The Following forms are only provided on the CD and only as PDF forms:

Advance Health Care Directives (51 forms)
      All 50 states and District of Columbia
Living Wills (51 forms)
      All 50 states and District of Columbia

Introduction to Powers of Attorney Simplified

In each chapter of this book you will find an introductory section that will give you an overview of the types of situations in which the forms in that chapter will generally be used. Following that overview, there will be a brief explanation of the specific uses for each form. Finally, for each form, there is a listing of the information that must be compiled to complete the form. The preferable manner for using these forms is to use the enclosed Forms-on-CD. Instructions for using the Forms-on-CD are included later in this chapter. However, it is perfectly acceptable to prepare these forms directly from the book by making a copy of the form, filling in the information that is necessary, and then retyping the form in its entirety (on your computer) and printing it out on clean white letter-sized paper.

Before you prepare any of the forms for use, you should carefully read the introductory information and instructions in the chapter where the particular form is contained. Try to be as detailed and specific as possible as you fill in these forms. The more precise the description, the less likelihood that later disputes may develop over what was actually intended by the language chosen. The careful preparation and use of the legal forms in this book should provide you with the proper documents for most power of attorney situations. If in doubt as to whether a particular form will work in a specific application, please consult a competent lawyer.

💡 Toolkit Tip!

Check your state's listing in the Appendix (which is located in the back of this book) to see any specific state requirements for your Powers of Attorney.

Installation Instructions for Installing Forms-on-CD

Installation Instructions for PCs

1. Insert the enclosed CD in your computer.
2. The installation program will start automatically. Follow the onscreen dialogue and make your appropriate choices.
3. If the CD installation does not start automatically, click on START, then RUN, then BROWSE, and select your CD drive, and then select the file "Install.exe." Finally, click OK to run the installation program.
4. During the installation program, you will be prompted as to whether or not you wish to install the Adobe Acrobat Reader® program. This software program is necessary to view and fill in the PDF (potable document format) forms that are included on the Forms-on-CD. If you do not already have the Adobe Acrobat Reader® program installed on your hard drive, you will need to select the full installation that will install the program on your computer.

Installation Instructions for MACs®

1. Insert the enclosed CD in your computer.
2. Copy the folder "Forms for Macs" to your hard drive. All of the PDF and text-only forms are included in this folder.
3. If you do not already have the Adobe Acrobat Reader® program installed on your hard drive, you will need to download the version of this software that is appropriate for your particular MAC operating system from www.adobe.com. Note: The latest versions of the MAC operating system (OS-X) have PDF capabilities built into it.

Instructions for Using Forms-on-CD

☀ Toolkit Tip!

MAC users will need to download Adobe Acrobat Reader directly from www.adobe.com.

All of the forms that are included in this book have been provided on the Forms-on-CD for your use if you have access to a computer. If you have completed the Forms-on-CD installation program, all of the forms will have been copied to your computer's hard drive. By default, these files are installed in the C:\Powers of Attorney\Forms folder which is created by the installation program. (Note for MAC users: see instructions on previous page). Opening the Forms folder will provide you with access to folders for each of the topics corresponding to chapters in the book. Within each chapter, the forms are provided in two separate formats:

Text forms may be opened, prepared, and printed from within your own word processing program (such as Microsoft Word®, or WordPerfect®). The text forms all have the file extension: .txt. These forms are located in the TEXT FORMS folders supplied for each chapter's forms. You will need to use the forms in this format if you will be making changes to any of the text on the forms.

PDF forms may be filled in on your computer screen and printed out on any printer. This particular format provides the most widely-used format for accessing computer files. Files in this format may be opened as images on your computer and printed out on any printer. The files in PDF format all have the file extension: .pdf. Although this format provides the easiest method for completing the forms, the forms in this format can not be altered (other than to fill in the information required on the blanks provided). To access the PDF forms, please see below. If you wish to alter the language in any of the forms, you will need to access the forms in their text-only versions. To access these text-only forms, please also see page 13.

To Access PDF Forms

1. You must have already installed the Adobe Acrobat Reader® program to your computer's hard drive. This program is installed automatically by the installation

program. (MAC users will need to install this program via www.adobe.com).

2. On your computer's desktop, you will find a shortcut icon labeled "Acrobat Reader®." Using your mouse, left double-click on this icon. This will open the Acrobat Reader® program. When the Acrobat Reader® program is opened for the first time, you will need to accept the Licensing Agreement from Adobe in order to use this program. Click "Accept" when given the option to accept or decline the Agreement.

Toolkit Tip!

Use the 'PDF' forms that are provided on the CD if you wish to simply fill in and print out the form that you select.

3. Once the Acrobat Reader® program is open on your computer, click on FILE (in the upper left-hand corner of the upper taskbar). Then click on OPEN in the drop down menu. Depending on which version of Windows or other operating system you are using, a box will open which will allow you to access files on your computer's hard drive. The files for power of attorney forms are located on your computer's "C" drive, under the folder "Powers of Attorney." In this folder, you will find a subfolder "Forms." (Note: if you installed the forms folder on a different drive, access the forms on that particular drive).

4. If you desire to work with one of the forms, you should then left double-click your mouse on the sub-folder: "Forms." A list of form topics (corresponding to the chapters in the book) will appear and you should then left double-click your mouse on the topic of your choice. This will open two folders: one for text forms and one for PDF forms. Left double click your mouse on the PDF forms folder and a list of the PDF forms for that topic should appear. Left double-click your mouse on the form of your choice. This will open the appropriate form within the Acrobat Reader® program.

To Fill in and Use PDF Forms

1. Once you have opened the appropriate form in the Acrobat Reader® program, filling in the form is a simple process. A 'hand tool' icon will be your cursor in the Acrobat Reader® program. Move the 'hand tool' cursor to the first blank space

that will need to be completed on the form. A vertical line or "I-beam" should appear at the beginning of the first space on a form that you will need to fill in. You may then begin to type the necessary information in the space provided. When you have filled in the first blank space, hit the TAB key on your keyboard. This will move the 'hand' cursor to the next space which must be filled in. Please note that some of the spaces in the forms must be completed by hand, specifically the signature blanks.

2. Move through the form, completing each required space, and hitting TAB to move to the next space to be filled in. For details on the information required for each blank on the forms, please read the instructions in this book. When you have completed all of the fill-ins, you may print out the form on your computer's printer. (Please note: hitting TAB after the last fill-in will return you to the first page of the form.)

3. If you wish to save a completed form, you should save it with a new name for the file. This way will allow you to save the original form in its unchanged format for later use if necessary.

> **☼ Toolkit Tip!**
> Filled-in PDF forms can be printed out and saved in the Adobe Acrobat Reader ® software program.

To Access and Complete Text Forms

For your convenience, all of the forms in this book (except the state-specific forms) are also provided as text-only forms which may be altered and saved. To open and use any of the text forms:

1. First, open your preferred word processing program. Then click on FILE (in the upper left-hand corner of the upper taskbar). Then click on OPEN in the drop down menu. Depending on which version of Windows or other operating system you are using, a box will open which will allow you to access files on your computer's hard drive. The files for power of attorney forms are located on your computer's "C" drive, under the folder "Powers of Attorney." In this folder, you will find a sub-folder: "Forms."

2. If you desire to work with one of the forms, you should then left double-click your mouse on the sub-folder: "Forms." A list of form topics (corresponding to the chapters in the book) will appear and you should then left double-click your mouse on the topic of your choice. This will open two folders: one for text forms and one for PDF forms. Left double-click your mouse on the text forms folder and a list of the text forms for that topic should appear. Left double-click your mouse on the form of your choice. This will open the appropriate form within your word processing program.

3. You may now fill in the necessary information while the text-only file is open in your word processing program. You may need to adjust margins and/or line endings of the form to fit your particular word processing program. Note that there is an asterisk (*) in every location in these forms where information will need to be included. Replace each asterisk with the necessary information. When the form is complete, you may print out the completed form and you may save the completed form. If you wish to save the completed form, you should rename the form so that your hard drive will retain an unaltered version of the original form.

☼Toolkit Tip!

Text forms are the forms you should use if you will be making changes to any of the text on the forms.

Technical Support

Please also note that Nova Publishing Company cannot provide legal advice regarding the effect or use of the forms in this book or on the CD. For questions about installing the Forms-on-CD and software, you may call Nova Technical Support at 1-800-748-1175 or access the Nova Publishing Website for support at www.novapublishing.com.

For any questions relating to Adobe Acrobat Reader®, please access Adobe Technical Support at www.adobe.com/support/main.html or you may search for assistance in the HELP area of Adobe Acrobat Reader® (located in approximately the center of the top line of the program's desktop).

Note regarding legal updates: Although power of attorney law is relatively stable and the information provided in this book is based on the most current state statutes, laws regarding business start-up are subject to constant change. In the Appendix of this book on the enclosed CD are provided internet addresses for each state's legislature and statutes. These sites may be accessed to check if any of the laws have changed since the publication of this book. In addition, the Nova Publishing website also provides legal updates for information that has changed since the publication of any Nova titles.

> **‿ơ‿ Toolkit Tip!**
>
> Check online at *www.nova publishing. com* for any updates to the legal information in this book.

Chapter 1

Understanding Powers of Attorney

A power of attorney is simply a document that is used to allow one person to give authority to another person to act on their behalf. The person signing the power of attorney (generally referred to as the *principal*) grants legal authority to another to "stand in their shoes" and act legally for them. The person who receives the such authority is called an *attorney-in-fact*. This title and the power of attorney form *does not* mean that the person receiving the power has to be a lawyer. If you appoint your spouse or a trusted relative or friend, then that person is your "attorney-in-fact". Think of the term "attorney-in-fact" as actually meaning "agent." Using a power of attorney, you will be appointing an "agent" to act in your place for some activities, perhaps relating to financial actions or perhaps relating to health care decisions, or any of a number of other possible actions that your "agent" may perform. The word 'attorney' in the context of a power of attorney or an attorney-in-fact is *not* related to the generally accepted notion of an 'attorney' as a lawyer.

Uses of Powers of Attorney

Power of attorney forms are useful documents for many occasions. They can be used to authorize someone else to

sign certain documents if you can not be present when the signatures are necessary. They can be used to authorize someone to handle any or all of the following possible matters:

Real estate transactions;
Goods and services transactions;
Stock, bond, share and commodity transactions;
Banking transactions;
Business operating transactions;
Insurance transactions;
Estate transactions;
Legal claims and litigation;
Personal relationships and affairs;
Benefits from military service;
Records, reports and statements;
Retirement benefit transactions;
Making gifts to a spouse, children, parents and other descendants;
Tax matters;
And, more recently, all personal decisions relating to health care.

Definition:

Power of Attorney: Document that authorizes one person to act for another in certain situations.

Traditionally, banking and real estate matters were the most typical type of actions handled with powers of attorney. Increasingly, however, all manner of affairs are being handled with the prudent use of a power of attorney.

Power of Attorney Definitions

There are many types of power of attorney forms and it is easy to confuse the terminology that is used to describe them. Here are a few definitions to help you understand powers of attorney:

Advance Health Care Directive: A comprehensive form for providing for your health care wishes that generally combines a *living will*, a *durable health care power of attorney*, designation of primary physician, and an organ donation form.

Agent: A person that is appointed in a power of attorney document to act on behalf of another person. Also referred to as an *attorney-in-fact*.

Attorney-in-Fact: A person that is appointed in a power of attorney document to act on behalf of another person. This person *does not* have to be an attorney. Also referred to as an *agent*.

Child Care Power of Attorney: A power of attorney that allows the *principal* to appoint someone to make limited child care decisions regarding a child of the *principal* (generally, limited to providing consent to emergency medical care and/or authority to enroll a child in school).

Designation Of Primary Physician: This form provides a method to make known your choice of primary physician in the event that you are unable to communicate your desires.

Durable Health Care Power of Attorney: A specialized power of attorney that allows the *principal* to appoint someone (the *attorney-in-fact* or *agent*) to make health care and medical decisions for them if they are unable to communicate their own wishes or decisions to health care providers. This type of form is intended to take effect only upon the principal's incapacitation.

Durable Power of Attorney for Financial Affairs: A power of attorney that is not affected by the disability or incapacity of the person that signed it (the *principal*). Note that durable powers of attorney for financial affairs can be of two distinct types: 1) it may take effect immediately and remain in effect *even if* the principal should become incapacitated, or 2) it may *only* take effect if the principal should become incapacitated (this is technically referred to as a *springing power of attorney*).

Financial Power of Attorney: Generally, any power of attorney (other than a *durable health care power of attorney*) that allows the *attorney-in-fact* or *agent* to make financial decisions or take financial action on behalf of the *principal*.

General Power of Attorney: This type of power of attorney allows the *principal* to select among a list of powers and grant the *agent* any or all of the listed powers. If a *principal* wishes to grant unlimited authority to an *agent* however, an *unlimited power of attorney* should be used.

Limited Power of Attorney: This type of power of attorney is a grant of authority to another person (the *attorney-in-fact* or *agent*) that is limited in scope or duration (for example, to handle a real estate closing on a certain date).

Living Will: A document that allows you to make end-of-life decisions in advance of medical situations that may leave you unable to communicate your wishes regarding the use of artificial life support systems. Often a living will is part of an *advance health care directive*.

Notary: A notary public is a public official whose duty it is to verify signatures on documents. Most banks provide notary services. All power of attorney forms in this book require notarization.

Organ Donation: This form provides a method to make known your decisions regarding organ donations under the Anatomical Gifts Act legislation that has been adopted by all 50 states and Washington D.C.

Power of Attorney: A legal document that allows one person (the *principal,* generally, you) to appoint another (the *attorney-in-fact* or *agent*) to act on their behalf.

Principal: The person who authorizes another person to act on their behalf using a power of attorney. Generally, this person is you.

Springing Power of Attorney: A type of durable power of attorney that only takes effect upon the incapacity of the *principal* (it springs into effect on the happening of that event). Can also be prepared (by a lawyer) to take effect on the happening of some other type of event.

Successor Attorney-in-Fact: A person that is appointed in a power of attorney document to act on behalf of another person if the original attorney-in-fact is unable or unwilling to act. This person *does not* have to be an attorney.

Unlimited Power of Attorney: Generally, any power of attorney that allows the *attorney-in-fact* or *agent* to make any and all decisions or take any and all action (except health care

> ### ☀️ Toolkit Tip!
> The Appendix of this book contains details of each state's specific laws relating to powers of attorney. Check your state's listing before you prepare any documents.

decisions and actions) on behalf of the *principal*. Each of he *unlimited powers of attorney* provided in this book contain an extremely detailed list of the powers and authority that the *principal* grants to the *agent*. It is intended to cover any and all possible decisions and actions that the *agent* might be called upon to make or perform on behalf of the *principal*.

Types of Powers of Attorney

Toolkit Tip!

There are many different types of powers of attorney. Make sure that you understand their use and that you select the correct one for your particular situation.

Let's take a look at the various different types of powers of attorney. (Note that the plural for power of attorney is "powers of attorney" and not "power of attorneys." That is because the legal document is actually creating a "power," the ability for someone else to act on your behalf. The legal document provides them with the "power" to do so.) The following will be a very brief explanation of the types of powers of attorney. Each specific chapter will contain a more detailed description of each type of power of attorney. You should read through this list carefully to determine which type of power of attorney is most appropriate in your particular circumstances. At the end of this chapter, a chart detailing the different types of powers of attorney is provided. Here are the various types of powers of attorney that are included in this book:

General Power of Attorney: Chapter 2 contains a basic power of attorney that allows you to authorize your agent (your "attorney in fact") to handle a few or all of your financial and/or business transactions. With this form, you are giving another person the right to manage some or perhaps all of your financial and/or business matters on your behalf. They are given the power to act exactly as you could. This can be a very powerful grant of authority to someone else to act on your behalf. The person appointed must be someone that you fully trust to handle your affairs. This power of attorney is not valid if you become disabled or incapacitated. You must use a 'durable' power of attorney for that purpose (see below and Chapters 5 and 6 for information on durable powers of attorney for financial affairs). It also can *not* be used for health care decisions.

Unlimited Power of Attorney: In Chapter 3, you will find a power of attorney that grants your agent (your "attorney in fact") full and complete power to handle all of your business and financial affairs. With this form, you are giving another person the right to manage any and all of your financial and/or business matters on your behalf. They are given the power to act exactly as you could. This particular power of attorney form is very extensive as it lists in great detail all of the powers that your agent (attorney-in-fact) is authorized to exercise. This is an extremely powerful grant of authority to someone else to act on your behalf. The person appointed must be someone that you fully trust to handle your affairs. This power of attorney is not valid if you become disabled or incapacitated. You must use a 'durable' power of attorney for that purpose (see below and Chapters 5 and 6 for durable powers of attorney for financial affairs). It also can *not* be used for health care decisions.

> **⚡ Warning!**
>
> Unlimited powers of attorney are extremely powerful legal documents that allow your chosen "attorney-in-fact full control over your property and finances.

Limited Power of Attorney: Chapter 4 contains a power of attorney that grants your agent (your "attorney in fact") only the exact power to handle the matter that you specifically spell out in the document. The power granted may be limited time-wise (the power to act only on a certain day, for example), geographically (handle financial affairs only in Texas, for example), transactionally (handle only insurance affairs, for example). With this form, you are giving another person the right to handle a particular financial and/or business matter on your behalf. They are given the power to act exactly as you could in the specific situation. This can be is a very powerful grant of authority to someone else to act on your behalf. The person appointed must be someone that you fully trust to handle your affairs. This power of attorney is not valid if you become disabled or incapacitated. You must use a 'durable' power of attorney for that purpose (see below and Chapters 5 and 6). It also can *not* be used for health care decisions.

Limited Power of Attorney for Real Estate: This power of attorney, also contained in Chapter 4, is a type of limited power of attorney that is specifically written to allow you to grant someone the authority to handle a specific real estate transaction, for example, a real estate closing. With this form, you are giving another person the right to handle a particular financial and/or business matter relating to real estate on your behalf. They are given the power to act exactly as you could in the specific situation. This power of attorney is not valid if you become disabled or incapacitated. You must use a 'durable' power of attorney for that purpose (see below and Chapters 5 and 6). This form also can *not* be used for health care decisions.

Limited Power of Attorney for Child Care: Also contained in Chapter 4, this power of attorney is a type of limited power of attorney that is specifically written to allow you to grant someone the authority to consent to medical treatment of a minor child, enroll a child in a school, or exercise other child care powers. With this form, you are giving another person the right to handle a particular child care matter on your behalf. They are given the power to act exactly as you could in the specific situation related to child care.

Durable Unlimited Power of Attorney for Financial Affairs (effective immediately): Chapter 5 provides four different durable powers of attorney for financial affairs. The term "durable" means that this type of power of attorney is not affected by your health. In other words, a durable power of attorney remains in effect even if you become disabled and/or incapacitated (or goes into effect only when you become disabled and/or incapacitated). A durable unlimited power of attorney for financial affairs allows you to appoint someone to handle your financial affairs during a period that you are unable to handle them yourself. This is a power of attorney that grants your agent (your "attorney in fact") full and complete power to handle all of your business and financial affairs. With this form, you are giving another person the right to manage your financial and/or business matters on your behalf. They are given the power to act exactly as you could. The person appointed must be someone that you fully trust to handle your affairs. This particular durable power of attorney is effective immediately (as opposed to a durable power of attorney that *only* becomes effective upon your disability—see below). This type of power of attorney, however, can *not* be used for health care decisions. You must use a 'durable health care power of attorney' for that purpose. Compare this type of durable power of attorney (that takes effect immediately and remains in effect even if the principal is incapacitated) with the following type of durable power of attorney (that only takes effect upon the principal's incapacity or disability). Please note that this form provides a release for your attorney-in-fact to receive your

☼ Toolkit Tip!

Durable powers of attorney can be used for either financial/ property situations or for health care situations. To use them for both situations requires two separate documents.

medical records under the federal HIPAA regulations relating to the privacy of health care records. This does not confer any authority for your attorney-in-fact to make health care decisions on your behalf. The HIPAA release is for the purpose of allowing your attorney-in-fact to have access to your medical files for the purpose of paying or examining medical bills and charges.

Durable Unlimited Power of Attorney for Financial Affairs (effective on disability): Another type of durable power of attorney found in Chapter 5, this is a power of attorney that grants your agent (your "attorney in fact") full and complete power to handle all of your business and financial affairs, but only when and if you become incapacitated and unable to handle your own affairs. The term "durable" means that this type of power of attorney is not affected by your health. In other words, a durable power of attorney, such as this, is valid if you become disabled and/or incapacitated. This power of attorney is effective *only* upon your disability (as opposed to a durable power of attorney that becomes effective immediately and remains in effect regardless of your disability or incapacity—see above). This type of durable power of attorney requires that a physician certify that you are unable to handle your own affairs before your chosen agent (attorney-in-fact) takes control of your financial affairs. A durable unlimited power of attorney for financial affairs allows you to appoint someone to handle your financial affairs during a period that you are unable to handle them yourself. This type of power of attorney, however, can *not* be used for health care decisions. You must use a 'durable health care power of attorney' for that purpose. Please note that this form provides a release for your attorney-in-fact to receive your medical records under the federal HIPAA regulations relating to the privacy of health care records. This does not confer any authority for your attorney-in-fact to make health care decisions on your behalf. The HIPAA release is for the purpose of allowing your attorney-in-fact to have access to your medical files for the purpose of paying or examining medical bills and charges.

Durable General Power of Attorney for Financial Affairs (effective immediately): Also found in Chapter 5, this a power of attorney that allows you to authorize your agent (your "attorney in fact") to handle a few or all of your financial

> **♀Toolkit Tip!**
>
> This book provides instructions and forms for both (1) unlimited and (2) general durable powers of attorney for financial affairs.

and/or business transactions. With this form, you are giving another person the right to manage some or perhaps all of your financial and/or business matters on your behalf. They are given the power to act exactly as you could. This can be a very powerful grant of authority to someone else to act on your behalf. The person appointed must be someone that you fully trust to handle your affairs. This particular durable power of attorney is effective immediately (as opposed to a durable power of attorney that *only* becomes effective upon your disability—see below). This type of power of attorney, however, can *not* be used for health care decisions. You must use a 'durable health care power of attorney' for that purpose. Compare this type of durable power of attorney (that takes effect immediately and remains in effect even if the principal is incapacitated) with the following type of durable power of attorney (that only takes effect upon the principal's incapacity or disability). Please note that this form provides a release for your attorney-in-fact to receive your medical records under the federal HIPAA regulations relating to the privacy of health care records. This does not confer any authority for your attorney-in-fact to make health care decisions on your behalf. The HIPAA release is for the purpose of allowing your attorney-in-fact to have access to your medical files for the purpose of paying or examining medical bills and charges.

Durable General Power of Attorney for Financial Affairs (effective on disability): Another type of durable power of attorney found in Chapter 5, this is a power of attorney that grants your agent (your "attorney in fact") to handle a few or all of your financial and/or business transactions, but only when and if you become incapacitated and unable to handle your own affairs. They are given the power to act exactly as you could, but only in those situations that you select. This can be a very powerful grant of authority to someone else to act on your behalf. The person appointed must be someone that you fully trust to handle your affairs. The term "durable" means that this type of power of attorney is not affected by your health. In other words, a durable power of attorney, such as this, is valid if you become disabled and/or incapacitated. This power of attorney is effective *only* upon your disability (as opposed to a durable power of attorney that becomes effective immediately and remains in effect regardless of your disability or incapacity—

see above). This type of durable power of attorney requires that a physician certify that you are unable to handle your own affairs before your chosen agent (attorney-in-fact) takes control of your financial affairs. A durable general power of attorney for financial affairs allows you to appoint someone to handle your certain of your financial affairs during a period that you are unable to handle them yourself. This type of power of attorney, however, can *not* be used for health care decisions. You must use a 'durable health care power of attorney' for that purpose. Please note that this form provides a release for your attorney-in-fact to receive your medical records under the federal HIPAA regulations relating to the privacy of health care records. This does not confer any authority for your attorney-in-fact to make health care decisions on your behalf. The HIPAA release is for the purpose of allowing your attorney-in-fact to have access to your medical files for the purpose of paying or examining medical bills and charges.

State Specific Durable Powers of Attorney: Chapter 6 of this book provides state-specific versions of durable powers of attorney for financial affairs. While the forms provided in Chapter 5 of this book (durable powers of attorney for financial affairs) are legally-valid in all states, some states provide their own particular form for a durable power of attorney. You may choose to use one of the generic forms provided in Chapter 5 or you may choose to use the state-specific forms provided in Chapter 6. Please check the Appendix for your state listing to determine if your state has a state-specific form for this purpose.

Durable Health Care Power of Attorney: Chapter 7 provides a durable health care power of attorney. This is a specialized type of power of attorney that has been developed to allow you to authorize another person to make all of your health care decisions for you in the event that you become disabled or incapacitated and unable to make such decisions for yourself. This is a very powerful document that, in some cases, grants someone else the power of life or death over you. This document allows the person you designate to make health care decisions whenever you are unable to communicate your own desires. As such, it is much more powerful than a living will (which generally provides a statement of your wishes should you be terminally ill

---

♀ Toolkit Tip!

All of the powers of attorney forms in this book are legally-valid in all states and Washington D.C.

⚡ Warning!

Do NOT sign any power of attorney form if you do not understand the details and impact of the document. You should see a lawyer if you do not understand the details of any legal form that you propose to sign.

or in a persistent vegetative state). Note that this is also a type of "durable" power of attorney in that it is effective even if you incapacitated and are unable to communicate your wishes and desires regarding your health care choices.

Advance Health Care Directives: Explained in Chapter 9, these forms are provided only on the CD that is enclosed with this book. An advance health care directive is a legal document that has been developed in most states that incorporates various health care matters into a single comprehensive form. These documents contain the following forms: living will, appointment of health care agent (a health care power of attorney), designation of primary physician, and organ donation. Please see the instructions for advance health care directives in Chapter 9 if you are interested in this type of form.

Living Will: This type of form allows you to make end-of-life decisions in advance of medical situations that may leave you unable to communicate your wishes regarding the use of artificial life support systems. A basic living will form is provided in Chapter 10. In addition, state-specific living will forms are provided on the CD that accompanies this book. In addition, a living will is also part of the *advance health care directives* provided by this book.

Designation Of Primary Physician Form: This form is provided in Chapter 11 and also is part of the *advance health care directives* provided by this book. This form provides a method to make known your choice of primary physician in the event that you are unable to communicate your desires.

Organ Donation Form: This form is provided in Chapter 12 and also is part of the *advance health care directives* provided by this book. This form provides a method to make known your decisions regarding organ donations under the Anatomical Gifts Act legislation that has been adopted by all 50 states and Washington D.C.

Revocation of Power of Attorney: Chapter 8 provides a form that may be used to revoke any of the powers of attorney in this book. Chapter 8 also contains a revocation specifically tailored to revoke a durable health care power of attorney. In addition,

> **☀️Toolkit Tip!**
>
> A living will, although not technically a power of attorney, allows you to communicate your wishes in the event that you are unable to communicate them yourself at some time in the future.

instructions for a revocation of advance health care directive are contained in Chapter 9 and this form is contained on the enclosed CD.

Additional Information for Power of Attorney: At the end of this chapter is provided a form that may be used with any of the power of attorney forms in this book (except the durable health care power of attorney. A similar form is provided in Chapter 7 for use with that form). This form may be used to include additional information and/or instructions for the attorney-in-fact.

Agent's Certification of the Validity of Power of Attorney and Agent's Authority: Finally, also included at the end of this chapter, is a form that may be used to verify an agent's authority to act under a particular power of attorney. This form may be presented to a financial institution in order to have a better chance that an agent's actions under a specific power of attorney will be accepted by the institution.

Toolkit Tip!

Remember to check your state's listing in the Appendix to see if there are any details of your state's laws that may apply in your particular circumstances.

Selecting your Attorney-in-Fact (or Agent)

The person that you decide to choose as your attorney-in-fact or agent to act on your behalf must be someone that you trust implicitly. Depending on the type of power of attorney that you may use, this person will have a tremendous amount of authority over either your financial affairs or your health care decisions, or both. For any power of attorney, you will need to select someone that you know very well. Most often, you will select your spouse, if you are married. A trusted sibling or adult child may be another safe choice. For financial and business affairs, you will need someone who has the ability to understand such affairs and make prudent decisions on your behalf and in your best interests. For health care decisions, you will need to select someone who can understand medical situations and who has the ability to act solely on your behalf, without letting their own personal desires impact their decisions.

With the forms in this book, you are granting the appointed agent very broad powers to handle your affairs. You may give your agent the maximum power under law to perform the following specific acts on your behalf: all acts relating to any and all of your financial and/or business affairs, including all banking and financial institution transactions, all real estate transactions, all insurance and annuity transactions, all claims and litigation, and all business transactions. Your attorney-in-fact (agent) is granted full power to act on your behalf in the same manner as if you were personally present. This is not a power that should be conferred lightly. Very serious thought should be given to both who you appoint as your attorney-in-fact (the person you authorize to act on your behalf) and to any specific directions that you may want to give to that person regarding financial decisions. You do not have to appoint anyone to handle your financial or health care affairs on your behalf, but it is often very useful to do so.

By accepting their appointment, your agent agrees to act in your best interest as he or she considers advisable. For financial powers of attorney, your appointed agent agrees to keep your assets separate from their own and to exercise reasonable prudence in handling your affairs. The appointed agent also agrees to keep full and accurate records of any actions or transactions taken on your behalf. They also agree to keep any receipts regarding any transactions. Any power of attorney, whether for financial matters or health care, may be revoked at any time and is automatically revoked on your death.

Toolkit Tip!

You should always select a "successor" attorney-in-fact in case your main choice is unavailable or unwilling to serve in the future.

The forms in this book will allow you to select an alternate or successor agent, that is, someone to act on your behalf if the main agent that you have selected is not available. It is a good idea to do so, since there may be circumstances beyond your control that would prevent your first choice of agent from acting. Your successor or alternate agent must also be someone whom your trust totally to handle your affairs, either financial or health care.

Additionally, you may wish to appoint two or more agents to act at the same time. Generally, however, this is not a good idea, as the agents may not be able to agree on a course of action and such conflicts can render the power of attorney useless. If you do desire to appoint more than one agent, you may wish to simply prepare two or more separate powers of attorney and allow your chosen agents to act separately. However, unless your multiple agents know each other well and are willing to act together in unison, this also may not be such a good idea. It is preferable to appoint a single agent and then appoint successor or alternate agents who would only have authority to act if your main choice for agent is unable or unwilling to act.

At the beginning of each of the documents are notices regarding the use of the particular type of power of attorney. They clearly explain the importance of caution in the use of this form and are applicable to all states. Please read each carefully to decide which of these forms are appropriate for your situation. Please note that the four durable power of attorney forms and the health care power of attorney form provide a release for your attorney-in-fact to receive your medical records under the federal HIPAA regulations relating to the privacy of health care records. This does not confer any authority for your attorney-in-fact to make health care decisions on your behalf. The HIPAA release is for the purpose of allowing your attorney-in-fact to have access to your medical files for the purpose of paying or examining medical bills and charges.

Please also note that the state-specific advance health care forms in Chapter 9 *do not* contain a durable power of attorney for financial affairs. If you wish to have this type of document as part of your advance health care plans, you will need to complete either one of the durable power of attorney forms in Chapter 5 or a state-specific durable power of attorney form in Chapter 6.

> **⚡ Warning!**
>
> Selecting your "attorney-in-fact" can be one of the most important decisions of your life. The person you select may have either control of your property and finances or the power to make life and death health care decisions. They may, indeed, have both powers.

Methods for Completing Your Powers of Attorney

Please note that there are two distinct methods provided in this book for completing a power of attorney using this book. Either method is legal and either method may be selected. There are different reasons for choosing each method and these are outlined below:

Prepare Individual Forms

You may choose to complete one or more of the generic forms that are contained in Chapters 2 through 5, and Chapter 7. This method may be chosen if:

> • You desire to custom-tailor one or more of the forms to more closely fit your individual wishes and desires concerning the use of your power of attorney, or

> • The details of the state-specific forms (explained below) do not fit your individual desires concerning the use of your power of attorney.

In a few states, the legislatures have not developed specific language for one or more of the forms. These instances are noted under the state's heading in the appendix of this book. In such situations, you should use the individual generic forms (in Chapters 2-5, and 7) for those states. Any such forms have been prepared following guidelines and requirements set out by the particular state's legislature.

These forms are provided on the enclosed CD in two separate formats: either as PDF forms that may be filled in on your computer, but not altered, or as text forms that may be carefully altered to more closely fit your individual wishes and desires. The individual forms have been prepared to meet the minimum legal requirements in all states and are legally-valid in all states. Please see the detailed instructions in the introduction of this book concerning how to complete either the PDF or text versions of these individual forms.

Prepare State-Specific Forms

The second method is to prepare a state-specific form in either Chapter 6, 9, or 10. A '*state-specific form*' is a form that has been taken directly from the laws of your particular state or is based on the legislative requirements of a particular state. The legal effects of the language in such a document have been approved by the legislature of the state. This provides an advantage in that the legal language in such a 'statutory' form is generally familiar to most financial institutions (or health care providers, in the case of advance health care directives) in the particular state and they know that such language has been approved. This does not mean, however, that other 'non-statutory' forms are not legally valid in the state as well.

All states specifically provide, in their legislation regarding powers of attorney, that power of attorney forms other than those contained in the statute itself are legally-valid. Anyone may use a 'non-statutory' legal form, such as those in Chapters 2 through 5 and Chapter 7, with language that they find appropriate to their own situation, as long as the document meets certain minimum legal standards for a particular state. All of the forms in this book meet such required legal standards.

The state-specific advance health care directives that are explained in Chapter 9 of this book and are found on the CD (in fillable PDF format) have also been prepared directly from the language and/or legislative guidance found in the statutes of each individual state. They are designed as a complete advance health care directive containing all appropriate forms. Any such forms have been prepared following any guidelines set out by the state's legislature.

Witness and Notary Requirements

All states have provided protections to ensure the validity of the powers of attorney. They have also provided legal protections against persons using undue influence to force or coerce someone into signing a power of attorney—by requiring the use of witnesses to signatures and/or the use of a notary public to acknowledge the signature.

All of the forms included in this book, including all of the state-specific forms, are designed to be notarized. This is a requirement in most states for most forms and has been made mandatory on all of the forms in this book. The purpose of notarization in this instance is to add another level of protection against coercion or undue pressure being exerted to force anyone to sign any of these legal forms against their wishes. Sadly, such undue pressure has been applied in some cases to force senior citizens to sign legal documents against their own wishes. The requirement that one sign a document in front of a notary and in front of two additional witnesses can significantly lessen the opportunity for such abuse.

Preparing and Signing Your Power of Attorney

① Select the appropriate form from the included forms in Chapters 2-5, and 7 or select a state-specific form for your state from Chapters 6, 9, and 10. Carefully read through the entire form selected. You may wish to make two copies of the form(s) that you choose. This will allow you to use one form as a draft copy and the other form for a final copy that you, your witnesses, and a notary will sign.

② For all forms, make the appropriate choices in each section where indicated by initialing the designated place or filling in the appropriate information. Depending on which form that you use, you may have many choices to initial or you may have no choices to initial. Please carefully read through the paragraphs and clauses that require choices to be certain that you understand the choices that you will be making. If you wish to add additional instructions or limitations in the places indicated on the form, please type or clearly print your instructions. Note: If you wish to add extensive additional instructions to any form, you will need to do so in two ways: a) the preferred method would be to use the text-formatted forms on the CD and insert such additional instructions directly into the form, or b) if you choose to use the PDF-formatted forms, you may add additional instructions by adding the phrase "See additional sheet which is attached to this document and incorporated by reference." A form for "Additional Information for Power of Attorney" is located at the end of this chapter. Please see the instructions for that form at the end of this chapter.

③ Finally, you will need to complete the signature and witness/notary sections of your forms. When you have a completed original with no erasures or corrections, staple all of the pages together in the upper left-hand corner. Do not sign this document or fill in the date yet. You should now assemble your witnesses and a notary public to witness your signature.

④ In front of all of the witnesses and the notary public, the following should take place in the order shown:

(a) There is no requirement that the witnesses (or notary) know any of the terms of your power of attorney or other legal forms, or that they read your power of attorney or legal forms. All that is necessary is that they observe you sign your power of attorney and that they also sign the power of attorney as witnesses in each other's presence. You will sign your legal form at the end where indicated, exactly as your name is written on the form, in ink using a pen. At this time, if you are using a form requiring initials in some spaces, you should also initial your choices as to which sections you have chosen. You will also need to fill in the date. Once you have signed and completed all of the necessary information, pass your legal form to the first witness, who should sign the acknowledgment where indicated and also print his or her name (in the witness section prior to the witness signature area).

(b) After the first witness has signed, have the legal form passed to the second witness, who should also sign the acknowledgment where indicated and print his or her name (in the witness section prior to the witness signature area).

(c) Throughout this ceremony, you and all of the witnesses must remain together. The final step is for the notary public to sign in the space where indicated and complete the notarization block on the form.

(d) If you have chosen individuals to act as either your health care agent (health care power of attorney) or as your attorney-in-fact for financial affairs (any other powers of attorney) and any successors agents, you should have them sign the form at the end where shown acknowledging that they accept their appointment. Note that these signature generally do not need to be witnessed or notarized.

⑤ When this step is completed, the individual legal form that you have signed is a valid legal document. Have several photo-copies made and, if appropriate, deliver a copy to any financial institutions that you intend to honor your power of attorney. (If you have completed a durable health care power of attorney or advance health care directive, provide your attending physician with a copy to have placed in your medical records file.) You should also provide a copy to any person who was selected as either your health care agent or your attorney-in-fact for financial affairs. You may also desire to give a copy to the person you have chosen as the executor of your will, your clergy, and your spouse or other trusted relative.

Important Note: Although most states have passed laws that require that persons or financial institutions honor the state-specific statutory forms that are provided in this book, not all institutions will do so. Unfortunately, many financial institutions will require the use of their own power of attorney form.

Finally, after the following Power of Attorney Chart, you will find two additional forms that may be used with any of the power of attorney forms in this book: Additional Information for Power of Attorney form and Agent's Certification of the Validity of Power of Attorney and Agent's Authority.

Power of Attorney Chart:

Use this chart to determine your specific power of attorney needs

Type of Power of Attorney	Effective for Financial Affairs	Effective for Health Care Decisions	Effective Immediately	Effective if Incapacitated
Unlimited Power of Attorney	YES, for *any and all* financial and business affairs	NO	YES	NO
General Power of Attorney	YES, but *may* be limited to specific situations	NO	YES	NO
Limited Power of Attorney	YES, but must be limited to specific situations	NO	YES, but may be restricted to certain dates	NO
Limited Power of Attorney for Real Estate	YES, but limited to real estate transactions	NO	YES, but may be restricted to certain dates	NO
Limited Power of Attorney for Child Care	NO, limited to child care situations	YES, but limited to consent to emergency medical care	YES	YES, if child is incapacitated
Durable Unlimited or General Power of Attorney (effective immediately)	YES, may be for *any and/or all* financial and business affairs	NO	YES	YES
Durable Unlimited or General Power of Attorney (effective upon disability)	YES, may be for *any and/or all* financial and business affairs	NO	NO, only effective upon incapacity of principal	YES, only becomes effective upon incapacity
Durable Health Care Power of Attorney	NO, only effective for health care decisions	YES, only effective for health care decisions	NO, only effective upon incapacity of principal	YES, only becomes effective upon incapacity

Instructions for Additional Information for Power of Attorney

If you need to add additional pages to your power of attorney document, please use the form titled "Additional Information for Power of Attorney" which is provided on the following page and on the CD. If you need to use additional pages, be certain that you initial and date each added page and that you clearly label each additional page regarding which paragraph or section of the form to which it pertains. You should also note in the form itself that you are using additional pages by printing or writing "See attached Additional Information page, which is incorporated by reference" in the section of the form where you wish to insert additional instructions or information. Note that this form should be attached to the original power of attorney document prior to the signing and notarization of the original document.

To complete this document, fill in the following information:

① Date of original power of attorney
② Name and address of person who originally granted power (principal)
③ Name and address of person granted power (attorney-in-fact)
④ Detailed statement of any additional information or instructions in power of attorney (Be certain that you note the paragraph or section of the original power of attorney where the additional information or instructions will apply).
⑤ Initials of principal and date of power of attorney

Additional Information for Power of Attorney

The following information is incorporated by reference and is to be considered as a part of the Power of Attorney, dated ① _____
_____, under which the following principal ② _____
_____, appointed the following
attorney-in-fact to act on his or her behalf ③
_____.

Principal must initial and date below and insert additional information here:
④

⑤ Initials of Principal _____   Date _____

Instructions for Agent's Certification of the Validity of Power of Attorney and Agent's Authority

This form is useful to authenticate an agent's authority to act under a power of attorney. It may be required by a financial or other institution in order for the agent's actions to be accepted as acts on behalf of the principal. The purpose of this form is to have the agent (attorney-in-fact) certify that the power of attorney is still valid and in effect. This certification will provide the institution with the agent's promise that, as far as he or she knows, the power of attorney is still valid and the agent has full authority to act under the particular power of attorney. Note that a copy of the original power of attorney should be attached to this form.

To complete this form, please fill in the following information:

① State and county in which certification is notarized

② Name of person who was originally granted the power by the principal (attorney-in-fact)

③ Name of person who originally granted the power to the agent (principal)

④ Date of original power of attorney

⑤ Agent's signature, date of signing of certification, agent's printed name and address

⑥ Notary block to be completed by notary

⑦ Name of person who prepared the form

Agent's Certification of the Validity of Power of Attorney and Agent's Authority

①
State of _____

County of_____

②I, _____, ③ certify that _____
_____signed a Power of Attorney (a copy of the Power of Attorney is attached to this certification) on ④_____ (date), naming the undersigned as an agent or successor agent.

I further certify that to my knowledge:

(1) the Principal is alive and has not revoked the Power of Attorney or my authority to act under the Power of Attorney and that the Power of Attorney remains in full force and effect;

(2) if the Power of Attorney was drafted to become effective upon the happening of an event or contingency that such event or contingency has occurred; and

(3) if I was named as a successor agent that the initial or predecessor agent is no longer able to serve.

⑤

_____   _____
Agent's signature   Date

_____
Agent's printed name

_____
Agent's address

Notary Acknowledgment

①
State of _____

County of_____

This document was acknowledged before me on _____ (date), by _____(name of Agent).

_____
Signature of Notary   (Seal, if any)
My commission expires: _____

⑥
This document prepared by: _____

Chapter 2

General Power of Attorney

A general power of attorney allows you to authorize your agent (your "attorney in fact") to handle a few or all of your financial and/or business transactions. The choice of which powers to bestow upon your agent is entirely yours and is made by placing your initials next to the authorized powers on the document at the time of your signing the form. With this form, you are giving another person the right to manage your financial and/or business matters on your behalf. They are given the power to act exactly as you could. This, of course, is a very powerful grant of authority to someone else to act on your behalf. The person appointed must be someone that you fully trust to handle your affairs. The authority granted by this power of attorney may be revoked by you at any time and is automatically revoked if you die or become incapacitated or incompetent. If there is anything about this form that you do not understand, you should ask a lawyer to explain it to you. This power of attorney contains an important notice prior to the form itself. Please read this notice carefully before you complete this form.

When Should You Use a General Power of Attorney?

A general power of attorney allows you to select any or all of a range of powers that you wish for your agent (attorney-in-fact) to have. This type of power of attorney can be used to authorize someone else to sign certain documents if you can not be present when the signatures are necessary. They can be used to authorize someone to handle any or all of the following possible matters:

Real estate transactions; Goods and services transactions; Stock, bond, share and Commodity transactions; Banking transactions; Business operating transactions; Insurance transactions; Estate transactions; Legal claims and litigation; Personal relationships and affairs; Benefits from military service; Records, reports and statements; Retirement benefit transactions; Making gifts to a spouse, children, parents and other descendants; Tax matters.

Additionally, you may also authorize your attorney-in-fact to delegate any or all of the above powers to someone that your appointed attorney-in-fact selects. This option should only be taken if you trust your appointed attorney-in-fact totally to make such a decision only with your best interests in mind.

A general power of attorney is most useful if you wish to grant your agent some, but not all of the possible powers available to an agent. If you wish to grant full and complete authority to your agent, you should use an *unlimited power of attorney* instead. An unlimited power of attorney provides that your agent will have total authority to act your behalf for all financial and/or business matters (but not for health care decisions). Unlimited powers of attorney are further explained in Chapter. 3 If you wish to provide a very limited power to your agent, you may wish to use a *limited power of attorney* instead of a general power of attorney. A limited power of attorney allows you to limit the power granted to a specific action or a specific date range. Limited powers of attorney are detailed in Chapter 4. A general power of attorney is not valid if you become disabled or incapacitated. You must use a *'durable' power of attorney* for that purpose. Durable powers of attorney are dealt with in Chapters 5 and 6. In addition, a general power of attorney also can *not* be used for health care decisions. You must use a *durable health care power of attorney* for that purpose. Durable health care powers of attorney are the subject of Chapter 7.

☀️Toolkit Tip!

You may, if you so choose, elect to use a durable general power of attorney, which will remain in effect if you become incapacitated (or go into effect only when you become incapacitated). Please see Chapter 5 for more details.

To complete your general power of attorney, please follow the instructions below. To use the form on the enclosed CD, simply fill in the required information in either the text or PDF versions of this form.

Instructions for General Power of Attorney

① Name and address of person granting power (principal)
② Name and address of person granted power (attorney-in-fact)
③ Initial each of the specific powers that you wish your attorney-in-fact to have. If you wish your attorney-in-fact to have full authority to do anything that you yourself could do, simply initial line (q). Cross out any items that you do not choose. Note: if you wish to have your attorney-in-fact to have full authority, you may wish to use the *unlimited power of attorney* form instead).
④ Name and address of successor to person originally granted power (successor attorney-in-fact) (optional-if not used, write n/a in this space)
⑤ Date
⑥ Printed name of principal, date of signing of power of attorney, and signature of principal (signed in front of notary public)
⑦ Printed names and signatures of witnesses (signed in front of notary public)
⑧ Notary acknowledgement should be completed by the notary public
⑨ Printed name, date, and signature of attorney-in-fact (need not be witnessed or notarized)
⑩ Printed name, date, and signature of successor attorney-in-fact (optional-if not used, write N/A in this space) (need not be witnessed or notarized)

General Power of Attorney

Notice: This is an important document. Before signing this document, you should know these important facts. By signing this document, you are not giving up any powers or rights to control your finances and property yourself. In addition to your own powers and rights, you may be giving another person, your attorney-in-fact, broad powers to handle your finances and property. This general power of attorney may give the person whom you designate (your "attorney-in-fact") broad powers to handle your finances and property, which may include powers to encumber, sell or otherwise dispose of any real or personal property without advance notice to you or approval by you. THE POWERS GRANTED WILL NOT EXIST AFTER YOU BECOME DISABLED, OR INCAPACITATED. This document does not authorize anyone to make medical or other health care decisions for you. If you own complex or special assets such as a business, or if there is anything about this form that you do not understand, you should ask a lawyer to explain this form to you before you sign it. If you wish to change your general power of attorney, you must complete a new document and revoke this one. You may revoke this document at any time by destroying it, by directing another person to destroy it in your presence or by signing a written and dated statement expressing your intent to revoke this document. If you revoke this document, you should notify your attorney-in-fact and any other person to whom you have given a copy of the form. You also should notify all parties having custody of your assets. These parties have no responsibility to you unless you actually notify them of the revocation. If your attorney-in-fact is your spouse and your marriage is annulled, or you are divorced after signing this document, this document is invalid. Since some 3rd parties or some transactions may not permit use of this document, it is advisable to check in advance, if possible, for any special requirements that may be imposed. You should sign this form only if the attorney-in-fact you name is reliable, trustworthy and competent to manage your affairs. This form must be signed by the Principal (the person appointing the attorney-in-fact), witnessed by two persons other than the notary public, and acknowledged by a notary public.

I, _____(printed name),
of (address)_____,
as principal, to grant a general power of attorney to, and do hereby appoint:
_____ (printed name),
of (address)_____,
my attorney-in-fact to act in my name, place and stead in any way which I myself could do, if I were personally present, with respect to the following matters to the extent that I am permitted by law to act through an agent. The powers chosen below shall have the full force and effect given to them by their full enumeration as laid out in the text of the Power of Attorney Act of the laws of the State of _____: (Place your initials before each item that you select and cross out each item that you do not select)

_____ (a) real estate transactions;

_____ (b) goods and services transactions;

_____ (c) bond, share and commodity transactions;

_____ (d) banking transactions;

_____ (e) business operating transactions;

_____ (f) insurance transactions;

_____ (g) estate transactions;

_____ (h) claims and litigation;

_____ (i) personal relationships and affairs;

_____ (j) benefits from military service;

_____ (k) records, reports and statements;

_____ (l) retirement benefit transactions;

_____ (m) making gifts to my spouse, children and more remote descendants, and parents;

_____ (n) tax matters;

_____ (o) all other matters;

_____ (p) full and unqualified authority to my attorney-in-fact to delegate any or all of the foregoing powers to any person or persons whom my attorney-in-fact shall select;

_____ (q) unlimited power and authority to act in all of the above situations (a) through (p)

If the attorney-in-fact named above is unable or unwilling to serve, I appoint
_____ (printed name),
of (address) _____ ,
to be my attorney-in-fact for all purposes hereunder.

To induce any third party to rely upon this power of attorney, I agree that any third party receiving a signed copy or facsimile of this power of attorney may rely upon such copy, and that revocation or termination of this power of attorney shall be ineffective as to such third party until actual notice or knowledge of such revocation or termination shall have been received by such third party. I, for myself and for my heirs, executors, legal representatives and assigns, agree to indemnify and hold harmless any such third party from any and all claims that may arise against such third party by reason of such third party having relied on the provisions of this power of attorney. **THIS POWER OF ATTORNEY SHALL NOT BE EFFECTIVE IN THE EVENT OF MY FUTURE DISABILITY OR INCAPACITY.** This power of attorney may be revoked by me at any time and is automatically revoked upon my death. My attorney-in-fact shall no be compensated for his or her services nor shall my attorney-in-fact be liable to me, my estate, heirs, successors, or assigns for acting or refraining from acting under this document, except for willful misconduct or gross negligence.

Dated: _____

Signature and Declaration of Principal

I, _____ (printed name) , the principal, sign my name to this power of attorney this _____ day of _____ and, being first duly sworn, do declare to the undersigned authority that I sign and execute this instrument as my power of attorney and that I sign it willingly, or willingly direct another to sign for me, that I execute it as my free and voluntary act for the purposes expressed in the power of attorney and that I am eighteen years of age or older, of sound mind and under no constraint or undue influence.

_____
Signature of Principal

Witness Attestation

I, _____ (printed name), the first witness, and I, _____ (printed name), the second witness, sign my name to the foregoing power of attorney being first duly sworn and do declare to the undersigned authority that the principal signs and executes this instrument as his/her power of attorney and that he\she signs it willingly, or willingly directs another to sign for him/her, and that I, in the presence and hearing of the principal, sign this power of attorney as witness to the principal's signing and that to the best of my knowledge the principal is eighteen years of age or older, of sound mind and under no constraint or undue influence.

_____
Signature of First Witness

_____
Signature of Second Witness

Notary Acknowledgment

State of _____
County of _____
Subscribed, sworn to and acknowledged before me by
_____, the Principal,
and subscribed and sworn to before me by
_____ and
_____, the witnesses,
this _____ day of _____ .

_____
Notary Signature
Notary Public,
In and for the County of _____
State of _____
My commission expires: _____ Seal

Acknowledgment and Acceptance of Appointment as Attorney-in-Fact

I, _____ , (printed name)
have read the attached power of attorney and am the person identified as the attorney-in-fact
for the principal. I hereby acknowledge that I accept my appointment as attorney-in-fact and
that when I act as agent I shall exercise the powers for the benefit of the principal; I shall keep
the assets of the principal separate from my assets; I shall exercise reasonable caution and
prudence; and I shall keep a full and accurate record of all actions, receipts and disbursements
on behalf of the principal.

_____   _____
Signature of Attorney-in-Fact   Date

Acknowledgment and Acceptance of Appointment as Successor Attorney-in-Fact

I, _____ , (printed name)
have read the attached power of attorney and am the person identified as the successor
attorney-in-fact for the principal. I hereby acknowledge that I accept my appointment as
successor attorney-in-fact and that, in the absence of a specific provision to the contrary in the
power of attorney, when I act as agent I shall exercise the powers for the benefit of the principal;
I shall keep the assets of the principal separate from my assets; I shall exercise reasonable
caution and prudence; and I shall keep a full and accurate record of all actions, receipts and
disbursements on behalf of the principal.

_____   _____
Signature of Successor Attorney-in-Fact   Date

Chapter 3

Unlimited Power of Attorney

An unlimited power of attorney should be used only in situations where you desire to authorize another person to act for you in *any and all* transactions. The grant of power under this document is unlimited. However, the powers you grant with this document cease to be effective should you become disabled or incompetent. This form gives the person whom you designate as your "attorney-in-fact" extremely broad powers to handle your property during your lifetime, which may include powers to mortgage, sell, or otherwise dispose of any real or personal property without advance notice to you or approval by you. This document does not authorize anyone to make medical or other health care decisions. You must execute a durable health care power of attorney to do this. The authority granted by this power of attorney may be revoked by you at any time and is automatically revoked if you die or become incapacitated or incompetent. If there is anything about this form that you do not understand, you should ask a lawyer to explain it to you. This power of attorney contains an important notice prior to the form itself.

When Should You Use an Unlimited Power of Attorney?

An unlimited power of attorney authorizes your agent to handle *any and all* of your financial and business affairs, including all of the following possible matters:

Real estate transactions; Personal property and goods and services transactions; Stock, bond, share and commodity transactions; Banking and financial institution transactions; Business operating transactions; Insurance and annuity transactions; Estate, trust, and other transactions where the principal is a beneficiary; Legal claims and litigation; Personal and family maintenance; Benefits from social security, medicare, medicaid, or civil or military service; Records, reports and statements; Retirement benefit transactions; Tax matters; Delegation of the agent's authority to others; and any and all other matters.

All of the above mentioned powers that are granted to your agent are spelled out in great detail in this particular power of attorney form. This is the most extensive and detailed power of attorney form that is provided. It should only be used if you are absolutely certain that the agent you choose is fully and totally trustworthy and able to exercise these broad powers in your best interest. The detailed powers that are listed in this form are taken from the Uniform Statutory Form Power of Attorney Act that has been legislatively adopted by many states. Please note that the "delegation of the agent's authority to others" provision in this document grants your chosen agent the power to delegate any of his or her powers to another person of his or her own choosing.

If you do not wish your agent to have this authority, or you wish to limit your agent's power under any of the other powers which are enumerated in this document, you should use instead a *general power of attorney*. A general power of attorney will allow you to pick and choose which of these powers you wish to grant to your agent. General powers of attorney are explained in Chapter 2. If you wish to provide a very limited power to your agent, you may wish to use a *limited power of attorney* instead of an unlimited power of attorney. A limited power of attorney allows you to limit the power granted to a specific action or a specific date range. Limited powers of attorney are covered in Chapter 4. An unlimited power of attorney is not valid if you become disabled or incapacitated. You must use a *'durable' financial power of attorney* for that purpose. Durable financial powers of attorney are detailed in Chapters 5 and 6. In addition,

> **☼Toolkit Tip!**
>
> Unlimited powers of attorney are extremely powerful legal documents. If you do not understand the full power of this type of document, please consult an attorney.

an unlimited power of attorney also can *not* be used for health care decisions. You must use a *durable health care power of attorney* for that purpose. Durable health care powers of attorney are explained in Chapter 7.

To complete your unlimited power of attorney, please follow the instructions below. To use the form on the enclosed CD, simply fill in the required information in either the text or PDF versions of this form.

Instructions for Unlimited Power of Attorney

① Name and address of person granting power (principal)

② Name and address of person granted power (attorney-in-fact)

③ Name and address of successor to person originally granted power (successor attorney-in-fact) (optional-if not used, write N/A in this space)

④ Date

⑤ Printed name of principal, date of signing of power of attorney, and signature of principal (signed in front of notary public)

⑥ Printed names and signatures of witnesses (signed in front of notary public)

⑦ Notary acknowledgement should be completed by the notary public

⑧ Printed name, date, and signature of attorney-in-fact (need not be witnessed or notarized)

⑨ Printed name, date, and signature of successor attorney-in-fact (optional-if not used, write N/A in this space) (need not be witnessed or notarized)

Unlimited Power of Attorney

Notice: This is an important document. Before signing this document, you should know these important facts. By signing this document, you are not giving up any powers or rights to control your finances and property yourself. In addition to your own powers and rights, you are giving another person, your attorney-in-fact, broad powers to handle your finances and property. This unlimited power of attorney will give the person whom you designate (your "attorney-in-fact") broad powers to handle your finances and property, which includes powers to encumber, sell or otherwise dispose of any real or personal property without advance notice to you or approval by you. THE POWERS GRANTED WILL NOT EXIST AFTER YOU BECOME DISABLED, OR INCAPACITATED. This document does not authorize anyone to make medical or other health care decisions for you. If you own complex or special assets such as a business, or if there is anything about this form that you do not understand, you should ask a lawyer to explain this form to you before you sign it. If you wish to change your unlimited power of attorney, you must complete a new document and revoke this one. You may revoke this document at any time by destroying it, by directing another person to destroy it in your presence or by signing a written and dated statement expressing your intent to revoke this document. If you revoke this document, you should notify your attorney-in-fact and any other person to whom you have given a copy of the form. You also should notify all parties having custody of your assets. These parties have no responsibility to you unless you actually notify them of the revocation. If your attorney-in-fact is your spouse and your marriage is annulled, or you are divorced after signing this document, this document is invalid. Since some 3rd parties or some transactions may not permit use of this document, it is advisable to check in advance, if possible, for any special requirements that may be imposed. You should sign this form only if the attorney-in-fact you name is reliable, trustworthy and competent to manage your affairs. This form must be signed by the Principal (the person appointing the attorney-in-fact), witnessed by two persons other than the notary public, and acknowledged by a notary public.

I, _____(printed name),
of (address)_____,
as principal, do grant an unlimited power of attorney to, and do hereby appoint:
_____(printed name),
of (address)_____,
my attorney-in-fact and do grant him or her unlimited power and authority to act in my name, place and stead in any way which I myself could do, if I were personally present, with respect to all of the following matters to the extent that I am permitted by law to act through an agent:

IN GENERAL, the principal authorizes the agent to: (1) demand, receive, and obtain by litigation or otherwise, money or other thing of value to which the principal is, may become, or claims to be entitled, and conserve, invest, disburse, or use anything so received for the purposes intended; (2) contract in any manner with any person, on terms agreeable to the agent, to accomplish a purpose of a transaction, and perform, rescind, reform, release, or modify the contract or another contract made by or on behalf of the principal; (3) execute, acknowledge, seal, and deliver a deed, revocation, mortgage, security agreement, lease, notice, check, promissory note, electronic funds transfer, release, or other instrument or communication the agent considers desirable to accomplish a purpose of a transaction, including creating a schedule of the principal's property and attaching it to the power of attorney; (4) prosecute, defend, submit to arbitration or mediation, settle, and propose or accept a compromise with respect to, a claim existing in favor of or against the principal or intervene in litigation relating to the claim; (5) seek on the principal's behalf the assistance of a court to carry out an act authorized by the principal in the power of attorney; (6) engage, compensate, and discharge an attorney, accountant, expert witness, or other assistant; (7) keep appropriate records of each transaction, including an accounting of receipts and disbursements; (8) prepare, execute, and file a record, report, or other document the agent considers desirable to safeguard or promote the principal's interest under a statute or governmental regulation; (9) reimburse the agent for expenditures properly made by the agent in exercising the powers granted by the power of attorney; and (10) in general, do any other lawful act with respect to the power and all property related to the power.

WITH RESPECT TO REAL PROPERTY, the principal authorizes the agent to: (1) accept as a gift or as security for an extension of credit, reject, demand, buy, lease, receive, or otherwise acquire, an interest in real property or a right incident to real property; (2) sell, exchange, convey with or without covenants, quitclaim, release, surrender, mortgage, retain title for security, encumber, partition, consent to partitioning, subdivide, apply for zoning, rezoning, or other governmental permits, plat or consent to platting, develop, grant options concerning, lease, sublease, or otherwise dispose of, an interest in real property or a right incident to real property; (3) release, assign, satisfy, or enforce by litigation or otherwise, a mortgage, deed of trust, conditional sale contract, encumbrance, lien, or other claim to real property which exists or is asserted; (4) manage or conserve an interest in real property or a right incident to real property, owned or claimed to be owned by the principal, including: (a) insuring against a casualty, liability, or loss; (b) obtaining or regaining possession, or protecting the interest or right, by litigation or otherwise; (c) paying, compromising, or contesting taxes or assessments, or applying for and receiving refunds in connection with them; and (d) purchasing supplies, hiring assistance or labor, and making repairs or alterations to the real property; (5) use, develop, alter, replace, remove, erect, or install structures or other improvements upon real property in or incident to which the principal has, or claims to have, an interest or right; (6) participate in a reorganization with respect to real property or a legal entity that owns an interest in or right incident to real property and receive and hold, directly or indirectly, shares of stock or obligations, or other evidences of ownership or debt, received in a plan of reorganization, and act with respect to them, including: (a) selling or otherwise disposing of them; (b) exercising or selling an option, conversion, or similar right with respect to them; and (c) voting them in person or by proxy; (7) change the form of title of an interest in or right incident to real property, and (8) dedicate to public use, with or without consideration, easements or other real property in which the principal has, or claims to have, an interest.

WITH RESPECT TO TANGIBLE PERSONAL PROPERTY, the principal authorizes the agent to: (1) accept as a gift or as security for an extension of credit, reject, demand, buy, receive, or otherwise acquire ownership or possession of tangible personal property or an interest in tangible personal property; (2) sell, exchange, convey with or without covenants, release, surrender, create a security interest in, grant options concerning, lease, sublease to others, or otherwise dispose of tangible personal property or an interest in tangible personal property; (3) release, assign, satisfy, or enforce by litigation or otherwise, a security interest, lien, or other claim on behalf of the principal, with respect to tangible personal property or an interest in tangible personal property; (4) manage or conserve tangible personal property or an interest in tangible personal property on behalf of the principal, including: (a) insuring against casualty, liability, or loss; (b) obtaining or regaining possession, or protecting the property or interest, by litigation or otherwise; (c) paying, compromising, or contesting taxes or assessments or applying for and receiving refunds in connection with taxes or assessments; (d) moving from place to place; (e) storing for hire or on a gratuitous bailment; and (f) using, altering, and making repairs or alterations; and (5) change the form of title of an interest in tangible personal property.

WITH RESPECT TO TRANSACTIONS CONCERNING STOCKS AND BONDS, the principal authorizes the agent to: (1) buy, sell, and exchange stocks, bonds, mutual funds, and all other types of securities and financial instruments, whether held directly or indirectly, except commodity futures contracts and call and put options on stocks and stock indexes, (2) receive certificates and other evidences of ownership with respect to securities, (3) exercise voting rights with respect to securities in person or by proxy, enter into voting trusts, and consent to limitations on the right to vote.

WITH RESPECT TO TRANSACTIONS CONCERNING COMMODITIES AND OPTIONS, the principal authorizes the agent to: (1) buy, sell, exchange, assign, settle, and exercise commodity futures contracts and call and put options on stocks and stock indexes traded on a regulated option exchange, and (2) establish, continue, modify, and terminate option accounts with a broker.

WITH RESPECT TO TRANSACTIONS CONCERNING BANKS AND OTHER FINANCIAL INSTITUTIONS, the principal authorizes the agent to: (1) continue, modify, and terminate an account or other banking arrangement made by or on behalf of the principal; (2) establish, modify, and terminate an account or other banking arrangement with a bank, trust company, savings and loan association, credit union, thrift company, brokerage firm, or other financial institution selected by the agent; (3) rent a safe deposit box or space in a vault; (4) contract for other services available from a financial institution as the agent considers desirable; (5) withdraw by check, order, or otherwise money or property of the principal deposited with or left in the custody of a financial institution; 6) receive bank statements, vouchers, notices, and similar documents from a financial institution and act with respect to them; (7) enter a safe deposit box or vault and withdraw or add to the contents; (8) borrow money at an interest rate agreeable to the agent and pledge as security personal property of the principal necessary in order to borrow, pay, renew, or extend the time of payment of a debt of the principal; (9) make, assign, draw, endorse, discount, guarantee, and negotiate promissory notes, checks, drafts, and other negotiable or nonnegotiable paper of the principal, or payable to the principal or the principal's order, transfer money, receive the cash or other proceeds of those transactions, accept a draft drawn by a person upon the principal, and pay it when due; (10) receive for the principal and act upon a sight draft, warehouse receipt, or other negotiable or nonnegotiable instrument; (11) apply for, receive, and use letters of credit, credit and debit cards, and traveler's checks from a financial institution and give an indemnity or other agreement in connection with letters of credit; and (12) consent to an extension of the time of payment with respect to commercial paper or a financial transaction with a financial institution.

WITH RESPECT TO OPERATING A BUSINESS, the principal authorizes the agent to: (1) operate, buy, sell, enlarge, reduce, and terminate a business interest; (2) act for a principal, subject to the terms of a partnership agreement or operating agreement, to: (a) perform a duty or discharge a liability and exercise a right, power, privilege, or option that the principal has, may have, or claims to have, under the partnership agreement or operating agreement, whether or not the principal is a partner in a partnership or member of a limited liability company; (b) enforce the terms of the partnership agreement or operating agreement by litigation or otherwise; and (c) defend, submit to arbitration, settle, or compromise litigation to which the principal is a party because of membership in a partnership or limited liability company; (3) exercise in person or by proxy, or enforce by litigation or otherwise, a right, power, privilege, or option the principal has or claims to have as the holder of a bond, share, or other instrument of similar character and defend, submit to arbitration or mediation, settle, or compromise litigation to which the principal is a party because of a bond, share, or similar instrument; (4) with respect to a business controlled by the principal: (a) continue, modify, renegotiate, extend, and terminate a contract made by or on behalf of the principal with respect to the business before execution of the power of attorney; (b) determine: (i) the location of its operation; (ii) the nature and extent of its business; (iii) the methods of manufacturing, selling, merchandising, financing, accounting, and advertising employed in its operation; (iv) the amount and types of insurance carried; and (v) the mode of engaging, compensating, and dealing with its accountants, attorneys, other agents, and employees; (c) change the name or form of organization under which the business is operated and enter into a partnership agreement or operating agreement with other persons or organize a corporation or other business entity to take over all or part of the operation of the business; and (d) demand and receive money due or claimed by the principal or on the principal's behalf in the operation of the business, and control and disburse the money in the operation of the business; (5) put additional capital into a business in which the principal has an interest; (6) join in a plan of reorganization, consolidation, or merger of the business; (7) sell or liquidate a business or part of it at the time and upon the terms the agent considers desirable; (8) establish the value of a business under a buy-out agreement to which the principal is a party; (9) prepare, sign, file, and deliver reports, compilations of information, returns, or other papers with respect to a business which are required by a governmental agency or instrumentality or which the agent considers desirable, and make related payments; and (10) pay, compromise, or contest taxes or assessments and perform any other act that the agent considers desirable to protect the principal from illegal or unnecessary taxation, fines, penalties, or assessments with respect to a business, including attempts to recover, in any manner permitted by law, money paid before or after the execution of the power of attorney.

WITH RESPECT TO INSURANCE AND ANNUITIES, the principal authorizes the agent to: (1) continue, pay the premium or assessment on, modify, rescind, release, or terminate a contract procured by or on behalf of the principal which insures or provides an annuity to either the principal or another person, whether or not the principal is a beneficiary under the contract; (2) procure new, different, and additional contracts of insurance and annuities for the principal and the principal's spouse, children, and other dependents, and select the amount, type of insurance or annuity, and mode of payment; (3) pay the premium or assessment on, modify, rescind, release, or terminate a contract of insurance or annuity procured by the agent; (4) apply for and receive a loan on the security of a contract of insurance or annuity; (5) surrender and receive the cash surrender value; (6) exercise an election; (7) change the manner of paying premiums; (8) change or convert the type of insurance or annuity, with respect to which the principal has or claims to have a power described in this section; (9) apply for and procure government aid to guarantee or pay premiums of a contract of insurance on the life of the principal; (10) collect, sell, assign, hypothecate, borrow upon, or pledge the interest of the principal in a contract of insurance or annuity; and (11) pay from proceeds or otherwise, compromise or contest, and apply for refunds in connection with, a tax or assessment levied by a taxing authority with respect to a contract of insurance or annuity or its proceeds or liability accruing by reason of the tax or assessment.

WITH RESPECT TO ESTATES, TRUSTS, AND OTHER RELATIONSHIPS IN WHICH THE PRINCIPAL IS A BENEFICIARY, the principal authorizes the agent to act for the principal in all matters that affect a trust, probate estate, guardianship, conservatorship, escrow, custodianship, or other fund from which the principal is, may become, or claims to be entitled, as a beneficiary, to a share or payment, including to: (1) accept, reject, disclaim, receive, receipt for, sell, assign, release, pledge, exchange, or consent to a reduction in or modification of a share in or payment from the fund; (2) demand or obtain by litigation or otherwise money or other thing of value to which the principal is, may become, or claims to be entitled by reason of the fund; (3) initiate, participate in, and oppose litigation to ascertain the meaning, validity, or effect of a deed, will, declaration of trust, or other instrument or transaction affecting the interest of the principal; (4) initiate, participate in, and oppose litigation to remove, substitute, or surcharge a fiduciary; (5) conserve, invest, disburse, and use anything received for an authorized purpose; and (6) transfer an interest of the principal in real property, stocks, bonds, accounts with financial institutions or securities intermediaries, insurance, annuities, and other property, to the trustee of a revocable trust created by the principal as settlor.

WITH RESPECT TO CLAIMS AND LITIGATION, the principal authorizes the agent to: (1) assert and prosecute before a court or administrative agency a claim, a claim for relief, cause of action, counterclaim, offset, or defense against an individual, organization, or government, including actions to recover property or other thing of value, to recover damages sustained by the principal, to eliminate or modify tax liability, or to seek an injunction, specific performance, or other relief; (2) bring an action to determine adverse claims, intervene in litigation, and act as amicus curiae; (3) in connection with litigation, procure an attachment, garnishment, libel, order of arrest, or other preliminary, provisional, or intermediate relief and use an available procedure to effect or satisfy a judgment, order, or decree; (4) in connection with litigation, perform any lawful act, including acceptance of tender, offer of judgment, admission of facts, submission of a controversy on an agreed statement of facts, consent to examination before trial, and binding the principal in litigation; (5) submit to arbitration or mediation, settle, and propose or accept a compromise with respect to a claim or litigation; (6) waive the issuance and service of process upon the principal, accept service of process, appear for the principal, designate persons upon whom process directed to the principal may be served, execute and file or deliver stipulations on the principal's behalf, verify pleadings, seek appellate review, procure and give surety and indemnity bonds, contract and pay for the preparation and printing of records and briefs, receive and execute and file or deliver a consent, waiver, release, confession of judgment, satisfaction of judgment, notice, agreement, or other instrument in connection with the prosecution, settlement, or defense of a claim or litigation; (7) act for the principal with respect to bankruptcy or insolvency, whether voluntary or involuntary, concerning the principal or some other person, or with respect to a reorganization, receivership, or application for the appointment of a receiver or trustee which affects an interest of the principal in property or other thing of value; and (8) pay a judgment against the principal or a settlement made in connection with litigation and receive and conserve money or other thing of value paid in settlement of or as proceeds of a claim or litigation.

WITH RESPECT TO PERSONAL AND FAMILY MAINTENANCE, the principal authorizes the agent to: (1) perform the acts necessary to maintain the customary standard of living of the principal, the principal's spouse, children, and other individuals customarily or legally entitled to be supported by the principal, including providing living quarters by purchase, lease, or other contract, or paying the operating costs, including interest, amortization payments, repairs, and taxes, on premises owned by the principal and occupied by those individuals; (2) provide for the individuals described under (1) normal domestic help, usual vacations and travel expenses, and funds for shelter, clothing, food, appropriate education, and other current living costs; (3) pay on behalf of the individuals described under (1) expenses for necessary medical, dental, and surgical care, hospitalization, and custodial care; (4) act as the principal's personal representative pursuant to sections 1171 through 1179 of the Social Security Act, 42 U.S.C. Section 1320d (sections 262 and 264 of Public Law 104-191) [or successor provisions] and applicable regulations, in making decisions related to the past, present, or future payment for the provision of health care consented to by the principal or anyone authorized under the law of this state to consent to health care on behalf of the principal; (5) continue any provision made by the principal, for the individuals described under (1), for automobiles or other means of transportation, including registering, licensing, insuring, and replacing them; (6) maintain or open charge accounts for the convenience of the individuals described under (1) and open new accounts the agent considers desirable to accomplish a lawful purpose; and (7) continue payments incidental to the membership or affiliation of the principal in a church, club, society, order, or other organization or to continue contributions to those organizations.

WITH RESPECT TO BENEFITS FROM SOCIAL SECURITY, MEDICARE, MEDICAID, OTHER GOVERNMENTAL PROGRAMS, OR CIVIL OR MILITARY SERVICE, the principal authorizes the agent to: (1) execute vouchers in the name of the principal for allowances and reimbursements payable by the United States or a foreign government or by a state or subdivision of a state to the principal, including allowances and reimbursements for transportation of the individuals described in Section 212(1), and for shipment of their household effects; (2) take possession and order the removal and shipment of property of the principal from a post, warehouse, depot, dock, or other place of storage or safekeeping, either governmental or private, and execute and deliver a release, voucher, receipt, bill of lading, shipping ticket, certificate, or other instrument for that purpose; (3) prepare, file, and prosecute a claim of the principal to a benefit or assistance, financial or otherwise, to which the principal claims to be entitled under a statute or governmental regulation; (4) prosecute, defend, submit to arbitration or mediation, settle, and propose or accept a compromise with respect to any benefit or assistance the principal may be entitled to receive under a statute or governmental regulation; and (5) receive the financial proceeds of a claim of the type described in paragraph (3) and conserve, invest, disburse, or use anything so received for a lawful purpose.

WITH RESPECT TO RETIREMENT PLANS, the principal authorizes the agent to: (1) select a payment option under a retirement plan in which the principal participates, including a plan for a self-employed individual; (2) make voluntary contributions to those plans; (3) exercise the investment powers available under a self-directed retirement plan; (4) make a rollover of benefits into another retirement plan; (5) if authorized by the plan, borrow from, sell assets to, purchase assets from, or request distributions from the plan; and (6) waive the right of the principal to be a beneficiary of a joint or survivor annuity if the principal is a spouse who is not employed.

WITH RESPECT TO TAX MATTERS, the principal authorizes the agent to: (1) prepare, sign, and file federal, state, local, and foreign income, gift, payroll, Federal Insurance Contributions Act, and other tax returns, claims for refunds, requests for extension of time, petitions regarding tax matters, and any other tax-related documents, including receipts, offers, waivers, consents, including consents and agreements under the Internal Revenue Code, 26 U.S.C. Section 2032A [or successor provisions], closing agreements, and any power of attorney required by the Internal Revenue Service or other taxing authority with respect to a tax year upon which the statute of limitations has not run and the following 25 tax years; (2) pay taxes due, collect refunds, post bonds, receive confidential information, and contest deficiencies determined by the Internal Revenue Service or other taxing authority; (3) exercise any election available to the principal under federal, state, local, or foreign tax law; and (4) act for the principal in all tax matters for all periods before the Internal Revenue Service, and any other taxing authority.

WITH RESPECT TO GIFTS, the principal authorizes the agent to make gifts of any of the principal's property to individuals or organizations within the limits of the annual exclusion under the Internal Revenue Code, 26 U.S.C. Section 2503(b) [or successor provisions], as the agent determines to be in the principal's best interest based on all relevant factors, including: (1) the value and nature of the principal's property; (2) the principal's foreseeable obligations and need for maintenance; 3) minimization of income, estate, inheritance, generation-skipping transfer or gift taxes; (4) eligibility for public benefits or assistance under a statute or governmental regulation; and (5) the principal's personal history of making or joining in making gifts.

WITH RESPECT TO DELEGATION OF AGENCY AUTHORITY, the principal authorizes the agent to delegate revocably by writing or other record to one or more persons a power granted to the agent by the principal.

If the attorney-in-fact named above is unable or unwilling to serve, I appoint
_____ (printed name),
of (address) _____ ,
to be my attorney-in-fact for all purposes hereunder.

To induce any third party to rely upon this power of attorney, I agree that any third party receiving a signed copy or facsimile of this power of attorney may rely upon such copy, and that revocation or termination of this power of attorney shall be ineffective as to such third party until actual notice or knowledge of such revocation or termination shall have been received by such third party. I, for myself and for my heirs, executors, legal representatives and assigns, agree to indemnify and hold harmless any such third party from any and all claims that may arise against such third party by reason of such third party having relied on the provisions of this power of attorney. **THIS POWER OF ATTORNEY SHALL NOT BE EFFECTIVE IN THE EVENT OF MY FUTURE DISABILITY OR INCAPACITY.** This power of attorney may be revoked by me at any time and is automatically revoked upon my death. My attorney-in-fact shall no be compensated for his or her services nor shall my attorney-in-fact be liable to me, my estate, heirs, successors, or assigns for acting or refraining from acting under this document, except for willful misconduct or gross negligence.

Dated: _____

Signature and Declaration of Principal

I, _____ (printed name), the principal, sign my name to this power of attorney this _____day of _____ and, being first duly sworn, do declare to the undersigned authority that I sign and execute this instrument as my power of attorney and that I sign it willingly, or willingly direct another to sign for me, that I execute it as my free and voluntary act for the purposes expressed in the power of attorney and that I am eighteen years of age or older, of sound mind and under no constraint or undue influence.

_____
Signature of Principal

Witness Attestation

I, _____ (printed name), the first witness, and I, _____ (printed name), the second witness, sign my name to the foregoing power of attorney being first duly sworn and do declare to the undersigned authority that the principal signs and executes this instrument as his/her power of attorney and that he\she signs it willingly, or willingly directs another to sign for him/her, and that I, in the presence and hearing of the principal, sign this power of attorney as witness to the principal's signing and that to the best of my knowledge the principal is eighteen years of age or older, of sound mind and under no constraint or undue influence.

_____
Signature of First Witness

_____
Signature of Second Witness

Notary Acknowledgment

State of _____

County of _____

Subscribed, sworn to and acknowledged before me by _____,

the Principal, and subscribed and sworn to before me by _____,

and _____, the witnesses, this _____ day of

_____ .

_____

Notary Signature

Notary Public, In and for the County of _____

State of _____

My commission expires: _____ Seal

Acknowledgment and Acceptance of Appointment as Attorney-in-Fact

I, _____, (printed name) have read
the attached power of attorney and am the person identified as the attorney-in-fact for the
principal. I hereby acknowledge that I accept my appointment as attorney-in-fact and that when
I act as agent I shall exercise the powers for the benefit of the principal; I shall keep the assets
of the principal separate from my assets; I shall exercise reasonable caution and prudence;
and I shall keep a full and accurate record of all actions, receipts and disbursements on behalf
of the principal.

_____   _____

Signature of Attorney-in-Fact   Date

Acknowledgment and Acceptance of Appointment as Successor Attorney-in-Fact

I, _____, (printed name) have read the
attached power of attorney and am the person identified as the successor attorney-in-fact for
the principal. I hereby acknowledge that I accept my appointment as successor attorney-in-fact
and that, in the absence of a specific provision to the contrary in the power of attorney, when I
act as agent I shall exercise the powers for the benefit of the principal; I shall keep the assets of
the principal separate from my assets; I shall exercise reasonable caution and prudence; and
I shall keep a full and accurate record of all actions, receipts and disbursements on behalf of
the principal.

_____   _____

Signature of Successor Attorney-in-Fact   Date

Chapter 4

Limited Powers of Attorney

This type of document provides for a *limited* grant of authority to another person. It should be used in those situations when you need to authorize another person to act for you in a specific transaction or transactions. The type of acts that you authorize the other person to perform should be spelled out in detail to avoid confusion (for example, to sign any necessary forms to open a bank account). If desired, the dates when the power of attorney will be valid may also be specified. The authority that you grant with a limited power of attorney may be revoked by you at any time and is automatically revoked if you die or become incapacitated or incompetent. This document does not authorize the appointed attorney-in-fact to make any decisions relating to medical or health care. If there is anything about these forms that you do not understand, you should ask a lawyer to explain it to you. These powers of attorney contain an important notice prior to the form itself.

When Should You Use a Limited Power of Attorney?

A limited power of attorney allows you to select a specific power that you wish for your agent (attorney-in-fact) to have. This type of power of attorney can be used to authorize someone else to sign certain documents if you can not be present when the signatures are necessary. They can be used to authorize someone to handle any of the following possible matters:

Real estate transactions; goods and services transactions; stock, bond, share and commodity transactions; banking transactions; business operating transactions; insurance transactions; estate transactions; legal claims and litigation; personal relationships and affairs; benefits from military service; records, reports and statements; retirement benefit transactions; making gifts to a spouse, children, parents and other descendants; tax matters; and certain child care decisions, such as consent to emergency medical care.

A limited power of attorney is most useful if you wish to grant your agent only some, but not all of the possible powers available to an agent or if you wish to limit the time period that the powers that you grant are authorized to be used. If you wish to grant full and complete authority to your agent, you may wish to use an *unlimited power of attorney* instead. An unlimited power of attorney provides that your agent will have total authority to act on your behalf for all financial and/or business matters (but not for health care decisions). Unlimited powers of attorney are explained in Chapter 3. If you wish to provide a range of powers to your agent, you may wish to use a *general power of attorney* instead of a limited power of attorney. General powers of attorney are detailed in Chapter 2. A limited power of attorney is not valid if you become disabled or incapacitated. You must use a *'durable' financial power of attorney* for that purpose. Durable financial powers of attorney are outlined in Chapters 5 and 6. In addition, a limited power of attorney also can *not* be used for health care decisions. You must use a *durable health care power of attorney* for that purpose. See Chapter 7.

Included in this chapter are 3 separate limited power of attorney forms for your use. The first document is a general limited power of attorney form that can be used to describe the particular power or time period that you would like to authorize someone to act on your behalf. The second type of limited power of attorney is designed to be used specifically in real estate transactions to authorize another person to act on your behalf; for example, during a real estate closing. The final type of limited power of attorney that is presented is for use in child care situations to authorize another to act on a parent's behalf with respect to a minor child.

☼ Toolkit Tip!

Limited powers of attorney can not be used to authorize another person to make health care decisions on your behalf. You must use a durable health care power of attorney to achieve that result.

Instructions for Limited Power of Attorney

To complete a general limited power of attorney, please follow the instructions that follow. To use the form on the enclosed CD, simply fill in the required information in either the text or PDF versions of this form.

① Name and address of person granting power (principal)
② Name and address of person granted power (attorney-in-fact)
③ List specific acts that you want your attorney-in-fact to perform (be as detailed as possible)
④ Name and address of successor to person originally granted power (successor attorney-in-fact) (optional-if not used, write N/A in this space.)
⑤ Date
⑥ Printed name of principal, date of signing of power of attorney, and signature of principal (signed in front of notary public)
⑦ Printed names and signatures of witnesses (signed in front of notary public)
⑧ Notary acknowledgement should be completed by the notary public
⑨ Printed name, date, and signature of attorney-in-fact (need not be witnessed or notarized)
⑩ Printed name, date, and signature of successor attorney-in-fact (optional-if not used, write N/A in this space) (need not be witnessed or notarized)

Limited Power of Attorney

Notice: This is an important document. Before signing this document, you should know these important facts. By signing this document, you are not giving up any powers or rights to control your finances and property yourself. In addition to your own powers and rights, you may be giving another person, your attorney-in-fact, broad powers to handle your finances and property. This limited power of attorney may give the person whom you designate (your "attorney-in-fact") broad powers to handle your finances and property, which may include powers to encumber, sell or otherwise dispose of any real or personal property without advance notice to you or approval by you. THE POWERS GRANTED WILL NOT EXIST AFTER YOU BECOME DISABLED, OR INCAPACITATED. This document does not authorize anyone to make medical or other health care decisions for you. If you own complex or special assets such as a business, or if there is anything about this form that you do not understand, you should ask a lawyer to explain this form to you before you sign it. If you wish to change your limited power of attorney, you must complete a new document and revoke this one. You may revoke this document at any time by destroying it, by directing another person to destroy it in your presence or by signing a written and dated statement expressing your intent to revoke this document. If you revoke this document, you should notify your attorney-in-fact and any other person to whom you have given a copy of the form. You also should notify all parties having custody of your assets. These parties have no responsibility to you unless you actually notify them of the revocation. If your attorney-in-fact is your spouse and your marriage is annulled, or you are divorced after signing this document, this document is invalid. Since some 3rd parties or some transactions may not permit use of this document, it is advisable to check in advance, if possible, for any special requirements that may be imposed. You should sign this form only if the attorney-in-fact that you appoint is reliable, trustworthy and competent to manage your affairs. This form must be signed by the Principal (the person appointing the attorney-in-fact), witnessed by two persons other than the notary public, and acknowledged by a notary public.

I, _____ (printed name),
of (address)_____,
as principal, do grant a limited and specific power of attorney to, and do hereby appoint
_____ (printed name),
of (address)_____,
to act as my attorney-in-fact and to have the full power and authority to perform only the following acts on my behalf to the same extent that I could do so personally if I were personally present, with respect to the following matter to the extent that I am permitted by law to act through an agent: (list specific acts and/or restrictions)

If the attorney-in-fact named above is unable or unwilling to serve, I appoint
_____ (printed name),
of (address) _____ ,
to be my attorney-in-fact for all purposes hereunder.

To induce any third party to rely upon this power of attorney, I agree that any third party receiving a signed copy or facsimile of this power of attorney may rely upon such copy, and that revocation or termination of this power of attorney shall be ineffective as to such third party until actual notice or knowledge of such revocation or termination shall have been received by such third party. I, for myself and for my heirs, executors, legal representatives and assigns, agree to indemnify and hold harmless any such third party from any and all claims that may arise against such third party by reason of such third party having relied on the provisions of this power of attorney.

This power of attorney shall not be effective in the event of my future disability or incapacity. This limited grant of authority does not authorize my attorney-in-fact to make any decisions regarding my medical or health care. This power of attorney may be revoked by me at any time and is automatically revoked upon my death. My attorney-in-fact shall not be compensated for his or her services nor shall my attorney-in-fact be liable to me, my estate, heirs, successors, or assigns for acting or refraining from acting under this document, except for willful misconduct or gross negligence. My attorney-in-fact accepts this appointment and agrees to act in my best interest as he or she considers advisable. This grant of authority shall include the power and authority to perform any incidental acts which may be reasonably required in order to perform the specific acts stated above.

Dated: _____

Signature and Declaration of Principal

I, _____ (printed name), the principal, sign my name to this power of attorney this _____ day of _____ and, being first duly sworn, do declare to the undersigned authority that I sign and execute this instrument as my power of attorney and that I sign it willingly, or willingly direct another to sign for me, that I execute it as my free and voluntary act for the purposes expressed in the power of attorney and that I am eighteen years of age or older, of sound mind and under no constraint or undue influence.

_____
Signature of Principal

Witness Attestation

I, _____ (printed name), the first witness, and I, _____ (printed name), the second witness, sign my name to the foregoing power of attorney being first duly sworn and do declare to the undersigned authority that the principal signs and executes this instrument as his/her power of attorney and that he\she signs it willingly, or willingly directs another to sign for him/her, and that I, in the presence and hearing of the principal, sign this power of attorney as witness to the principal's signing and that to the best of my knowledge the principal is eighteen years of age or older, of sound mind and under no constraint or undue influence.

_____
Signature of First Witness

_____
Signature of Second Witness

Notary Acknowledgment

State of _____
County of _____
Subscribed, sworn to and acknowledged before me by _____,
the Principal, and subscribed and sworn to before me by _____, and
_____, the witnesses, this _____
day of _____ .

_____
Notary Signature
Notary Public,
In and for the County of _____
State of _____
My commission expires: _____ Seal

Acknowledgment and Acceptance of Appointment as Attorney-in-Fact

I, _____, (printed name)
have read the attached power of attorney and am the person identified as the attorney-in-fact
for the principal. I hereby acknowledge that I accept my appointment as attorney-in-fact and
that when I act as agent I shall exercise the powers for the benefit of the principal; I shall keep
the assets of the principal separate from my assets; I shall exercise reasonable caution and
prudence; and I shall keep a full and accurate record of all actions, receipts and disbursements
on behalf of the principal.

_____   _____
Signature of Attorney-in-Fact   Date

Acknowledgment and Acceptance of Appointment as Successor Attorney-in-Fact

I, _____, (printed name)
have read the attached power of attorney and am the person identified as the successor
attorney-in-fact for the principal. I hereby acknowledge that I accept my appointment as
successor attorney-in-fact and that, in the absence of a specific provision to the contrary in the
power of attorney, when I act as agent I shall exercise the powers for the benefit of the principal;
I shall keep the assets of the principal separate from my assets; I shall exercise reasonable
caution and prudence; and I shall keep a full and accurate record of all actions, receipts and
disbursements on behalf of the principal.

_____   _____
Signature of Successor Attorney-in-Fact   Date

Instructions for Limited Power of Attorney for Real Estate

① Name and address of person granting power (principal)

② Name and address of person granted power (attorney-in-fact)

③ List specific acts (relating to real estate only) that you want your attorney-in fact to perform. (Be as detailed as possible. You should include an exact legal description of the real estate covered by the power of attorney. You should also include an exact date or dates for the power of attorney to be effective, if desired. An example might be: "Authority to sign any and all documents, on behalf of the principal, relating to the real estate closing to be held on June 4, 2008, for the following described real estate: Parcel 123 of the Smith Subdivision, as described on Warranty Deed recorded on Page 234 of Book 56 in Jones County, Missouri").

④ Name and address of successor to person originally granted power (successor attorney-in-fact) (optional-if not used, write N/A in this space.)

⑤ Date

⑥ Printed name of principal, date of signing of power of attorney, and signature of principal (signed in front of notary public)

⑦ Printed names and signatures of witnesses (signed in front of notary public)

⑧ Notary acknowledgement should be completed by the notary public

⑨ Printed name, date, and signature of attorney-in-fact (need not be witnessed or notarized)

⑩ Printed name, date, and signature of successor attorney-in-fact (optional-if not used, write N/A in this space) (need not be witnessed or notarized)

Limited Power of Attorney for Real Estate

Notice: This is an important document. Before signing this document, you should know these important facts. By signing this document, you are not giving up any powers or rights to control your finances and property yourself. In addition to your own powers and rights, you may be giving another person, your attorney-in-fact, broad powers to handle your finances and property. This limited power of attorney may give the person whom you designate (your "attorney-in-fact") broad powers to handle your finances and property, which may include powers to encumber, sell or otherwise dispose of any real or personal property without advance notice to you or approval by you. THE POWERS GRANTED WILL NOT EXIST AFTER YOU BECOME DISABLED, OR INCAPACITATED. This document does not authorize anyone to make medical or other health care decisions for you. If you own complex or special assets such as a business, or if there is anything about this form that you do not understand, you should ask a lawyer to explain this form to you before you sign it. If you wish to change your limited power of attorney, you must complete a new document and revoke this one. You may revoke this document at any time by destroying it, by directing another person to destroy it in your presence or by signing a written and dated statement expressing your intent to revoke this document. If you revoke this document, you should notify your attorney-in-fact and any other person to whom you have given a copy of the form. You also should notify all parties having custody of your assets. These parties have no responsibility to you unless you actually notify them of the revocation. If your attorney-in-fact is your spouse and your marriage is annulled, or you are divorced after signing this document, this document is invalid. Since some 3rd parties or some transactions may not permit use of this document, it is advisable to check in advance, if possible, for any special requirements that may be imposed. You should sign this form only if the attorney-in-fact that you appoint is reliable, trustworthy and competent to manage your affairs. This form must be signed by the Principal (the person appointing the attorney-in-fact), witnessed by two persons other than the notary public, and acknowledged by a notary public.

① I, _____ (printed name),
of (address)_____,
as principal, do grant a limited and specific power of attorney to, and do hereby appoint

②_____ (printed name),
of (address)_____,
to act as my attorney-in-fact and to have the full power and authority to perform only the following acts on my behalf to the same extent that I could do so personally if I were personally present, with respect to the following real estate matter to the extent that I am permitted by law to act through an agent: (list specific acts) ③

If the attorney-in-fact named above is unable or unwilling to serve, I appoint ④_____ (printed name), of (address) _____
_____ , to be my attorney-in-fact for all purposes hereunder.

To induce any third party to rely upon this power of attorney, I agree that any third party receiving a signed copy or facsimile of this power of attorney may rely upon such copy, and that revocation or termination of this power of attorney shall be ineffective as to such third party until actual notice or knowledge of such revocation or termination shall have been received by such third party. I, for myself and for my heirs, executors, legal representatives and assigns, agree to indemnify and hold harmless any such third party from any and all claims that may arise against such third party by reason of such third party having relied on the provisions of this power of attorney.

This power of attorney shall not be effective in the event of my future disability or incapacity. This limited grant of authority does not authorize my attorney-in-fact to make any decisions regarding my medical or health care. This power of attorney may be revoked by me at any time and is automatically revoked upon my death. My attorney-in-fact shall not be compensated for his or her services nor shall my attorney-in-fact be liable to me, my estate, heirs, successors, or assigns for acting or refraining from acting under this document, except for willful misconduct or gross negligence. My attorney-in-fact accepts this appointment and agrees to act in my best interest as he or she considers advisable. This grant of authority shall include the power and authority to perform any incidental acts which may be reasonably required in order to perform the specific acts stated above.

⑤
Dated: _____

Signature and Declaration of Principal

⑥

I, _____ (printed name), the principal, sign my name to this power of attorney this _____ day of _____ and, being first duly sworn, do declare to the undersigned authority that I sign and execute this instrument as my power of attorney and that I sign it willingly, or willingly direct another to sign for me, that I execute it as my free and voluntary act for the purposes expressed in the power of attorney and that I am eighteen years of age or older, of sound mind and under no constraint or undue influence.

_____
Signature of Principal

Witness Attestation

⑦

I, _____ (printed name), the first witness, and I, _____ (printed name), the second witness, sign my name to the foregoing power of attorney being first duly sworn and do declare to the undersigned authority that the principal signs and executes this instrument as his/her power of attorney and that he\she signs it willingly, or willingly directs another to sign for him/her, and that I, in the presence and hearing of the principal, sign this power of attorney as witness to the principal's signing and that to the best of my knowledge the principal is eighteen years of age or older, of sound mind and under no constraint or undue influence.

_____
Signature of First Witness

_____
Signature of Second Witness

Notary Acknowledgment

⑧

State of _____ County of _____
Subscribed, sworn to and acknowledged before me by _____
_____ principal, and subscribed and sworn to before me by ____
_____, and _____,
the witnesses, this _____ day of _____ .

_____
Notary Public Signature
In and for the County of _____ State of _____
My commission expires: _____ Seal

Acknowledgment and Acceptance of Appointment as Attorney-in-Fact

⑨

I, _____, (printed name) have read the attached power of attorney and am the person identified as the attorney-in-fact for the principal. I hereby acknowledge that I accept my appointment as attorney-in-fact and that when I act as agent I shall exercise the powers for the benefit of the principal; I shall keep the assets of the principal separate from my assets; I shall exercise reasonable caution and prudence; and I shall keep a full and accurate record of all actions, receipts and disbursements on behalf of the principal.

_____   _____
Signature of Attorney-in-Fact   Date

Acknowledgment and Acceptance of Appointment as Successor Attorney-in-Fact

⑩

I, _____, (printed name) have read the attached power of attorney and am the person identified as the successor attorney-in-fact for the principal. I hereby acknowledge that I accept my appointment as successor attorney-in-fact and that, in the absence of a specific provision to the contrary in the power of attorney, when I act as agent I shall exercise the powers for the benefit of the principal; I shall keep the assets of the principal separate from my assets; I shall exercise reasonable caution and prudence; and I shall keep a full and accurate record of all actions, receipts and disbursements on behalf of the principal.

_____   _____
Signature of Successor Attorney-in-Fact   Date

Instructions for Limited Power of Attorney for Child Care

1. Name and address of person granting power (principal)
2. Name, age, and address of the child over whom you wish the attorney-in-fact to have authority
3. Name and address of person granted the power (attorney-in-fact or agent)
4. Initial the specific acts that you want your attorney-in-fact to perform. Note: only three child care actions are permitted using this type of power of attorney: 1) the authority to consent to emergency medical care for the child and/or 2) the authority to enroll the child in a school or child care facility and/or 3) the authority to exercise the same parental rights that you may exercise. You may initial any or all of these powers. If you wish your attorney-in-fact to have all of these powers, you should initial all three of the spaces. Please also note that if you have more than one child that you wish to grant someone else authority to make such decisions for, you must prepare a separate limited power of attorney for child care for each child.
5. Name and address of successor to person originally granted power (successor attorney-in-fact) (optional-if not used, write N/A in this space.)
6. Date
7. Printed name of principal, date of signing of power of attorney, and signature of principal (signed in front of notary public)
8. Printed names and signatures of witnesses (signed in front of notary public)
9. Notary acknowledgement should be completed by the notary public
10. Printed name, date, and signature of attorney-in-fact (need not be witnessed or notarized)
11. Printed name, date, and signature of successor attorney-in-fact (optional-if not used, write N/A in this space) (need not be witnessed or notarized)

Limited Power of Attorney for Child Care

Notice: This is an important document. Before signing this document, you should know these important facts. By signing this document, you are not giving up any powers or rights to provide child care consent or make child care decisions yourself. In addition to your own powers and rights, you may be giving another person, your attorney-in-fact, powers to provide consent to emergency medical care for a child and/or authority to enroll a child in a school or child care facility and/or authority to exercise additional parental rights. THE POWERS GRANTED WILL NOT EXIST AFTER YOU BECOME DISABLED, OR INCAPACITATED. If there is anything about this form that you do not understand, you should ask a lawyer to explain this form to you before you sign it. If you wish to change your limited power of attorney, you must complete a new document and revoke this one. You may revoke this document at any time by destroying it, by directing another person to destroy it in your presence or by signing a written and dated statement expressing your intent to revoke this document. If you revoke this document, you should notify your attorney-in-fact and any other person to whom you have given a copy of the form. These parties have no responsibility to you unless you actually notify them of the revocation. Since some 3rd parties or some transactions may not permit use of this document, it is advisable to check in advance, if possible, for any special requirements that may be imposed. You should sign this form only if the attorney-in-fact that you appoint is reliable, trustworthy and competent to manage make the child care decisions that you are authorizing them to make. This form must be signed by the Principal (the person appointing the attorney-in-fact), witnessed by two persons other than the notary public, and acknowledged by a notary public.

① I, _____ (printed name),
of (address)_____,
as principal, and as parent of the following child,
② _____(printed name of child),
_____ (age of child), of (address)_____
_____

do grant a limited and specific power of attorney to, and do hereby appoint
③_____ (printed name),
of (address)_____,

to act as my attorney-in-fact and to have the full power and authority to perform only the following acts *that bear my initials,* on my behalf to the same extent that I could do so personally if I were personally present, with respect to the following matter to the extent that I am permitted by law to act through an agent:

④

_____ to consent to any necessary medical treatment for the above child, including any emergency medical treatment, surgery, medication, hospitalization, or any other necessary medical treatment; that may be required;

_____ to enroll and/or withdraw the above child from any school or child care facility;

_____ to exercise the same parental rights that I may personally exercise regarding the care, custody and control of the above child;

If the attorney-in-fact named above is unable or unwilling to serve, I appoint

⑤_____ (printed name),

of (address) _____ ,

to be my attorney-in-fact for all purposes hereunder.

To induce any third party to rely upon this power of attorney, I agree that any third party receiving a signed copy or facsimile of this power of attorney may rely upon such copy, and that revocation or termination of this power of attorney shall be ineffective as to such third party until actual notice or knowledge of such revocation or termination shall have been received by such third party. I, for myself and for my heirs, executors, legal representatives and assigns, agree to indemnify and hold harmless any such third party from any and all claims that may arise against such third party by reason of such third party having relied on the provisions of this power of attorney. This power of attorney shall not be effective in the event of my future disability or incapacity. This power of attorney may be revoked by me at any time and is automatically revoked upon my death. My attorney-in-fact shall not be compensated for his or her services, nor shall my attorney-in-fact be liable to me, my estate, heirs, successors, or assigns for acting or refraining from acting under this document, except for willful misconduct or gross negligence. My attorney-in-fact accepts this appointment and agrees to act in my and my child's best interest as he or she considers advisable. This grant of authority shall include the power and authority to perform any incidental acts which may be reasonably required in order to perform the specific acts stated above.

⑥
Dated: _____

Signature and Declaration of Principal

⑦
I, _____ (printed name),
the principal, sign my name to this power of attorney this _____day of
_____ and, being first duly sworn, do declare to the undersigned
authority that I sign and execute this instrument as my power of attorney and
that I sign it willingly, or willingly direct another to sign for me, that I execute
it as my free and voluntary act for the purposes expressed in the power of
attorney and that I am eighteen years of age or older, of sound mind and
under no constraint or undue influence.

_____
Signature of Principal

Witness Attestation

⑧
I, _____ (printed name),
the first witness, and I, _____ (printed name),
the second witness, sign my name to the foregoing power of attorney being
first duly sworn and do declare to the undersigned authority that the principal
signs and executes this instrument as his/her power of attorney and that he\
she signs it willingly, or willingly directs another to sign for him/her, and that
I, in the presence and hearing of the principal, sign this power of attorney
as witness to the principal's signing and that to the best of my knowledge
the principal is eighteen years of age or older, of sound mind and under no
constraint or undue influence.

_____
Signature of First Witness

_____
Signature of Second Witness

Notary Acknowledgment

⑨

State of _____ County of _____

Subscribed, sworn to and acknowledged before me by _____,

the Principal, and subscribed and sworn to before me by _____

_____, and _____, the

witnesses, this _____ day of _____ .

_____

Notary Public Signature

In and for the County of _____ State of _____

My commission expires: _____Seal

Acknowledgment and Acceptance of Appointment as Attorney-in-Fact

⑩

I, _____, (printed
name) have read the attached power of attorney and am the person identified
as the attorney-in-fact for the principal. I hereby acknowledge that I accept my
appointment as attorney-in-fact and that when I act as agent I shall exercise the
powers for the benefit of the principal; I shall keep the assets of the principal
separate from my assets; I shall exercise reasonable caution and prudence; and
I shall keep a full and accurate record of all actions, receipts and disbursements
on behalf of the principal.

_____   _____

Signature of Attorney-in-Fact   Date

Acknowledgment and Acceptance of Appointment as Successor Attorney-in-Fact

⑪

I, _____, (printed name)
have read the attached power of attorney and am the person identified as the
successor attorney-in-fact for the principal. I hereby acknowledge that I accept
my appointment as successor attorney-in-fact and that, in the absence of a
specific provision to the contrary in the power of attorney, when I act as agent I
shall exercise the powers for the benefit of the principal; I shall keep the assets
of the principal separate from my assets; I shall exercise reasonable caution
and prudence; and I shall keep a full and accurate record of all actions, receipts
and disbursements on behalf of the principal.

_____   _____

Signature of Successor Attorney-in-Fact   Date

Chapter 5

Durable Powers of Attorney for Financial Affairs

A durable power of attorney for financial affairs is a specific type of power of attorney that gives another person the authority to sign legal papers, transact business, buy or sell property, etc., and is only effective in one of two scenarios: (1) it may be written so that it *remains* in effect *even* if a person becomes disabled or incompetent, or (2) one that *only* goes into effect *if and when* a person becomes disabled or incompetent (this is technically known as a "springing" power of attorney that "springs" into effect if a certain event takes place; in this case, one's incapacity). A *durable unlimited power of attorney for financial affairs* provides that your agent will have total authority to act on your behalf *only* for any and all financial and/or business matters. A *durable general power of attorney for financial affairs* allows you to choose which specific powers you wish your appointed agent to exercise. A durable power of attorney for financial affairs does not confer authority on another person to make health care decisions on someone else's behalf. Only a *durable health care power of attorney* can do that. Please see Chapter 7 for information regarding durable health care powers of attorney.

There are four separate durable power of attorney for financial affairs forms detailed in this chapter: (1) one is a durable unlimited power of attorney for financial affairs that remains in effect if you become incapacitated; (2) one is a durable unlimited power of attorney for financial affairs that only goes

ᐡ Toolkit Tip!

There are two types of durable financial powers of attorney: 1) one that goes into effect immediately and remains in effect upon the makers incapacitation, and 2) one that *only* goes into effect upon the maker's incapacitation.

into in effect if you become incapacitated; (3) one is a durable general power of attorney for financial affairs that remains in effect if you become incapacitated; and (4) one is a durable general power of attorney for financial affairs that only goes into in effect if you become incapacitated. In addition, there are also state-specific durable powers of attorney for certain states that are explained further in Chapter 6 and are also contained on the enclosed CD.

When Should You Use a Durable Power of Attorney for Financial Affairs?

A *durable power of attorney for financial affairs* allows you to appoint an agent (who is then referred to as an 'attorney-in-fact') to handle your financial affairs during a period that you are unable to handle them yourself. With this form, you are giving another person the right to manage your financial and business matters on your behalf. They are given the power to act as you could, if you were able. If there is someone available who can be trusted implicitly to act on your behalf, the appointment of such a person can eliminate many problems that may arise if you are unable to handle your own affairs.

The appointment of an agent for your financial affairs allows for the paying of bills, writing of checks, etc. while you are unable to do so yourself. With the forms in this book, you may be granting the appointed agent very broad powers to handle your affairs. Using a durable *unlimited* power of attorney for financial affairs, you will give your agent the maximum power under law to perform any and all acts relating to any and all of your financial and/or business affairs. Your attorney-in-fact (agent) is granted full power to act on your behalf in the same manner as if you were personally present. Using a durable *general* power of attorney for financial affairs, you will only grant your agent (attorney-in-fact) those specific powers that you choose on the form itself.

The person you appoint (remember: attorney-in-fact) will (with an unlimited version) and may (with a general version) have the authority to handle real estate transactions; goods and services transactions; stock, bond, share and commodity transactions;

> ## ⊘ Definition:
> ## Attorney-in-Fact:
> The designation given to the person that you appoint in your financial power of attorney. This does *not* mean that the person has to be an attorney.

banking transactions; business operating transactions; insurance transactions; estate transactions; legal claims and litigation; personal relationships and affairs; benefits from military service; records, reports and statements; retirement benefit transactions; making gifts to a spouse, children, parents and other descendants (if any); and tax matters.

> ### ⚡ Warning!
>
> If you decide to use the durable un-limited power of attorney that goes into effect immediately, remember that as soon as you sign this form, your appointed attorney-in-fact will share with you total control over your finances.

You should appoint someone whom you trust completely. This is not a power that should be conferred lightly. Very serious thought should be given to both who you appoint as your attorney-in-fact (the person you authorize to act on your behalf) and to any specific directions that you may want to give to that person regarding financial decisions. You do not have to appoint anyone to handle your financial affairs, but it is often very useful to do so.

By accepting their appointment, your agent agrees to act in your best interest as he or she considers advisable. A durable power of attorney for financial matters may be revoked by you at any time and is automatically revoked on your death.

If you wish to limit the powers that you give to your agent, you may wish to use a durable *general power of attorney* instead of a durable unlimited power of attorney. However, because of its limited scope, this type of power of attorney is often not as practical in situations when a *durable* power of attorney is generally used, that is, when you are incapacitated and unable to handle any of your own affairs.

The first durable unlimited power of attorney for financial affairs that is provided immediately appoints your chosen attorney-in-fact and provides that such appointment and powers will remain in effect *even if* you become incapacitated. The second durable unlimited power of attorney for financial affairs that is provided will become effective *only* upon your incapacitation, as certified by your primary physician or, if your primary physician is not available, by any other attending physician. Neither of these durable unlimited powers of attorney grant any power or authority to your designated attorney-in-fact regarding health care decisions. Only the *durable health care power of attorney* can confer those powers (explained in Chapter 7). You may, of course, choose to select the very same person to act as both your health care representative and your agent for financial affairs.

The same holds true for the two durable general powers of attorney that are provided: the first one immediately appoints your chosen attorney-in-fact and provides that such appointment and powers remain in effect even if you later become incapacitated. The second form provides that your attorney-in-fact shall only have powers if and when you later become incapacitated, as certified by your primary physician or, if your primary physician is not available, by any other attending physician. Again, please note that neither of these durable general powers of attorney grant any power or authority to your designated attorney-in-fact regarding health care decisions. Only the *durable health care power of attorney* can confer those powers (explained in Chapter 7).

At the beginning of each of the documents are notices regarding the use of a durable power of attorney. They clearly explain the importance of caution in the use of this form and are applicable to all states. Please read each carefully to decide which of these forms are appropriate for your situation.

Please note that the forms in the book provide a release for your attorney-in-fact to receive your medical records under the federal HIPAA regulations relating to the privacy of health care records. This does not confer any authority for your attorney-in-fact to make health care decisions on your behalf. The HIPAA release is for the purpose of allowing your attorney-in-fact to have access to your medical files for the purpose of paying or examining medical bills and charges.

State-Specific Power of Attorney Forms

Although, the forms provided in this chapter are legally-valid in all states, some states provide their own particular form for a durable power of attorney. You may choose to use a state-specific form if they are provided for your state or you may use the forms in this chapter. A '*state-specific statutory form*' is a form that has been taken directly from the laws of your particular state. The legal effects of the language in such a document have been approved by the legislature of the state. This provides an advantage in that the legal language in such a 'statutory' form is generally familiar to most financial institutions in the particular state and they know that such language has been approved.

Toolkit Tip!
If you live in the states noted below, you may wish to compare the state-specific form for your state (provided in Chapter 6 and also on the CD) with the forms in this chapter and select the one that best fits your particular situation.

☼ Toolkit Tip!

Note that the forms in this chapter are provided on the CD in both text-only and PDF formats.

This does not mean, however, that other 'non-statutory' forms are not legally valid in the state as well. All states specifically provide, in their legislation regarding powers of attorney, that power of attorney forms other than those contained in the statute itself are legally valid. All of the forms in this book meet such required legal standards.

The following states have developed state-specific statutory forms for durable powers of attorney and they are explained further in Chapter 6 and also included on the enclosed CD:

Alaska, Arkansas, California, Colorado, Connecticut, District of Columbia, Georgia, Illinois, Minnesota, Montana, Nebraska, New Hampshire, New Mexico, New York, North Carolina, Oklahoma, Pennsylvania, Rhode Island, Texas, and Wisconsin

In all other states, the legislatures have not developed specific forms for durable powers of attorney. In such situations, you may use the individual durable unlimited or general power of attorney forms provided in this chapter which have been prepared following any required legal requirements. These forms are also provided on the enclosed CD in both PDF and text formats.

Instructions for Durable Unlimited Power of Attorney for Financial Affairs - Effective Immediately

This Power of Attorney goes into effect immediately and remains in effect even upon your incapacitation.

This form should be used only in situations where you desire to authorize another person to act for you in *all* transactions immediately and you wish the power to remain in effect in the event that you become incapacitated and unable to handle your own affairs. The grant of power under this document is unlimited (except for health care decisions). This form gives the person whom you designate as your "attorney-in-fact" broad powers to handle your property during your lifetime, which may include powers to mortgage, sell, or otherwise dispose of any real or personal property without advance notice to you or approval by you. This document does not authorize anyone to make medical or other health care decisions. You must execute a health care power of attorney to accomplish this. This form does provide a HIPPA medical records privacy release that will allow the person that you appoint to access any hospital or medical bills or records on you behalf. This form also provides that you will also name a successor attorney-in-fact who will have the same powers as the original person appointed, but who will only have the powers if the original person appointed is unable to perform the necessary tasks required by the power of attorney. The authority granted by this power of attorney may be revoked by you at any time and is automatically revoked if you die. If there is anything about this form that you do not understand, you should ask a lawyer to explain it to you.

To complete this form, fill in the following:

①   Name and address of person granting power (principal)
②   Name and address of person granted power (attorney-in-fact)
③   Name and address of successor to person originally granted power (successor attorney-in-fact) (optional-if not used, write N/A in this space)
④   Printed name of principal, date of signature, and signature of principal (signed in front of notary public)
⑤   Witnesses printed names and signatures (signed in front of notary public)
⑥   Notary acknowledgement should be completed by the notary public
⑦   Printed name and signature of attorney-in-fact and successor attorney-in-fact (need not be witnessed or notarized)
⑧   Printed name and signature of attorney-in-fact and successor attorney-in-fact (optional-if not used, write N/A in this space) (need not be witnessed or notarized)

Durable Unlimited Power of Attorney For Financial Affairs (Effective Immediately)

NOTICE TO ADULT SIGNING THIS DOCUMENT: This is an important document. Before signing this document, you should know these important facts. By signing this document, you are not giving up any powers or rights to control your finances and property yourself. In addition to your own powers and rights, you are giving another person, your attorney-in-fact, broad powers to handle your finances and property, which may include powers to encumber, sell or otherwise dispose of any real or personal property without advance notice to you or approval by you. THE POWERS GRANTED UNDER THIS DOCUMENT ARE EFFECTIVE IMMEDIATELY AND WILL REMAIN IN EFFECT IF YOU BECOME DISABLED OR INCAPACITATED. This document does not authorize anyone to make medical or other health care decisions for you. If you own complex or special assets such as a business, or if there is anything about this form that you do not understand, you should ask a lawyer to explain this form to you before you sign it. If you wish to change your durable unlimited power of attorney, you must complete a new document and revoke this one. You have the right to revoke the designation of the attorney-in-fact and the right to revoke this entire document at any time and in any manner. You may revoke this document at any time by destroying it, by directing another person to destroy it in your presence or by signing a written and dated statement expressing your intent to revoke this document. If you revoke this document, you should notify your attorney-in-fact and any other person to whom you have given a copy of the form. You also should notify all parties having custody of your assets. These parties have no responsibility to you unless you actually notify them of the revocation. If your attorney-in-fact is your spouse and your marriage is annulled, or you are divorced after signing this document, this document may become invalid. Since some third parties or some transactions may not permit use of this document, it is advisable to check in advance, if possible, for any special requirements that may be imposed. You should sign this form only if the attorney-in- fact you name is reliable, trustworthy and competent to manage your affairs. Generally, you may designate any competent adult as the attorney-in-fact under this document.

① I, _____ (printed name),
of (address) _____,
as principal, ② do appoint _____ (printed name),
of (address) _____, as
my attorney-in-fact and do grant him or her unlimited power and authority to act in my name,

place and stead in any way which I myself could do, if I were personally present, with respect to all of the following matters to the extent that I am permitted by law to act through an agent:

IN GENERAL, the principal authorizes the agent to: (1) demand, receive, and obtain by litigation or otherwise, money or other thing of value to which the principal is, may become, or claims to be entitled, and conserve, invest, disburse, or use anything so received for the purposes intended; (2) contract in any manner with any person, on terms agreeable to the agent, to accomplish a purpose of a transaction, and perform, rescind, reform, release, or modify the contract or another contract made by or on behalf of the principal; (3) execute, acknowledge, seal, and deliver a deed, revocation, mortgage, security agreement, lease, notice, check, promissory note, electronic funds transfer, release, or other instrument or communication the agent considers desirable to accomplish a purpose of a transaction, including creating a schedule of the principal's property and attaching it to the power of attorney; (4) prosecute, defend, submit to arbitration or mediation, settle, and propose or accept a compromise with respect to, a claim existing in favor of or against the principal or intervene in litigation relating to the claim; (5) seek on the principal's behalf the assistance of a court to carry out an act authorized by the principal in the power of attorney; (6) engage, compensate, and discharge an attorney, accountant, expert witness, or other assistant; (7) keep appropriate records of each transaction, including an accounting of receipts and disbursements; (8) prepare, execute, and file a record, report, or other document the agent considers desirable to safeguard or promote the principal's interest under a statute or governmental regulation; (9) reimburse the agent for expenditures properly made by the agent in exercising the powers granted by the power of attorney; and (10) in general, do any other lawful act with respect to the power and all property related to the power.

WITH RESPECT TO REAL PROPERTY, the principal authorizes the agent to: (1) accept as a gift or as security for an extension of credit, reject, demand, buy, lease, receive, or otherwise acquire, an interest in real property or a right incident to real property; (2) sell, exchange, convey with or without covenants, quitclaim, release, surrender, mortgage, retain title for security, encumber, partition, consent to partitioning, subdivide, apply for zoning, rezoning, or other governmental permits, plat or consent to platting, develop, grant options concerning, lease, sublease, or otherwise dispose of, an interest in real property or a right incident to real property; (3) release, assign, satisfy, or enforce by litigation or otherwise, a mortgage, deed of trust, conditional sale contract, encumbrance, lien, or other claim to real property which exists or is asserted; (4) manage or conserve an interest in real property or a right incident to real property, owned or claimed to be owned by the principal, including: (a) insuring against a casualty, liability, or loss; (b) obtaining or regaining possession, or protecting the interest or right, by litigation or otherwise; (c) paying, compromising, or contesting taxes or assessments, or applying for and receiving refunds in connection with them; and (d) purchasing supplies, hiring assistance or labor, and making repairs or alterations to the real property; (5) use, develop, alter, replace, remove, erect, or install structures or other improvements upon real property in or incident to which the principal has, or claims to have, an interest or right; (6) participate in a reorganization with respect to real property or a legal entity that owns an interest in or right incident to real property and receive and hold, directly or indirectly, shares of stock or obligations, or other evidences of ownership or debt, received in a plan of reorganization, and act with respect to them, including: (a) selling or otherwise disposing of them; (b) exercising or selling an option, conversion, or similar right with respect to them; and (c) voting them in person or by proxy; (7) change the form of title of an interest in or right incident to real property, and (8) dedicate to public use, with or without consideration, easements or other real property in which the principal has, or claims to have, an interest.

WITH RESPECT TO TANGIBLE PERSONAL PROPERTY, the principal authorizes the agent to: (1) accept as a gift or as security for an extension of credit, reject, demand, buy, receive, or otherwise acquire ownership or possession of tangible personal property or an interest in tangible personal property; (2) sell, exchange, convey with or without covenants, release, surrender, create a security interest in, grant options concerning, lease, sublease to others, or otherwise dispose of tangible personal property or an interest in tangible personal property; (3) release, assign, satisfy, or enforce by litigation or otherwise, a security interest, lien, or other claim on behalf of the principal, with respect to tangible personal property or an interest in tangible personal property; (4) manage or conserve tangible personal property or an interest in tangible personal property on behalf of the principal, including: (a) insuring against casualty, liability, or loss; (b) obtaining or regaining possession, or protecting the property or interest, by litigation or otherwise; (c) paying, compromising, or contesting taxes or assessments or applying for and receiving refunds in connection with taxes or assessments; (d) moving from place to place; (e) storing for hire or on a gratuitous bailment; and (f) using, altering, and making repairs or alterations; and (5) change the form of title of an interest in tangible personal property.

WITH RESPECT TO TRANSACTIONS CONCERNING STOCKS AND BONDS, the principal authorizes the agent to: (1) buy, sell, and exchange stocks, bonds, mutual funds, and all other types of securities and financial instruments, whether held directly or indirectly, except commodity futures contracts and call and put options on stocks and stock indexes, (2) receive certificates and other evidences of ownership with respect to securities, (3) exercise voting rights with respect to securities in person or by proxy, enter into voting trusts, and consent to limitations on the right to vote.

WITH RESPECT TO TRANSACTIONS CONCERNING COMMODITIES AND OPTIONS, the principal authorizes the agent to: (1) buy, sell, exchange, assign, settle, and exercise commodity futures contracts and call and put options on stocks and stock indexes traded on a regulated option exchange, and (2) establish, continue, modify, and terminate option accounts with a broker.

WITH RESPECT TO TRANSACTIONS CONCERNING BANKS AND OTHER FINANCIAL INSTITUTIONS, the principal authorizes the agent to: (1) continue, modify, and terminate an account or other banking arrangement made by or on behalf of the principal; (2) establish, modify, and terminate an account or other banking arrangement with a bank, trust company, savings and loan association, credit union, thrift company, brokerage firm, or other financial institution selected by the agent; (3) rent a safe deposit box or space in a vault; (4) contract for other services available from a financial institution as the agent considers desirable; (5) withdraw by check, order, or otherwise money or property of the principal deposited with or left in the custody of a financial institution; 6) receive bank statements, vouchers, notices, and similar documents from a financial institution and act with respect to them; (7) enter a safe deposit box or vault and withdraw or add to the contents; (8) borrow money at an interest rate agreeable to the agent and pledge as security personal property of the principal necessary in order to borrow, pay, renew, or extend the time of payment of a debt of the principal; (9) make, assign, draw, endorse, discount, guarantee, and negotiate promissory notes, checks, drafts, and other negotiable or nonnegotiable paper of the principal, or payable to the principal or the principal's order, transfer money, receive the cash or other proceeds of those transactions, accept a draft drawn by a person upon the principal, and pay it when due; (10) receive for the principal and act upon a sight draft, warehouse receipt, or other negotiable or nonnegotiable instrument; (11) apply for, receive, and use letters of credit, credit and debit cards, and traveler's checks from a financial institution and give an indemnity or other agreement in connection with letters of credit; and (12) consent to an extension of the time of payment with respect to commercial paper or a financial transaction with a financial institution.

WITH RESPECT TO OPERATING A BUSINESS, the principal authorizes the agent to: (1) operate, buy, sell, enlarge, reduce, and terminate a business interest; (2) act for a principal, subject to the terms of a partnership agreement or operating agreement, to: (a) perform a duty or discharge a liability and exercise a right, power, privilege, or option that the principal has, may have, or claims to have, under the partnership agreement or operating agreement, whether or not the principal is a partner in a partnership or member of a limited liability company; (b) enforce the terms of the partnership agreement or operating agreement by litigation or otherwise; and (c) defend, submit to arbitration, settle, or compromise litigation to which the principal is a party because of membership in a partnership or limited liability company; (3) exercise in person or by proxy, or enforce by litigation or otherwise, a right, power, privilege, or option the principal has or claims to have as the holder of a bond, share, or other instrument of similar character and defend, submit to arbitration or mediation, settle, or compromise litigation to which the principal is a party because of a bond, share, or similar instrument; (4) with respect to a business controlled by the principal: (a) continue, modify, renegotiate, extend, and terminate a contract made by or on behalf of the principal with respect to the business before execution of the power of attorney; (b) determine: (i) the location of its operation; (ii) the nature and extent of its business; (iii) the methods of manufacturing, selling, merchandising, financing, accounting, and advertising employed in its operation; (iv) the amount and types of insurance carried; and (v) the mode of engaging, compensating, and dealing with its accountants, attorneys, other agents, and employees; (c) change the name or form of organization under which the business is operated and enter into a partnership agreement or operating agreement with other persons or organize a corporation or other business entity to take over all or part of the operation of the business; and (d) demand and receive money due or claimed by the principal or on the principal's behalf in the operation of the business, and control and disburse the money in the operation of the business; (5) put additional capital into a business in which the principal has an interest; (6) join in a plan of reorganization, consolidation, or merger of the business; (7) sell or liquidate a business or part of it at the time and upon the terms the agent considers desirable; (8) establish the value of a business under a buy-out agreement to which the principal is a party; (9) prepare, sign, file, and deliver reports, compilations of information, returns, or other papers with respect to a business which are required by a governmental agency or instrumentality or which the agent considers desirable, and make related payments; and (10) pay, compromise, or contest taxes or assessments and perform any other act that the agent considers desirable to protect the principal from illegal or unnecessary taxation, fines, penalties, or assessments with respect to a business, including attempts to recover, in any manner permitted by law, money paid before or after the execution of the power of attorney.

WITH RESPECT TO INSURANCE AND ANNUITIES, the principal authorizes the agent to: (1) continue, pay the premium or assessment on, modify, rescind, release, or terminate a contract procured by or on behalf of the principal which insures or provides an annuity to either the principal or another person, whether or not the principal is a beneficiary under the contract; (2) procure new, different, and additional contracts of insurance and annuities for the principal and the principal's spouse, children, and other dependents, and select the amount, type of insurance or annuity, and mode of payment; (3) pay the premium or assessment on, modify, rescind, release, or terminate a contract of insurance or annuity procured by the agent; (4) apply for and receive a loan on the security of a contract of insurance or annuity; (5)

surrender and receive the cash surrender value; (6) exercise an election; (7) change the manner of paying premiums; (8) change or convert the type of insurance or annuity, with respect to which the principal has or claims to have a power described in this section; (9) apply for and procure government aid to guarantee or pay premiums of a contract of insurance on the life of the principal; (10) collect, sell, assign, hypothecate, borrow upon, or pledge the interest of the principal in a contract of insurance or annuity; and (11) pay from proceeds or otherwise, compromise or contest, and apply for refunds in connection with, a tax or assessment levied by a taxing authority with respect to a contract of insurance or annuity or its proceeds or liability accruing by reason of the tax or assessment.

WITH RESPECT TO ESTATES, TRUSTS, AND OTHER RELATIONSHIPS IN WHICH THE PRINCIPAL IS A BENEFICIARY, the principal authorizes the agent to act for the principal in all matters that affect a trust, probate estate, guardianship, conservatorship, escrow, custodianship, or other fund from which the principal is, may become, or claims to be entitled, as a beneficiary, to a share or payment, including to: (1) accept, reject, disclaim, receive, receipt for, sell, assign, release, pledge, exchange, or consent to a reduction in or modification of a share in or payment from the fund; (2) demand or obtain by litigation or otherwise money or other thing of value to which the principal is, may become, or claims to be entitled by reason of the fund; (3) initiate, participate in, and oppose litigation to ascertain the meaning, validity, or effect of a deed, will, declaration of trust, or other instrument or transaction affecting the interest of the principal; (4) initiate, participate in, and oppose litigation to remove, substitute, or surcharge a fiduciary; (5) conserve, invest, disburse, and use anything received for an authorized purpose; and (6) transfer an interest of the principal in real property, stocks, bonds, accounts with financial institutions or securities intermediaries, insurance, annuities, and other property, to the trustee of a revocable trust created by the principal as settlor.

WITH RESPECT TO CLAIMS AND LITIGATION, the principal authorizes the agent to: (1) assert and prosecute before a court or administrative agency a claim, a claim for relief, cause of action, counterclaim, offset, or defense against an individual, organization, or government, including actions to recover property or other thing of value, to recover damages sustained by the principal, to eliminate or modify tax liability, or to seek an injunction, specific performance, or other relief; (2) bring an action to determine adverse claims, intervene in litigation, and act as amicus curiae; (3) in connection with litigation, procure an attachment, garnishment, libel, order of arrest, or other preliminary, provisional, or intermediate relief and use an available procedure to effect or satisfy a judgment, order, or decree; (4) in connection with litigation, perform any lawful act, including acceptance of tender, offer of judgment, admission of facts, submission of a controversy on an agreed statement of facts, consent to examination before trial, and binding the principal in litigation; (5) submit to arbitration or mediation, settle, and propose or accept a compromise with respect to a claim or litigation; (6) waive the issuance and service of process upon the principal, accept service of process, appear for the principal, designate persons upon whom process directed to the principal may be served, execute and file or deliver stipulations on the principal's behalf, verify pleadings, seek appellate review, procure and give surety and indemnity bonds, contract and pay for the preparation and printing of records and briefs, receive and execute and file or deliver a consent, waiver, release, confession of judgment, satisfaction of judgment, notice, agreement, or other instrument in connection with the prosecution, settlement, or defense of a claim or litigation; (7) act for the principal with respect to bankruptcy or insolvency, whether voluntary or involuntary, concerning the principal or some other person, or with respect to a reorganization, receivership, or application for the appointment of a receiver or trustee which affects an interest of the principal in property or other thing of value; and (8) pay a judgment against the principal or a settlement made in connection with litigation and receive and conserve money or other thing of value paid in settlement of or as proceeds of a claim or litigation.

WITH RESPECT TO PERSONAL AND FAMILY MAINTENANCE, the principal authorizes the agent to: (1) perform the acts necessary to maintain the customary standard of living of the principal, the principal's spouse, children, and other individuals customarily or legally entitled to be supported by the principal, including providing living quarters by purchase, lease, or other contract, or paying the operating costs, including interest, amortization payments, repairs, and taxes, on premises owned by the principal and occupied by those individuals; (2) provide for the individuals described under (1) normal domestic help, usual vacations and travel expenses, and funds for shelter, clothing, food, appropriate education, and other current living costs; (3) pay on behalf of the individuals described under (1) expenses for necessary medical, dental, and surgical care, hospitalization, and custodial care; (4) act as the principal's personal representative pursuant to sections 1171 through 1179 of the Social Security Act, 42 U.S.C. Section 1320d (sections 262 and 264 of Public Law 104-191) [or successor provisions] and applicable regulations, in making decisions related to the past, present, or future payment for the provision of health care consented to by the principal or anyone authorized under the law of this state to consent to health care on behalf of the principal; (5) continue any provision made by the principal, for the individuals described under (1), for automobiles or other means of transportation, including registering, licensing, insuring, and replacing them; (6) maintain or open charge accounts for the convenience of the individuals described under (1) and open new accounts the agent considers desirable to accomplish a lawful purpose; and (7) continue payments incidental to the membership or affiliation of the principal in a church, club, society, order, or other organization or to continue contributions to those organizations.

WITH RESPECT TO BENEFITS FROM SOCIAL SECURITY, MEDICARE, MEDICAID, OTHER GOVERNMENTAL PROGRAMS, OR CIVIL OR MILITARY SERVICE, the principal authorizes the agent to: (1) execute vouchers in the name of the principal for allowances and reimbursements payable by the United States or a foreign government or by a state or subdivision of a state to the principal, including allowances and reimbursements for transportation of the individuals described in Section 212(1), and for shipment of their household effects; (2) take possession and order the removal and shipment of property of the principal from a post, warehouse, depot, dock, or other place of storage or safekeeping, either governmental or private, and execute and deliver a release, voucher, receipt, bill of lading, shipping ticket, certificate, or other instrument for that purpose; (3) prepare, file, and prosecute a claim of the principal to a benefit or assistance, financial or otherwise, to which the principal claims to be entitled under a statute or governmental regulation; (4) prosecute, defend, submit to arbitration or mediation, settle, and propose or accept a compromise with respect to any benefit or assistance the principal may be entitled to receive under a statute or governmental regulation; and (5) receive the financial proceeds of a claim of the type described in paragraph (3) and conserve, invest, disburse, or use anything so received for a lawful purpose.

WITH RESPECT TO RETIREMENT PLANS, the principal authorizes the agent to: (1) select a payment option under a retirement plan in which the principal participates, including a plan for a self-employed individual; (2) make voluntary contributions to those plans; (3) exercise the investment powers available under a self-directed retirement plan; (4) make a rollover of benefits into another retirement plan; (5) if authorized by the plan, borrow from, sell assets to, purchase assets from, or request distributions from the plan; and (6) waive the right of the principal to be a beneficiary of a joint or survivor annuity if the principal is a spouse who is not employed.

WITH RESPECT TO TAX MATTERS, the principal authorizes the agent to: (1) prepare, sign, and file federal, state, local, and foreign income, gift, payroll,

Federal Insurance Contributions Act, and other tax returns, claims for refunds, requests for extension of time, petitions regarding tax matters, and any other tax-related documents, including receipts, offers, waivers, consents, including consents and agreements under the Internal Revenue Code, 26 U.S.C. Section 2032A [or successor provisions], closing agreements, and any power of attorney required by the Internal Revenue Service or other taxing authority with respect to a tax year upon which the statute of limitations has not run and the following 25 tax years; (2) pay taxes due, collect refunds, post bonds, receive confidential information, and contest deficiencies determined by the Internal Revenue Service or other taxing authority; (3) exercise any election available to the principal under federal, state, local, or foreign tax law; and (4) act for the principal in all tax matters for all periods before the Internal Revenue Service, and any other taxing authority.

WITH RESPECT TO GIFTS, the principal authorizes the agent to make gifts of any of the principal's property to individuals or organizations within the limits of the annual exclusion under the Internal Revenue Code, 26 U.S.C. Section 2503(b) [or successor provisions], as the agent determines to be in the principal's best interest based on all relevant factors, including: (1) the value and nature of the principal's property; (2) the principal's foreseeable obligations and need for maintenance; 3) minimization of income, estate, inheritance, generation-skipping transfer or gift taxes; (4) eligibility for public benefits or assistance under a statute or governmental regulation; and (5) the principal's personal history of making or joining in making gifts.

THIS POWER OF ATTORNEY SHALL BECOME EFFECTIVE IMMEDIATELY AND SHALL REMAIN IN FULL EFFECT UPON MY DISABILITY OR INCAPACITATION.

This power of attorney grants no power or authority regarding healthcare decisions to my designated attorney-in-fact.

③
If the attorney-in-fact named above is unable or unwilling to serve, then I appoint _____(printed name), of _____ (address), to be my successor attorney-in-fact for all purposes hereunder.

My attorney-in-fact is granted full and unlimited power to act on my behalf in the same manner as if I were personally present. My attorney-in-fact accepts this appointment and agrees to act in my best interest as he or she considers advisable. To induce any third party to rely upon this power of attorney, I agree that any third party receiving a signed copy or facsimile of this power of attorney may rely upon such copy, and that revocation or termination of this power of attorney shall be ineffective as to such third party until actual notice or knowledge of such revocation or termination shall have been received by such third party. I, for myself and for my heirs, executors, legal representatives and assigns, agree to indemnify and hold harmless any such third party from any and all claims that may arise against such third party by reason of such third party having relied on the provisions of this power of attorney. This power of attorney may be revoked by me at any time and is automatically revoked upon my death. My attorney-in-fact shall not be compensated for his or her services nor shall my attorney-in-fact be liable to me, my estate, heirs, successors, or assigns for acting or refraining from acting under this document, except for willful misconduct or gross negligence. Revocation of this document is not effective unless a third party has actual knowledge of such revocation.

I intend for my attorney-in-fact under this Power of Attorney to be treated as I would be with respect to my rights regarding the use and disclosure of my individually identifiable health information or other medical records. This release authority applies to any information governed by the Health Insurance Portability and Accountability Act of 1996 (aka HIPAA), 42 USC 1320d and 45 CFR 160-164.

④

Signature and Declaration of Principal

I, _____(printed name), the principal, sign my name to this power of attorney this _____day of _____and, being first duly sworn, do declare to the undersigned authority that I sign and execute this instrument as my power of attorney and that I sign it willingly, or willingly direct another to sign for me, that I execute it as my free and voluntary act for the purposes expressed in the power of attorney and that I am eighteen years of age or older, of sound mind and under no constraint or undue influence, and that I have read and understand the contents of the notice at the beginning of this document.

_____
Signature of Principal

⑤ **Witness Attestation**

I, _____ (printed name), the first witness, and I, _____ (printed name), the second witness, sign my name to the foregoing power of attorney being first duly sworn and do declare to the undersigned authority that the principal signs and executes this instrument as his/her power of attorney and that he/she signs it willingly, or willingly directs another to sign for him/her, and that I, in the presence and hearing of the principal, sign this power of attorney as witness to the principal's signing and that to the best of my knowledge the principal is eighteen years of age or older, of sound mind and under no constraint or undue influence.

_____
Signature of First Witness

_____
Signature of Second Witness

⑥ **Notary Acknowledgment**

The State of _____
County of _____

Subscribed, sworn to and acknowledged before me by
_____, the principal,
and subscribed and sworn to before me by
_____, the first witness, and
_____, the second witness
on this date _____.

_____
Notary Public Signature

Notary Public, In and for the County of _____
State of _____
My commission expires: _____
Notary Seal

⑦ Acknowledgment and Acceptance of Appointment as Attorney-in-Fact

I, _____, (printed name) have read the attached power of attorney and am the person identified as the attorney-in-fact for the principal. I hereby acknowledge that I accept my appointment as attorney-in-fact and that when I act as agent I shall exercise the powers for the benefit of the principal; I shall keep the assets of the principal separate from my assets; I shall exercise reasonable caution and prudence; and I shall keep a full and accurate record of all actions, receipts and disbursements on behalf of the principal.

_____   _____

Signature of Attorney-in-Fact   Date

⑧ Acknowledgment and Acceptance of Appointment as Successor Attorney-in-Fact

I, _____, (printed name) have read the attached power of attorney and am the person identified as the successor attorney-in-fact for the principal. I hereby acknowledge that I accept my appointment as successor attorney-in-fact and that, in the absence of a specific provision to the contrary in the power of attorney, when I act as agent I shall exercise the powers for the benefit of the principal; I shall keep the assets of the principal separate from my assets; I shall exercise reasonable caution and prudence; and I shall keep a full and accurate record of all actions, receipts and disbursements on behalf of the principal.

_____   _____

Signature of Successor Attorney-in-Fact   Date

Instructions for Durable Unlimited Power of Attorney for Financial Affairs - Effective on Incapacitation

This Power of Attorney goes into effect only upon your incapacitation as certified by your primary physician, or another physician, if your primary physician is not available.

This form should be used only in situations where you desire to authorize another person to act for you in all transactions but you desire that the powers granted will not take effect until you become incapacitated and unable to handle your own affairs. This documents also provides that your incapacitation must be certified by your primary physician, or another attending physician if your primary physician is not available.

The grant of power under this document is unlimited (except for health care decisions). This form gives the person whom you designate as your "attorney-in-fact" broad powers to handle your property during your incapacitation, which may include powers to mortgage, sell, or otherwise dispose of any real or personal property without advance notice to you or approval by you. This document does not authorize anyone to make medical or other health care decisions. You must execute a durable health care power of attorney to accomplish this.

This form does provide a HIPPA medical records privacy release that will allow the person that you appoint to access any hospital or medical bills or records on you behalf under the federal HIPAA regulations relating to the privacy of health care records.

This form also provides that you will also name a successor attorney-in-fact who will have the same powers as the original person appointed, but who will only have the powers if the original person appointed is unable to perform the necessary tasks required by the power of attorney. The authority granted by this power of attorney may be revoked by you at any time and is automatically revoked if you die. If there is anything about this form that you do not understand, you should ask a lawyer to explain it to you.

To complete this form, fill in the following:

① Name and address of person granting power (principal)
② Name and address of person granted power (attorney-in-fact)

③   Name and address of successor to person originally granted power (successor attorney-in-fact) (optional-if not used, write N/A in this space)

④   Printed name of principal, date of signature, and signature of principal (signed in front of notary public)

⑤   Witnesses printed names and signatures (signed in front of notary public)

⑥   Notary acknowledgement should be completed by the notary public

⑦   Printed name and signature of attorney-in-fact and successor attorney-in-fact (need not be witnessed or notarized)

⑧   Printed name and signature of attorney-in-fact and successor attorney-in-fact (optional-if not used, write N/A in this space) (need not be witnessed or notarized)

Durable Unlimited Power of Attorney For Financial Affairs (Effective Only Upon Incapacitation)

NOTICE TO ADULT SIGNING THIS DOCUMENT: This is an important document. Before signing this document, you should know these important facts. By signing this document, you are not giving up any powers or rights to control your finances and property yourself. In addition to your own powers and rights, you are giving another person, your attorney-in-fact, broad powers to handle your finances and property, which may include powers to encumber, sell or otherwise dispose of any real or personal property without advance notice to you or approval by you. THE POWERS GRANTED UNDER THIS DOCUMENT WILL ONLY GO INTO EFFECT IF YOU BECOME DISABLED OR INCAPACITATED, AS CERTIFIED BY YOUR PRIMARY PHYSICIAN, OR BY ANOTHER ATTENDING PHYSICIAN, IF YOUR PRIMARY PHYSICIAN IS NOT AVAILABLE. This document does not authorize anyone to make medical or other health care decisions for you. If you own complex or special assets such as a business, or if there is anything about this form that you do not understand, you should ask a lawyer to explain this form to you before you sign it. If you wish to change your durable unlimited power of attorney, you must complete a new document and revoke this one. You have the right to revoke the designation of the attorney-in-fact and the right to revoke this entire document at any time and in any manner. You may revoke this document at any time by destroying it, by directing another person to destroy it in your presence or by signing a written and dated statement expressing your intent to revoke this document. If you revoke this document, you should notify your attorney-in-fact and any other person to whom you have given a copy of the form. You also should notify all parties having custody of your assets. These parties have no responsibility to you unless you actually notify them of the revocation. If your attorney-in-fact is your spouse and your marriage is annulled, or you are divorced after signing this document, this document may become invalid. Since some third parties or some transactions may not permit use of this document, it is advisable to check in advance, if possible, for any special requirements that may be imposed. You should sign this form only if the attorney-in-fact you name is reliable, trustworthy and competent to manage your affairs. Generally, you may designate any competent adult as the attorney-in-fact under this document.

① I, _____(printed name),
of (address) _____, as principal,
② do appoint _____(printed name), of
(address) _____, as
my attorney-in-fact and do grant him or her unlimited power and authority to act in my name,

place and stead in any way which I myself could do, if I were personally present, with respect to all of the following matters to the extent that I am permitted by law to act through an agent:

IN GENERAL, the principal authorizes the agent to: (1) demand, receive, and obtain by litigation or otherwise, money or other thing of value to which the principal is, may become, or claims to be entitled, and conserve, invest, disburse, or use anything so received for the purposes intended; (2) contract in any manner with any person, on terms agreeable to the agent, to accomplish a purpose of a transaction, and perform, rescind, reform, release, or modify the contract or another contract made by or on behalf of the principal; (3) execute, acknowledge, seal, and deliver a deed, revocation, mortgage, security agreement, lease, notice, check, promissory note, electronic funds transfer, release, or other instrument or communication the agent considers desirable to accomplish a purpose of a transaction, including creating a schedule of the principal's property and attaching it to the power of attorney; (4) prosecute, defend, submit to arbitration or mediation, settle, and propose or accept a compromise with respect to, a claim existing in favor of or against the principal or intervene in litigation relating to the claim; (5) seek on the principal's behalf the assistance of a court to carry out an act authorized by the principal in the power of attorney; (6) engage, compensate, and discharge an attorney, accountant, expert witness, or other assistant; (7) keep appropriate records of each transaction, including an accounting of receipts and disbursements; (8) prepare, execute, and file a record, report, or other document the agent considers desirable to safeguard or promote the principal's interest under a statute or governmental regulation; (9) reimburse the agent for expenditures properly made by the agent in exercising the powers granted by the power of attorney; and (10) in general, do any other lawful act with respect to the power and all property related to the power.

WITH RESPECT TO REAL PROPERTY, the principal authorizes the agent to: (1) accept as a gift or as security for an extension of credit, reject, demand, buy, lease, receive, or otherwise acquire, an interest in real property or a right incident to real property; (2) sell, exchange, convey with or without covenants, quitclaim, release, surrender, mortgage, retain title for security, encumber, partition, consent to partitioning, subdivide, apply for zoning, rezoning, or other governmental permits, plat or consent to platting, develop, grant options concerning, lease, sublease, or otherwise dispose of, an interest in real property or a right incident to real property; (3) release, assign, satisfy, or enforce by litigation or otherwise, a mortgage, deed of trust, conditional sale contract, encumbrance, lien, or other claim to real property which exists or is asserted; (4) manage or conserve an interest in real property or a right incident to real property, owned or claimed to be owned by the principal, including: (a) insuring against a casualty, liability, or loss; (b) obtaining or regaining possession, or protecting the interest or right, by litigation or otherwise; (c) paying, compromising, or contesting taxes or assessments, or applying for and receiving refunds in connection with them; and (d) purchasing supplies, hiring assistance or labor, and making repairs or alterations to the real property; (5) use, develop, alter, replace, remove, erect, or install structures or other improvements upon real property in or incident to which the principal has, or claims to have, an interest or right; (6) participate in a reorganization with respect to real property or a legal entity that owns an interest in or right incident to real property and receive and hold, directly or indirectly, shares of stock or obligations, or other evidences of ownership or debt, received in a plan of reorganization, and act with respect to them, including: (a) selling or otherwise disposing of them; (b) exercising or selling an option, conversion, or similar right with respect to them; and (c) voting them in person or by proxy; (7) change the form of title of an interest in or right incident to real property, and (8) dedicate to public use, with or without consideration, easements or other real property in which the principal has, or claims to have, an interest.

WITH RESPECT TO TANGIBLE PERSONAL PROPERTY, the principal authorizes the agent to: (1) accept as a gift or as security for an extension of credit, reject, demand, buy, receive, or otherwise acquire ownership or possession of tangible personal property or an interest in tangible personal property; (2) sell, exchange, convey with or without covenants, release, surrender, create a security interest in, grant options concerning, lease, sublease to others, or otherwise dispose of tangible personal property or an interest in tangible personal property; (3) release, assign, satisfy, or enforce by litigation or otherwise, a security interest, lien, or other claim on behalf of the principal, with respect to tangible personal property or an interest in tangible personal property; (4) manage or conserve tangible personal property or an interest in tangible personal property on behalf of the principal, including: (a) insuring against casualty, liability, or loss; (b) obtaining or regaining possession, or protecting the property or interest, by litigation or otherwise; (c) paying, compromising, or contesting taxes or assessments or applying for and receiving refunds in connection with taxes or assessments; (d) moving from place to place; (e) storing for hire or on a gratuitous bailment; and (f) using, altering, and making repairs or alterations; and (5) change the form of title of an interest in tangible personal property.

WITH RESPECT TO TRANSACTIONS CONCERNING STOCKS AND BONDS, the principal authorizes the agent to: (1) buy, sell, and exchange stocks, bonds, mutual funds, and all other types of securities and financial instruments, whether held directly or indirectly, except commodity futures contracts and call and put options on stocks and stock indexes, (2) receive certificates and other evidences of ownership with respect to securities, (3) exercise voting rights with respect to securities in person or by proxy, enter into voting trusts, and consent to limitations on the right to vote.

WITH RESPECT TO TRANSACTIONS CONCERNING COMMODITIES AND OPTIONS, the principal authorizes the agent to: (1) buy, sell, exchange, assign, settle, and exercise commodity futures contracts and call and put options on stocks and stock indexes traded on a regulated option exchange, and (2) establish, continue, modify, and terminate option accounts with a broker.

WITH RESPECT TO TRANSACTIONS CONCERNING BANKS AND OTHER FINANCIAL INSTITUTIONS, the principal authorizes the agent to: (1) continue, modify, and terminate an account or other banking arrangement made by or on behalf of the principal; (2) establish, modify, and terminate an account or other banking arrangement with a bank, trust company, savings and loan association, credit union, thrift company, brokerage firm, or other financial institution selected by the agent; (3) rent a safe deposit box or space in a vault; (4) contract for other services available from a financial institution as the agent considers desirable; (5) withdraw by check, order, or otherwise money or property of the principal deposited with or left in the custody of a financial institution; 6) receive bank statements, vouchers, notices, and similar documents from a financial institution and act with respect to them; (7) enter a safe deposit box or vault and withdraw or add to the contents; (8) borrow money at an interest rate agreeable to the agent and pledge as security personal property of the principal necessary in order to borrow, pay, renew, or extend the time of payment of a debt of the principal; (9) make, assign, draw, endorse, discount, guarantee, and negotiate promissory notes, checks, drafts, and other negotiable or nonnegotiable paper of the principal, or payable to the principal or the principal's order, transfer money, receive the cash or other proceeds of those transactions, accept a draft drawn by a person upon the principal, and pay it when due; (10) receive for the principal and act upon a sight draft, warehouse receipt, or other negotiable or nonnegotiable instrument; (11) apply for, receive, and use letters of credit, credit and debit cards, and traveler's checks from a financial institution and give an indemnity or other agreement in connection with letters of credit; and (12) consent to an extension of the time of payment with respect to commercial paper or a financial transaction with a financial institution.

WITH RESPECT TO OPERATING A BUSINESS, the principal authorizes the agent to: (1) operate, buy, sell, enlarge, reduce, and terminate a business interest; (2) act for a principal, subject to the terms of a partnership agreement or operating agreement, to: (a) perform a duty or discharge a liability and exercise a right, power, privilege, or option that the principal has, may have, or claims to have, under the partnership agreement or operating agreement, whether or not the principal is a partner in a partnership or member of a limited liability company; (b) enforce the terms of the partnership agreement or operating agreement by litigation or otherwise; and (c) defend, submit to arbitration, settle, or compromise litigation to which the principal is a party because of membership in a partnership or limited liability company; (3) exercise in person or by proxy, or enforce by litigation or otherwise, a right, power, privilege, or option the principal has or claims to have as the holder of a bond, share, or other instrument of similar character and defend, submit to arbitration or mediation, settle, or compromise litigation to which the principal is a party because of a bond, share, or similar instrument; (4) with respect to a business controlled by the principal: (a) continue, modify, renegotiate, extend, and terminate a contract made by or on behalf of the principal with respect to the business before execution of the power of attorney; (b) determine: (i) the location of its operation; (ii) the nature and extent of its business; (iii) the methods of manufacturing, selling, merchandising, financing, accounting, and advertising employed in its operation; (iv) the amount and types of insurance carried; and (v) the mode of engaging, compensating, and dealing with its accountants, attorneys, other agents, and employees; (c) change the name or form of organization under which the business is operated and enter into a partnership agreement or operating agreement with other persons or organize a corporation or other business entity to take over all or part of the operation of the business; and (d) demand and receive money due or claimed by the principal or on the principal's behalf in the operation of the business, and control and disburse the money in the operation of the business; (5) put additional capital into a business in which the principal has an interest; (6) join in a plan of reorganization, consolidation, or merger of the business; (7) sell or liquidate a business or part of it at the time and upon the terms the agent considers desirable; (8) establish the value of a business under a buy-out agreement to which the principal is a party; (9) prepare, sign, file, and deliver reports, compilations of information, returns, or other papers with respect to a business which are required by a governmental agency or instrumentality or which the agent considers desirable, and make related payments; and (10) pay, compromise, or contest taxes or assessments and perform any other act that the agent considers desirable to protect the principal from illegal or unnecessary taxation, fines, penalties, or assessments with respect to a business, including attempts to recover, in any manner permitted by law, money paid before or after the execution of the power of attorney.

WITH RESPECT TO INSURANCE AND ANNUITIES, the principal authorizes the agent to: (1) continue, pay the premium or assessment on, modify, rescind, release, or terminate a contract procured by or on behalf of the principal which insures or provides an annuity to either the principal or another person, whether or not the principal is a beneficiary under the contract; (2) procure new, different, and additional contracts of insurance and annuities for the principal and the principal's spouse, children, and other dependents, and select the amount, type of insurance or annuity, and mode of payment; (3) pay the premium or assessment on, modify, rescind, release, or terminate a contract of insurance or annuity procured by the agent; (4) apply for and receive a loan on the security of a contract of insurance or annuity; (5) surrender and receive the cash surrender value; (6) exercise an election; (7) change the manner of paying premiums; (8) change or convert the type of insurance or annuity, with respect to which the principal has or claims to have a power described in this section; (9) apply for and procure government aid to guarantee or pay premiums of a contract of insurance on the life of the principal; (10) collect, sell, assign, hypothecate, borrow upon, or pledge the interest of the principal in a contract of insurance or annuity; and (11) pay from proceeds or otherwise, compromise or contest, and apply for refunds in connection with, a tax or assessment levied by a taxing authority with respect to a contract of insurance or annuity or its proceeds or liability accruing by reason of the tax or assessment.

WITH RESPECT TO ESTATES, TRUSTS, AND OTHER RELATIONSHIPS IN WHICH THE PRINCIPAL IS A BENEFICIARY, the principal authorizes the agent to act for the principal in all matters that affect a trust, probate estate, guardianship, conservatorship, escrow, custodianship, or other fund from which the principal is, may become, or claims to be entitled, as a beneficiary, to a share or payment, including to: (1) accept, reject, disclaim, receive, receipt for, sell, assign, release, pledge, exchange, or consent to a reduction in or modification of a share in or payment from the fund; (2) demand or obtain by litigation or otherwise money or other thing of value to which the principal is, may become, or claims to be entitled by reason of the fund; (3) initiate, participate in, and oppose litigation to ascertain the meaning, validity, or effect of a deed, will, declaration of trust, or other instrument or transaction affecting the interest of the principal; (4) initiate, participate in, and oppose litigation to remove, substitute, or surcharge a fiduciary; (5) conserve, invest, disburse, and use anything received for an authorized purpose; and (6) transfer an interest of the principal in real property, stocks, bonds, accounts with financial institutions or securities intermediaries, insurance, annuities, and other property, to the trustee of a revocable trust created by the principal as settlor.

WITH RESPECT TO CLAIMS AND LITIGATION, the principal authorizes the agent to: (1) assert and prosecute before a court or administrative agency a claim, a claim for relief, cause of action, counterclaim, offset, or defense against an individual, organization, or government, including actions to recover property or other thing of value, to recover damages sustained by the principal, to eliminate or modify tax liability, or to seek an injunction, specific performance, or other relief; (2) bring an action to determine adverse claims, intervene in litigation, and act as amicus curiae; (3) in connection with litigation, procure an attachment, garnishment, libel, order of arrest, or other preliminary, provisional, or intermediate relief and use an available procedure to effect or satisfy a judgment, order, or decree; (4) in connection with litigation, perform any lawful act, including acceptance of tender, offer of judgment, admission of facts, submission of a controversy on an agreed statement of facts, consent to examination before trial, and binding the principal in litigation; (5) submit to arbitration or mediation, settle, and propose or accept a compromise with respect to a claim or litigation; (6) waive the issuance and service of process upon the principal, accept service of process, appear for the principal, designate persons upon whom process directed to the principal may be served, execute and file or deliver stipulations on the principal's behalf, verify pleadings, seek appellate review, procure and give surety and indemnity bonds, contract and pay for the preparation and printing of records and briefs, receive and execute and file or deliver a consent, waiver, release, confession of judgment, satisfaction of judgment, notice, agreement, or other instrument in connection with the prosecution, settlement, or defense of a claim or litigation; (7) act for the principal with respect to bankruptcy or insolvency, whether voluntary or involuntary, concerning the principal or some other person, or with respect to a reorganization, receivership, or application for the appointment of a receiver or trustee which affects an interest of the principal in property or other thing of value; and (8) pay a judgment against the principal or a settlement made in connection with litigation and receive and conserve money or other thing of value paid in settlement of or as proceeds of a claim or litigation.

WITH RESPECT TO PERSONAL AND FAMILY MAINTENANCE, the principal authorizes the agent to: (1) perform the acts necessary to maintain the customary standard of living of the principal, the principal's spouse, children, and other individuals customarily or legally entitled to be supported by the principal, including providing living quarters by purchase, lease, or other contract, or paying the operating costs, including interest, amortization payments, repairs, and taxes, on premises owned by the principal and occupied by those individuals; (2) provide for the individuals described under (1) normal domestic help, usual vacations and travel expenses, and funds for shelter, clothing, food, appropriate education, and other current living costs; (3) pay on behalf of the individuals described under (1) expenses for necessary medical, dental, and surgical care, hospitalization, and custodial care; (4) act as the principal's personal representative pursuant to sections 1171 through 1179 of the Social Security Act, 42 U.S.C. Section 1320d (sections 262 and 264 of Public Law 104-191) [or successor provisions] and applicable regulations, in making decisions related to the past, present, or future payment for the provision of health care consented to by the principal or anyone authorized under the law of this state to consent to health care on behalf of the principal; (5) continue any provision made by the principal, for the individuals described under (1), for automobiles or other means of transportation, including registering, licensing, insuring, and replacing them; (6) maintain or open charge accounts for the convenience of the individuals described under (1) and open new accounts the agent considers desirable to accomplish a lawful purpose; and (7) continue payments incidental to the membership or affiliation of the principal in a church, club, society, order, or other organization or to continue contributions to those organizations.

WITH RESPECT TO BENEFITS FROM SOCIAL SECURITY, MEDICARE, MEDICAID, OTHER GOVERNMENTAL PROGRAMS, OR CIVIL OR MILITARY SERVICE, the principal authorizes the agent to: (1) execute vouchers in the name of the principal for allowances and reimbursements payable by the United States or a foreign government or by a state or subdivision of a state to the principal, including allowances and reimbursements for transportation of the individuals described in Section 212(1), and for shipment of their household effects; (2) take possession and order the removal and shipment of property of the principal from a post, warehouse, depot, dock, or other place of storage or safekeeping, either governmental or private, and execute and deliver a release, voucher, receipt, bill of lading, shipping ticket, certificate, or other instrument for that purpose; (3) prepare, file, and prosecute a claim of the principal to a benefit or assistance, financial or otherwise, to which the principal claims to be entitled under a statute or governmental regulation; (4) prosecute, defend, submit to arbitration or mediation, settle, and propose or accept a compromise with respect to any benefit or assistance the principal may be entitled to receive under a statute or governmental regulation; and (5) receive the financial proceeds of a claim of the type described in paragraph (3) and conserve, invest, disburse, or use anything so received for a lawful purpose.

WITH RESPECT TO RETIREMENT PLANS, the principal authorizes the agent to: (1) select a payment option under a retirement plan in which the principal participates, including a plan for a self-employed individual; (2) make voluntary contributions to those plans; (3) exercise the investment powers available under a self-directed retirement plan; (4) make a rollover of benefits into another retirement plan; (5) if authorized by the plan, borrow from, sell assets to, purchase assets from, or request distributions from the plan; and (6) waive the right of the principal to be a beneficiary of a joint or survivor annuity if the principal is a spouse who is not employed.

WITH RESPECT TO TAX MATTERS, the principal authorizes the agent to: (1)

prepare, sign, and file federal, state, local, and foreign income, gift, payroll, Federal Insurance Contributions Act, and other tax returns, claims for refunds, requests for extension of time, petitions regarding tax matters, and any other tax-related documents, including receipts, offers, waivers, consents, including consents and agreements under the Internal Revenue Code, 26 U.S.C. Section 2032A [or successor provisions], closing agreements, and any power of attorney required by the Internal Revenue Service or other taxing authority with respect to a tax year upon which the statute of limitations has not run and the following 25 tax years; (2) pay taxes due, collect refunds, post bonds, receive confidential information, and contest deficiencies determined by the Internal Revenue Service or other taxing authority; (3) exercise any election available to the principal under federal, state, local, or foreign tax law; and (4) act for the principal in all tax matters for all periods before the Internal Revenue Service, and any other taxing authority.

WITH RESPECT TO GIFTS, the principal authorizes the agent to make gifts of any of the principal's property to individuals or organizations within the limits of the annual exclusion under the Internal Revenue Code, 26 U.S.C. Section 2503(b) [or successor provisions], as the agent determines to be in the principal's best interest based on all relevant factors, including: (1) the value and nature of the principal's property; (2) the principal's foreseeable obligations and need for maintenance; 3) minimization of income, estate, inheritance, generation-skipping transfer or gift taxes; (4) eligibility for public benefits or assistance under a statute or governmental regulation; and (5) the principal's personal history of making or joining in making gifts.

THIS POWER OF ATTORNEY SHALL ONLY BECOME EFFECTIVE UPON MY DISABILITY OR INCAPACITATION, AS CERTIFIED BY MY PRIMARY PHYSICIAN, OR IF MY PRIMARY PHYSICIAN IS NOT AVAILABLE, BY ANY OTHER ATTENDING PHYSICIAN.

This power of attorney grants no power or authority regarding healthcare decisions to my designated attorney-in-fact.

③

If the attorney-in-fact named above is unable or unwilling to serve, then I appoint

_____(printed name),

of _____ (address),

to be my successor attorney-in-fact for all purposes hereunder.

My attorney-in-fact is granted full and unlimited power to act on my behalf in the same manner as if I were personally present. My attorney-in-fact accepts this appointment and agrees to act in my best interest as he or she considers advisable. To induce any third party to rely upon this power of attorney, I agree that any third party receiving a signed copy or facsimile of this power of attorney may rely upon such copy, and that revocation or termination of this power of attorney shall be ineffective as to such third party until actual notice or knowledge of such revocation or termination shall have been received by such third party. I, for myself and for my heirs, executors, legal representatives and assigns, agree to indemnify and hold harmless any such third party from any and all claims that may arise against such third party by reason of such third party having relied on the provisions of this power of attorney. This power of attorney may be revoked by me at any time and is automatically revoked upon my death. My attorney-in-fact shall not be compensated for his or her services nor shall my attorney-in-fact be liable to me, my estate, heirs, successors, or assigns for acting or refraining from acting under this document, except for willful misconduct or gross negligence. Revocation of this document is not effective unless a third party has actual knowledge of such revocation.

I intend for my attorney-in-fact under this Power of Attorney to be treated as I would be with respect to my rights regarding the use and disclosure of my individually identifiable health information or other medical records. This release authority applies to any information governed by the Health Insurance Portability and Accountability Act of 1996 (aka HIPAA), 42 USC 1320d and 45 CFR 160-164.

④ **Signature and Declaration of Principal**
I, _____ (printed name), the principal, sign my name to this power of attorney this _____day of _____and, being first duly sworn, do declare to the undersigned authority that I sign and execute this instrument as my power of attorney and that I sign it willingly, or willingly direct another to sign for me, that I execute it as my free and voluntary act for the purposes expressed in the power of attorney and that I am eighteen years of age or older, of sound mind and under no constraint or undue influence ,and that I have read and understand the contents of the notice at the beginning of this document.

_____
Signature of Principal

⑤ Witness Attestation

I, _____ (printed name), the first witness, and I, _____ (printed name), the second witness, sign my name to the foregoing power of attorney being first duly sworn and do declare to the undersigned authority that the principal signs and executes this instrument as his/her power of attorney and that he/she signs it willingly, or willingly directs another to sign for him/her, and that I, in the presence and hearing of the principal, sign this power of attorney as witness to the principal's signing and that to the best of my knowledge the principal is eighteen years of age or older, of sound mind and under no constraint or undue influence.

_____ _____
Signature of First Witness   Signature of Second Witness

⑥ Notary Acknowledgment

The State of _____
County of _____

Subscribed, sworn to and acknowledged before me by
_____, the principal, and subscribed and sworn to before me by
_____, the first witness, and
_____,the second witness
on this date _____.

_____
Notary Public Signature
Notary Public, In and for the County of _____
State of _____
My commission expires: _____ Notary Seal

⑦ **Acknowledgment and Acceptance of Appointment as Attorney-in-Fact**

I, _____ (printed name) have read the attached power of attorney and am the person identified as the attorney-in-fact for the principal. I hereby acknowledge that I accept my appointment as attorney-in-fact and that when I act as agent I shall exercise the powers for the benefit of the principal; I shall keep the assets of the principal separate from my assets; I shall exercise reasonable caution and prudence; and I shall keep a full and accurate record of all actions, receipts and disbursements on behalf of the principal.

_____   _____

Signature of Attorney-in-Fact   Date

⑧ **Acknowledgment and Acceptance of Appointment as Successor Attorney-in-Fact**

I, _____ (printed name) have read the attached power of attorney and am the person identified as the successor attorney-in-fact for the principal. I hereby acknowledge that I accept my appointment as successor attorney-in-fact and that, in the absence of a specific provision to the contrary in the power of attorney, when I act as agent I shall exercise the powers for the benefit of the principal; I shall keep the assets of the principal separate from my assets; I shall exercise reasonable caution and prudence; and I shall keep a full and accurate record of all actions, receipts and disbursements on behalf of the principal.

_____   _____

Signature of Successor Attorney-in-Fact   Date

Instructions for Durable General Power of Attorney for Financial Affairs - Effective Immediately

This Power of Attorney goes into effect immediately and remains in effect even upon your incapacitation.

This form should be used only in situations where you desire to authorize another person to act for you in *specifically chosen* transactions immediately and you wish the power to be in effect immediately and to continue to remain in effect in the event that you become incapacitated and unable to handle your own affairs. The grant of power under this document is general and based upon your own choices as to the powers that you authorize, but may be unlimited if you so choose (except for health care decisions). Note: if you wish to have your attorney-in-fact to have full unlimited authority, you may wish to use the *durable unlimited power of attorney for financial affairs* form instead.

This form gives the person whom you designate as your "attorney-in-fact" broad powers to handle your property during your lifetime, which may include powers to mortgage, sell, or otherwise dispose of any real or personal property without advance notice to you or approval by you. This document does not authorize anyone to make medical or other health care decisions. You must execute a health care power of attorney to accomplish this. This form does provide a HIPPA medical records privacy release that will allow the person that you appoint to access any hospital or medical bills or records on you behalf.

This form also provides that you will also name a successor attorney-in-fact who will have the same powers as the original person appointed, but who will only have the powers if the original person appointed is unable to perform the necessary tasks required by the power of attorney. The authority granted by this power of attorney may be revoked by you at any time and is automatically revoked if you die. If there is anything about this form that you do not understand, you should ask a lawyer to explain it to you.

To complete this form, fill in the following:

① Name and address of person granting power (principal)
② Name and address of person granted power (attorney-in-fact)
③ Name of state in which you are signing this power of attorney
④ Initial each of the specific powers that you wish your attorney-in-fact to have.

If you wish your attorney-in-fact to have full authority to do anything that you yourself could do, simply initial line (q). Cross out each item that you do not select.

⑤ Name and address of successor to person originally granted power (successor attorney-in-fact) (optional-if not used, write n/a in this space)

⑥ Date

⑦ Printed name of principal, date of signing of power of attorney, and signature of principal (signed in front of notary public)

⑧ Printed names and signatures of witnesses (signed in front of notary public)

⑨ Notary acknowledgement should be completed by the notary public

⑩ Printed name, date, and signature of attorney-in-fact (need not be witnessed or notarized)

⑪ Printed name, date, and signature of successor attorney-in-fact (optional-if not used, write N/A in this space) (need not be witnessed or notarized)

Durable General Power of Attorney for Financial Affairs (Effective Immediately)

Notice: This is an important document. Before signing this document, you should know these important facts. By signing this document, you are not giving up any powers or rights to control your finances and property yourself. In addition to your own powers and rights, you may be giving another person, your attorney-in-fact, broad powers to handle your finances and property. This general power of attorney may give the person whom you designate (your "attorney-in-fact") broad powers to handle your finances and property, which may include powers to encumber, sell or otherwise dispose of any real or personal property without advance notice to you or approval by you. THE POWERS GRANTED UNDER THIS DOCUMENT ARE EFFECTIVE IMMEDIATELY AND WILL REMAIN IN EFFECT IF YOU BECOME DISABLED OR INCAPACITATED. This document does not authorize anyone to make medical or other health care decisions for you. If you own complex or special assets such as a business, or if there is anything about this form that you do not understand, you should ask a lawyer to explain this form to you before you sign it. If you wish to change your general power of attorney, you must complete a new document and revoke this one. You may revoke this document at any time by destroying it, by directing another person to destroy it in your presence or by signing a written and dated statement expressing your intent to revoke this document. If you revoke this document, you should notify your attorney-in-fact and any other person to whom you have given a copy of the form. You also should notify all parties having custody of your assets. These parties have no responsibility to you unless you actually notify them of the revocation. If your attorney-in-fact is your spouse and your marriage is annulled, or you are divorced after signing this document, this document is invalid. Since some 3rd parties or some transactions may not permit use of this document, it is advisable to check in advance, if possible, for any special requirements that may be imposed. You should sign this form only if the attorney-in-fact you name is reliable, trustworthy and competent to manage your affairs. This form must be signed by the Principal (the person appointing the attorney-in-fact), witnessed by two persons other than the notary public, and acknowledged by a notary public.

I, ①_____(printed name),
of (address)_____,
as principal, to grant a general power of attorney to, and do hereby appoint:
②_____ (printed name),
of (address)_____,
my attorney-in-fact to act in my name, place and stead in any way which I
myself could do, if I were personally present, with respect to the following
matters to the extent that I am permitted by law to act through an agent. The
powers chosen below shall have the full force and effect given to them by their
full enumeration as laid out in the text of the Power of Attorney Act of the laws
of the State of ③_____: (Place your initials before each
item that you select and cross out each item that you do not select)

④

_____ (a) real estate transactions;

_____ (b) goods and services transactions;

_____ (c) bond, share and commodity transactions;

_____ (d) banking transactions;

_____ (e) business operating transactions;

_____ (f) insurance transactions;

_____ (g) estate transactions;

_____ (h) claims and litigation;

_____ (i) personal relationships and affairs;

_____ (j) benefits from military service;

_____ (k) records, reports and statements;

_____ (l) retirement benefit transactions;

_____ (m) making gifts to my spouse, children and more remote descendants, and parents;

_____ (n) tax matters;

_____ (o) all other matters;

_____ (p) full and unqualified authority to my attorney-in-fact to delegate any or all of the foregoing powers to any person or persons whom my attorney-in-fact shall select;

_____ (q) unlimited power and authority to act in all of the above situations (a) through (p)

If the attorney-in-fact named above is unable or unwilling to serve, I appoint
⑤_____ (printed name), of (address) _____ , to be my attorney-in-fact for all purposes hereunder.

To induce any third party to rely upon this power of attorney, I agree that any third party receiving a signed copy or facsimile of this power of attorney may rely upon such copy, and that revocation or termination of this power of attorney shall be ineffective as to such third party until actual notice or knowledge of such revocation or termination shall have been received by such third party. I, for myself and for my heirs, executors, legal representatives and assigns, agree to indemnify and hold harmless any such third party from any and all claims that may arise against such third party by reason of such third party having relied on the provisions of this power of attorney.

THE POWERS GRANTED UNDER THIS DOCUMENT ARE EFFECTIVE IMMEDIATELY AND SHALL REMAIN IN FULL EFFECT EVEN IF I BECOME DISABLED OR INCAPACITATED.

This power of attorney may be revoked by me at any time and is automatically revoked upon my death. My attorney-in-fact shall no be compensated for his or her services nor shall my attorney-in-fact be liable to me, my estate, heirs, successors, or assigns for acting or refraining from acting under this document, except for willful misconduct or gross negligence.

Dated: ⑥ _____

Signature and Declaration of Principal

⑦

I, _____ (printed name) , the principal, sign my name to this power of attorney this _____ day of _____ and, being first duly sworn, do declare to the undersigned authority that I sign and execute this instrument as my power of attorney and that I sign it willingly, or willingly direct another to sign for me, that I execute it as my free and voluntary act for the purposes expressed in the power of attorney and that I am eighteen years of age or older, of sound mind and under no constraint or undue influence.

_____
Signature of Principal

Witness Attestation

⑧

I, _____ (printed name), the first witness, and I, _____ (printed name), the second witness, sign my name to the foregoing power of attorney being first duly sworn and do declare to the undersigned authority that the principal signs and executes this instrument as his/her power of attorney and that he\she signs it willingly, or willingly directs another to sign for him/her, and that I, in the presence and hearing of the principal, sign this power of attorney as witness to the principal's signing and that to the best of my knowledge the principal is eighteen years of age or older, of sound mind and under no constraint or undue influence.

_____
Signature of First Witness

_____
Signature of Second Witness

Notary Acknowledgment

⑨

State of _____

County of _____

Subscribed, sworn to and acknowledged before me by

_____, the Principal,

and subscribed and sworn to before me by

_____ and

_____, the witnesses,

this _____ day of _____ .

_____

Notary Signature

Notary Public, In and for the County of _____

State of _____

My commission expires: _____ Seal

Acknowledgment and Acceptance of Appointment as Attorney-in-Fact

⑩

I, _____, (printed name)
have read the attached power of attorney and am the person identified as
the attorney-in-fact for the principal. I hereby acknowledge that I accept my
appointment as attorney-in-fact and that when I act as agent I shall exercise
the powers for the benefit of the principal; I shall keep the assets of the
principal separate from my assets; I shall exercise reasonable caution and
prudence; and I shall keep a full and accurate record of all actions, receipts
and disbursements on behalf of the principal.

_____   _____

Signature of Attorney-in-Fact   Date

**Acknowledgment and Acceptance of Appointment as Successor
Attorney-in-Fact**

⑪

I, _____, (printed name)
have read the attached power of attorney and am the person identified as
the successor attorney-in-fact for the principal. I hereby acknowledge that I
accept my appointment as successor attorney-in-fact and that, in the absence

of a specific provision to the contrary in the power of attorney, when I act as agent I shall exercise the powers for the benefit of the principal; I shall keep the assets of the principal separate from my assets; I shall exercise reasonable caution and prudence; and I shall keep a full and accurate record of all actions, receipts and disbursements on behalf of the principal.

_____   _____
Signature of Successor Attorney-in-Fact   Date

Instructions for Durable General Power of Attorney for Financial Affairs - Effective on Incapacitation

This Power of Attorney goes into effect only upon your incapacitation as certified by your primary physician, or another physician, if your primary physician is not available.

This form should be used only in situations where you desire to authorize another person to act for you in *specifically chosen* transactions but you desire that the powers granted will not take effect until you become incapacitated and unable to handle your own affairs. This documents also provides that your incapacitation must be certified by your primary physician, or another attending physician if your primary physician is not available. The grant of power under this document is general and based upon your own choices as to the powers that you authorize, but may be unlimited if you so choose (except for health care decisions). Note: if you wish to have your attorney-in-fact to have full unlimited authority, you may wish to use the *durable unlimited power of attorney for financial affairs* form instead.

This form gives the person whom you designate as your "attorney-in-fact" broad powers to handle your property during your incapacitation, which may include powers to mortgage, sell, or otherwise dispose of any real or personal property without advance notice to you or approval by you. This document does not authorize anyone to make medical or other health care decisions. You must execute a durable health care power of attorney to accomplish this.

This form does provide a HIPPA medical records privacy release that will allow the person that you appoint to access any hospital or medical bills or records on you behalf under the federal HIPAA regulations relating to the privacy of health care records. This form also provides that you will also name a successor attorney-in-fact who will have the same powers as the original person appointed, but who will only have the powers if the original person appointed is unable to perform the necessary tasks required by the power of attorney.

The authority granted by this power of attorney may be revoked by you at any time and is automatically revoked if you die. If there is anything about this form that you do not understand, you should ask a lawyer to explain it to you.

To complete this form, fill in the following:

① Name and address of person granting power (principal)
② Name and address of person granted power (attorney-in-fact)
③ Name of state in which you are signing this power of attorney
④ Initial each of the specific powers that you wish your attorney-in-fact to have. If you wish your attorney-in-fact to have full authority to do anything that you yourself could do, simply initial line (q). Cross out each item that you do not select.
⑤ Name and address of successor to person originally granted power (successor attorney-in-fact) (optional-if not used, write n/a in this space)
⑥ Date
⑦ Printed name of principal, date of signing of power of attorney, and signature of principal (signed in front of notary public)
⑧ Printed names and signatures of witnesses (signed in front of notary public)
⑨ Notary acknowledgement should be completed by the notary public
⑩ Printed name, date, and signature of attorney-in-fact (need not be witnessed or notarized)
⑪ Printed name, date, and signature of successor attorney-in-fact (optional-if not used, write N/A in this space)(need not be witnessed or notarized)

Durable General Power of Attorney for Financial Affairs (Effective on Incapacitation)

Notice: This is an important document. Before signing this document, you should know these important facts. By signing this document, you are not giving up any powers or rights to control your finances and property yourself. In addition to your own powers and rights, you may be giving another person, your attorney-in-fact, broad powers to handle your finances and property. This general power of attorney may give the person whom you designate (your "attorney-in-fact") broad powers to handle your finances and property, which may include powers to encumber, sell or otherwise dispose of any real or personal property without advance notice to you or approval by you. THE POWERS GRANTED UNDER THIS DOCUMENT WILL ONLY GO INTO EFFECT IF YOU BECOME DISABLED OR INCAPACITATED, AS CERTIFIED BY YOUR PRIMARY PHYSICIAN, OR BY ANOTHER ATTENDING PHYSICIAN, IF YOUR PRIMARY PHYSICIAN IS NOT AVAILABLE. This document does not authorize anyone to make medical or other health care decisions for you. If you own complex or special assets such as a business, or if there is anything about this form that you do not understand, you should ask a lawyer to explain this form to you before you sign it. If you wish to change your general power of attorney, you must complete a new document and revoke this one. You may revoke this document at any time by destroying it, by directing another person to destroy it in your presence or by signing a written and dated statement expressing your intent to revoke this document. If you revoke this document, you should notify your attorney-in-fact and any other person to whom you have given a copy of the form. You also should notify all parties having custody of your assets. These parties have no responsibility to you unless you actually notify them of the revocation. If your attorney-in-fact is your spouse and your marriage is annulled, or you are divorced after signing this document, this document is invalid. Since some 3rd parties or some transactions may not permit use of this document, it is advisable to check in advance, if possible, for any special requirements that may be imposed. You should sign this form only if the attorney-in-fact you name is reliable, trustworthy and competent to manage your affairs. This form must be signed by the Principal (the person appointing the attorney-in-fact), witnessed by two persons other than the notary public, and acknowledged by a notary public.

I, ①_____(printed name),
of (address)_____,
as principal, to grant a general power of attorney to, and do hereby appoint:
②_____ (printed name),
of (address)_____,
my attorney-in-fact to act in my name, place and stead in any way which I myself could do, if I were personally present, with respect to the following matters to the extent that I am permitted by law to act through an agent. The powers chosen below shall have the full force and effect given to them by their full enumeration as laid out in the text of the Power of Attorney Act of the laws of the State of ③_____: (Place your initials before each item that you select and cross out each item that you do not select)

④

_____ (a) real estate transactions;

_____ (b) goods and services transactions;

_____ (c) bond, share and commodity transactions;

_____ (d) banking transactions;

_____ (e) business operating transactions;

_____ (f) insurance transactions;

_____ (g) estate transactions;

_____ (h) claims and litigation;

_____ (i) personal relationships and affairs;

_____ (j) benefits from military service;

_____ (k) records, reports and statements;

_____ (l) retirement benefit transactions;

_____ (m) making gifts to my spouse, children and more remote descendants, and parents;

_____ (n) tax matters;

_____ (o) all other matters;

_____ (p) full and unqualified authority to my attorney-in-fact to delegate any or all of the foregoing powers to any person or persons whom my attorney-in-fact shall select;

_____ (q) unlimited power and authority to act in all of the above situations (a) through (p)

If the attorney-in-fact named above is unable or unwilling to serve, I appoint
⑤_____ (printed name), of (address) _____ , to be my attorney-in-fact for all purposes hereunder.

To induce any third party to rely upon this power of attorney, I agree that any third party receiving a signed copy or facsimile of this power of attorney may rely upon such copy, and that revocation or termination of this power of attorney shall be ineffective as to such third party until actual notice or knowledge of such revocation or termination shall have been received by such third party. I, for myself and for my heirs, executors, legal representatives and assigns, agree to indemnify and hold harmless any such third party from any and all claims that may arise against such third party by reason of such third party having relied on the provisions of this power of attorney.

THIS POWER OF ATTORNEY SHALL ONLY BECOME EFFECTIVE UPON MY DISABILITY OR INCAPACITATION, AS CERTIFIED BY MY PRIMARY PHYSICIAN, OR IF MY PRIMARY PHYSICIAN IS NOT AVAILABLE, BY ANY OTHER ATTENDING PHYSICIAN.

This power of attorney may be revoked by me at any time and is automatically revoked upon my death. My attorney-in-fact shall no be compensated for his or her services nor shall my attorney-in-fact be liable to me, my estate, heirs, successors, or assigns for acting or refraining from acting under this document, except for willful misconduct or gross negligence.

Dated: ⑥_____

Signature and Declaration of Principal

I, ⑦_____(printed name)
, the principal, sign my name to this power of attorney this _____day
of _____ and, being first duly sworn, do declare to the undersigned
authority that I sign and execute this instrument as my power of attorney and
that I sign it willingly, or willingly direct another to sign for me, that I execute
it as my free and voluntary act for the purposes expressed in the power of
attorney and that I am eighteen years of age or older, of sound mind and under
no constraint or undue influence.

_____
Signature of Principal

Witness Attestation

⑧
I, _____ (printed name),
the first witness, and I, _____
(printed name), the second witness, sign my name to the foregoing power of
attorney being first duly sworn and do declare to the undersigned authority that
the principal signs and executes this instrument as his/her power of attorney
and that he\she signs it willingly, or willingly directs another to sign for him/
her, and that I, in the presence and hearing of the principal, sign this power
of attorney as witness to the principal's signing and that to the best of my
knowledge the principal is eighteen years of age or older, of sound mind and
under no constraint or undue influence.

_____
Signature of First Witness

_____
Signature of Second Witness

Notary Acknowledgment

⑨

State of _____

County of _____

Subscribed, sworn to and acknowledged before me by

_____, the Principal,

and subscribed and sworn to before me by

_____ and

_____, the witnesses,

this _____ day of _____ .

_____

Notary Signature
Notary Public,
In and for the County of _____
State of _____
My commission expires: _____ Seal

Acknowledgment and Acceptance of Appointment as Attorney-in-Fact

⑩

I, _____, (printed name)
have read the attached power of attorney and am the person identified as
the attorney-in-fact for the principal. I hereby acknowledge that I accept my
appointment as attorney-in-fact and that when I act as agent I shall exercise the
powers for the benefit of the principal; I shall keep the assets of the principal
separate from my assets; I shall exercise reasonable caution and prudence; and
I shall keep a full and accurate record of all actions, receipts and disbursements
on behalf of the principal.

_____   _____
Signature of Attorney-in-Fact   Date

**Acknowledgment and Acceptance of Appointment as Successor
Attorney-in-Fact**

⑪

I, _____, (printed name)
have read the attached power of attorney and am the person identified as the
successor attorney-in-fact for the principal. I hereby acknowledge that I accept

my appointment as successor attorney-in-fact and that, in the absence of a specific provision to the contrary in the power of attorney, when I act as agent I shall exercise the powers for the benefit of the principal; I shall keep the assets of the principal separate from my assets; I shall exercise reasonable caution and prudence; and I shall keep a full and accurate record of all actions, receipts and disbursements on behalf of the principal.

_____   _____

Signature of Successor Attorney-in-Fact   Date

Chapter 6

State Specific Durable Powers of Attorney

Although, the forms provided in Chapter 5 of this book (durable powers of attorney for financial affairs) are legally-valid in all states, some states provide their own particular form for a durable power of attorney. You may choose to use one of the generic forms provided in Chapter 5 or you may choose to use the state-specific forms provided in this chapter.

A 'state-specific statutory form' is a form that has been taken directly from the laws of your particular state. The legal effects of the language in such a document have been approved by the legislature of the state. This provides an advantage in that the legal language in such a 'statutory' form is generally familiar to most financial institutions in the particular state and they know that such language has been approved. This does not mean, however, that other 'non-statutory' forms are not legally valid in the state as well. All states specifically provide, in their legislation regarding powers of attorney, that power of attorney forms other than those contained in the statute itself are legally valid, as long as such documents meet certain legal requirements. Anyone may use a 'non-statutory' legal form, such as those in Chapters 2 through 5, with language that they find appropriate to their own situation, as long as the document meets certain minimum legal standards for a particular state. All of the forms in this book meet such required legal standards.

The following states have developed state-specific statutory forms for durable powers of attorney:

Alaska, Arkansas, California, Colorado, Connecticut, District of Columbia, Georgia, Illinois, Minnesota, Montana, Nebraska, New Hampshire, New Mexico, New York, North Carolina, Oklahoma, Pennsylvania, Rhode Island, Texas and Wisconsin

In all other states, the legislatures have not developed specific forms for durable powers of attorney. In such situations, you may use the individual durable power of attorney forms provided in Chapter 5. The forms in Chapter 5 have been prepared following any guidelines and all legal requirements for all 50 states and Washington D.C.

When Should You Use a State-Specific Durable Power of Attorney?

You should use the form in this chapter for your specific state if, after reading through the form, you feel that it meets your particular needs. The forms in this chapter have been taken directly from each state's statutes and, thus, are well known to financial institutions in the particular state. This makes these forms more readily acceptable to some institutions. However, if the forms in this chapter do not fit your particular needs, you should read through the four durable power of attorney forms in Chapter 5 and determine if those forms will be more acceptable in your situation. If so, you may use the form in Chapter 5.

Toolkit Tip!

You should, whenever possible, use the Power of Attorney form that your state provides. However, if your state-provided form does not meet your specific needs, you may use the forms provided in Chapter 5, which are also legally valid in all states, including those states that have their own state-specific forms.

ALASKA POWER OF ATTORNEY

The powers granted from the principal to the agent or agents in the following document are very broad. They may include the power to dispose, sell, convey, and encumber your real and personal property, and the power to make your health care decisions. Accordingly, the following document should only be used after careful consideration. If you have any questions about this document, you should seek competent advice. You may revoke this power of attorney at any time.

Section 1. Pursuant to A.S.13.26.338 - 13.26.353,

I,_____(Name of principal) , of _____
_____(Address of principal), do hereby appoint _____
_____as
(Name and address of agent or agents)

my attorney(s)-in-fact to act as I have checked below in my name, place and stead in any way which I myself could do, if I were personally present, with respect to the following matters, as each of them is defined in AS 13.26.344, to the full extent that I am permitted by law to act through an agent:

Section 2. The agent or agents you have appointed will have all the powers listed below **UNLESS** you draw a line through a category; **AND** initial the space before that category.

_____(A) Real estate transactions
_____(B) Transactions involving tangible personal property, chattels, and goods
_____(C) Bonds, shares, and commodities transactions
_____(D) Banking transactions
_____(E) Business operating transactions
_____(F) Insurance transactions
_____(G) Estate transactions
_____(H) Gift transactions
_____(I) Claims and litigation
_____(J) Personal relationships and affairs
_____(K) Benefits from government programs and military service
_____(L) (repealed)
_____(M) Records, reports, and statements
_____(N) Delegation
_____(O) All other matters, including those specified as follows:

_____

_____

_____

Section 3. If you have appointed more than one agent, check one of the following:

_____Each agent may exercise the powers conferred separately, without the consent of any other agent.

_____All agents shall exercise the powers conferred jointly, with the consent of all other agents.

DURABLE POWER OF ATTORNEY OPTIONS
(Sections 4, 5 and 6 allow you to choose whether or not you want this to be a durable power of attorney and when you want it to go into effect.)

Section 4. To indicate when this document shall become effective, check one of the following:

_____This document shall become effective upon the date of my signature.

_____This document shall become effective upon the date of my disability and shall not otherwise be affected by my disability.

Section 5. If you have indicated that this document shall become effective on the date of your signature check one of the following:

_____This document shall not be affected by my subsequent disability.

_____This document shall be revoked by my subsequent disability.

If you want this to be a durable power of attorney, do not limit the term of this document in Section 6.

Section 6. If you have indicated that this document shall become effective upon the date of your signature and want to limit the term of this document, complete the following:

This document shall only continue in effect for _____(_____) years from the date of my signature.

Section 7. Notice of revocation of the powers granted in this document.
You may revoke one or more of the powers granted in this document. Unless otherwise provided in this document, you may revoke a specific power granted in this power of attorney by completing a special power of attorney that includes the specific power in this document that you want to revoke. Unless otherwise provided in this document, you may revoke all the powers granted in this power of attorney by completing a subsequent power of attorney.

Additional Provisions

Section 8. If you have given an agent authority regarding health care services, complete the following:

_____I have executed a separate declaration under AS 13.52 known as an "Alaska Advance Health Care Directive."

_____I have not executed an "Alaska Advance Health Care Directive."

Section 9. You may designate an alternate attorney-in-fact. Any alternate you designate will be able to exercise the same powers as the agent(s) you named at the beginning of this document. If you wish to designate an alternate or alternates, complete the following:

If the agent(s) named at the beginning of this document is unable or unwilling to serve or continue to serve, then I appoint the following agent to serve with the same powers:

First alternate or successor attorney-in-fact_____

_____
(Name and address of alternate)
Second alternate or successor attorney-in-fact_____

_____
(Name and address of alternate)

Section 10. Notice to Third Parties

A third party who relies on the reasonable representations of an attorney-in-fact as to a matter relating to a power granted by a properly executed statutory power of attorney does not incur any liability to the principal or to the principals heirs, assigns, or estate as a result of permitting the attorney-in-fact to exercise the authority granted by the power of attorney. A third party who fails to honor a properly executed statutory form power of attorney may be liable to the principal, the attorney-in-fact, the principal's heirs, assigns, or estate for civil penalty, plus damages, costs, and fees associated with the failure to comply with the statutory form power of attorney. If the power of attorney is one which becomes effective upon the disability of the principal, the disability of the principal is established by an affidavit, as required by law.

In Witness Whereof, I have hereunto signed my name this _____ day of _____, 20____.

_____
(Signature of principal)

STATE OF ALASKA _____)
_____) ss.
_____ JUDICIAL DISTRICT)

Acknowledged before me at_____
on the_____day of_____, 20__.

_____
Signature of officer or notary. Serial number, if any; date commission expires.

TRANSLATION CLAUSE (if needed)

I certify that I have translated the provisions of the foregoing *Power of Attorney* from the English language to the
_____ language to the best of my ability.

_____
Translator

ARKANSAS STATUTORY POWER OF ATTORNEY

28-68-401. Statutory form of power of attorney.

(a) Form. The following statutory form of power of attorney is legally sufficient:

STATUTORY POWER OF ATTORNEY

NOTICE: THE POWERS GRANTED BY THIS DOCUMENT ARE BROAD AND SWEEPING. THEY ARE EXPLAINED IN THE UNIFORM STATUTORY FORM POWER OF ATTORNEY ACT. IF YOU HAVE ANY QUESTIONS ABOUT THESE POWERS, OBTAIN COMPETENT LEGAL ADVICE. THIS DOCUMENT DOES NOT AUTHORIZE ANYONE TO MAKE MEDICAL AND OTHER HEALTH-CARE DECISIONS FOR YOU. YOU MAY REVOKE THIS POWER OF ATTORNEY IF YOU LATER WISH TO DO SO.

I_____
_____(insert your name and address) appoint _____
_____ (insert the name and address of the person appointed) as my agent (attorney-in-fact) to act for me in any lawful way with respect to the following initialed subjects:

TO GRANT ALL OF THE FOLLOWING POWERS, INITIAL THE LINE IN FRONT OF (N) AND IGNORE THE LINES IN FRONT OF THE OTHER POWERS. TO GRANT ONE OR MORE, BUT FEWER THAN ALL, OF THE FOLLOWING POWERS, INITIAL THE LINE IN FRONT OF EACH POWER YOU ARE GRANTING. TO WITHHOLD A POWER, DO NOT INITIAL THE LINE IN FRONT OF IT. YOU MAY, BUT NEED NOT, CROSS OUT EACH POWER WITHHELD.

INITIAL
_____ (A) Real property transactions.
_____ (B) Tangible personal property transactions.
_____ (C) Stock and bond transactions.
_____ (D) Commodity and option transactions.
_____ (E) Banking and other financial institution transactions.
_____ (F) Business operating transactions.
_____ (G) Insurance and annuity transactions.
_____ (H) Estate, trust, and other beneficiary transactions.
_____ (I) Claims and litigation.
_____ (J) Personal and family maintenance.

_____(K) Benefits from social security, medicare, medicaid, or other governmental programs, or military service.
_____ (L) Retirement plan transactions.
_____ (M) Tax matters.
_____ (N) ALL OF THE POWERS LISTED ABOVE. YOU NEED NOT INITIAL ANY OTHER LINES IF YOU INITIAL LINE (N).

SPECIAL INSTRUCTIONS:

ON THE FOLLOWING LINES YOU MAY GIVE SPECIAL INSTRUCTIONS LIMITING OR EXTENDING THE POWERS GRANTED TO YOUR AGENT.

_____
_____
_____
_____

UNLESS YOU DIRECT OTHERWISE ABOVE, THIS POWER OF ATTORNEY IS EFFECTIVE IMMEDIATELY AND WILL CONTINUE UNTIL IT IS REVOKED.
This power of attorney will continue to be effective even though I become disabled, incapacitated, or incompetent.

STRIKE THE PRECEDING SENTENCE IF YOU DO NOT WANT THIS POWER OF ATTORNEY TO CONTINUE IF YOU BECOME DISABLED, INCAPACITATED, OR INCOMPETENT.

I agree that any third party who receives a copy of this document may act under it. Revocation of the power of attorney is not effective as to a third party until the third party learns of the revocation. I agree to indemnify the third party for any claims that arise against the third party because of reliance on this power of attorney.

Signed this _____ day of _____ , 20_____

_____
(Your Signature)

_____
(Your Social Security Number)

State of _____

County of _____

This document was acknowledged before me on _____ (Date) by
_____ (Name of principal)
_____(Signature of notarial officer)
_____ (Seal, if any)
_____(Title (and Rank))
_____
[My commission expires: _____]

BY ACCEPTING OR ACTING UNDER THE APPOINTMENT, THE AGENT ASSUMES THE FIDUCIARY AND OTHER LEGAL RESPONSIBILITIES OF AN AGENT.

(b) Requirements. A statutory power of attorney is legally sufficient under this subchapter, if the wording of the form complies substantially with subsection (a), the form is properly completed, and the signature of the principal is acknowledged.

(c) Grant of All Listed Powers. If the line in front of (N) of the form under subsection (a) is initialed, an initial on the line in front of any other power does not limit the powers granted by line (N).
History. Acts 1999, No. 1423, § 1.

CALIFORNIA UNIFORM STATUTORY FORM POWER OF ATTORNEY

THE POWERS YOU GRANT BELOW ARE EFFECTIVE EVEN IF YOU BECOME DISABLED OR INCOMPETENT

CAUTION: A DURABLE POWER OF ATTORNEY IS AN IMPORTANT LEGAL DOCUMENT. BY SIGNING THE DURABLE POWER OF ATTORNEY, YOU ARE AUTHORIZING ANOTHER PERSON TO ACT FOR YOU, THE PRINCIPAL. BEFORE YOU SIGN THIS DURABLE POWER OF ATTORNEY, YOU SHOULD KNOW THESE IMPORTANT FACTS: YOUR AGENT (ATTORNEY-IN-FACT) HAS NO DUTY TO ACT UNLESS YOU AND YOUR AGENT AGREE OTHERWISE IN WRITING. THIS DOCUMENT GIVES YOUR AGENT THE POWERS TO MANAGE, DISPOSE OF, SELL, AND CONVEY YOUR REAL AND PERSONAL PROPERTY, AND TO USE YOUR PROPERTY AS SECURITY IF YOUR AGENT BORROWS MONEY ON YOUR BEHALF. THIS DOCUMENT DOES NOT GIVE YOUR AGENT THE POWER TO ACCEPT OR RECEIVE ANY OF YOUR PROPERTY, IN TRUST OR OTHERWISE, AS A GIFT, UNLESS YOU SPECIFICALLY AUTHORIZE THE AGENT TO ACCEPT OR RECEIVE A GIFT. YOUR AGENT WILL HAVE THE RIGHT TO RECEIVE REASONABLE PAYMENT FOR SERVICES PROVIDED UNDER THIS DURABLE POWER OF ATTORNEY UNLESS YOU PROVIDE OTHERWISE IN THIS POWER OF ATTORNEY. THE POWERS YOU GIVE YOUR AGENT WILL CONTINUE TO EXIST FOR YOUR ENTIRE LIFETIME, UNLESS YOU STATE THAT THE DURABLE POWER OF ATTORNEY WILL LAST FOR A SHORTER PERIOD OF TIME OR UNLESS YOU OTHERWISE TERMINATE THE DURABLE POWER OF ATTORNEY.

THE POWERS YOU GIVE YOUR AGENT IN THIS DURABLE POWER OF ATTORNEY WILL CONTINUE TO EXIST EVEN IF YOU CAN NO LONGER MAKE YOUR OWN DECISIONS RESPECTING THE MANAGEMENT OF YOUR PROPERTY. YOU CAN AMEND OR CHANGE THIS DURABLE POWER OF ATTORNEY ONLY BY EXECUTING A NEW DURABLE POWER OF ATTORNEY OR BY EXECUTING AN AMENDMENT THROUGH THE SAME FORMALITIES AS AN ORIGINAL. YOU HAVE THE RIGHT TO REVOKE OR TERMINATE THIS DURABLE POWER OF ATTORNEY AT ANY TIME, SO LONG AS YOU ARE COMPETENT.

THIS DURABLE POWER OF ATTORNEY MUST BE DATED AND MUST BE ACKNOWLEDGED BEFORE A NOTARY PUBLIC OR SIGNED BY TWO WITNESSES. IF IT IS SIGNED BY TWO WITNESSES, THEY MUST WITNESS EITHER (1) THE SIGNING OF THE POWER OF ATTORNEY OR (2) THE PRINCIPAL'S SIGNING OR ACKNOWLEDGMENT OF HIS OR HER SIGNATURE. A DURABLE POWER OF ATTORNEY THAT MAY AFFECT REAL PROPERTY SHOULD BE ACKNOWLEDGED BEFORE A NOTARY PUBLIC SO THAT IT MAY EASILY BE RECORDED.

YOU SHOULD READ THIS DURABLE POWER OF ATTORNEY CAREFULLY. WHEN EFFECTIVE, THIS DURABLE POWER OF ATTORNEY WILL GIVE YOUR AGENT THE

RIGHT TO DEAL WITH PROPERTY THAT YOU NOW HAVE OR MIGHT ACQUIRE IN THE FUTURE. THE DURABLE POWER OF ATTORNEY IS IMPORTANT TO YOU. IF YOU DO NOT UNDERSTAND THE DURABLE POWER OF ATTORNEY, OR ANY PROVISION OF IT, THEN YOU SHOULD OBTAIN THE ASSISTANCE OF AN ATTORNEY OR OTHER QUALIFIED PERSON.

NOTICE TO PERSON ACCEPTING THE APPOINTMENT AS ATTORNEY-IN-FACT BY ACTING OR AGREEING TO ACT AS THE AGENT (ATTORNEY-IN-FACT) UNDER THIS POWER OF ATTORNEY YOU ASSUME THE FIDUCIARY AND OTHER LEGAL RESPONSIBILITIES OF AN AGENT. THESE RESPONSIBILITIES INCLUDE:

1. THE LEGAL DUTY TO ACT SOLELY IN THE INTEREST OF THE PRINCIPAL AND TO AVOID CONFLICTS OF INTEREST.

2. THE LEGAL DUTY TO KEEP THE PRINCIPAL'S PROPERTY SEPARATE AND DISTINCT FROM ANY OTHER PROPERTY OWNED OR CONTROLLED BY YOU. YOU MAY NOT TRANSFER THE PRINCIPAL'S PROPERTY TO YOURSELF WITHOUT FULL AND ADEQUATE CONSIDERATION OR ACCEPT A GIFT OF THE PRINCIPAL'S PROPERTY UNLESS THIS POWER OF ATTORNEY SPECIFICALLY AUTHORIZES YOU TO TRANSFER PROPERTY TO YOURSELF OR ACCEPT A GIFT OF THE PRINCIPAL'S PROPERTY. IF YOU TRANSFER THE PRINCIPAL'S PROPERTY TO YOURSELF WITHOUT SPECIFIC AUTHORIZATION IN THE POWER OF ATTORNEY, YOU MAY BE PROSECUTED FOR FRAUD AND/OR EMBEZZLEMENT. IF THE PRINCIPAL IS 65 YEARS OF AGE OR OLDER AT THE TIME THAT THE PROPERTY IS TRANSFERRED TO YOU WITHOUT AUTHORITY, YOU MAY ALSO BE PROSECUTED FOR ELDER ABUSE UNDER PENAL CODE SECTION 368. IN ADDITION TO CRIMINAL PROSECUTION, YOU MAY ALSO BE SUED IN CIVIL COURT. I HAVE READ THE FOREGOING NOTICE AND I UNDERSTAND THE LEGAL AND FIDUCIARY DUTIES THAT I ASSUME BY ACTING OR AGREEING TO ACT AS THE AGENT (ATTORNEY-IN-FACT) UNDER THE TERMS OF THIS POWER OF ATTORNEY.

DATE: _____

_____
(SIGNATURE OF AGENT)

_____
(PRINT NAME OF AGENT)

UNIFORM STATUTORY FORM POWER OF ATTORNEY
(California Probate Code Section 4401 Prob.)

NOTICE: THE POWERS GRANTED BY THIS DOCUMENT ARE BROAD AND SWEEPING. THEY ARE EXPLAINED IN THE UNIFORM STATUTORY FORM POWER OF ATTORNEY ACT (CALIFORNIA PROBATE CODE SECTIONS 4400 Prob. - 4465 Prob.).

IF YOU HAVE ANY QUESTIONS ABOUT THESE POWERS, OBTAIN COMPETENT LEGAL ADVICE. THIS DOCUMENT DOES NOT AUTHORIZE ANYONE TO MAKE MEDICAL AND OTHER HEALTH-CARE DECISIONS FOR YOU. YOU MAY REVOKE HIS POWER OF ATTORNEY IF YOU LATER WISH TO DO SO.

I, _____ (your name and address) appoint _____

_____

_____
(name and address of the person appointed, or of each person appointed if you want to designate more than one) as my agent (attorney-in-fact) to act for me in any lawful way with respect to the following initialed subjects:

TO GRANT ALL OF THE FOLLOWING POWERS, INITIAL THE LINE IN FRONT OF (N) AND IGNORE THE LINES IN FRONT OF THE OTHER POWERS.

TO GRANT ONE OR MORE, BUT FEWER THAN ALL, OF THE FOLLOWING POWERS, INITIAL THE LINE IN FRONT OF EACH POWER YOU ARE GRANTING.

TO WITHHOLD A POWER, DO NOT INITIAL THE LINE IN FRONT OF IT. YOU MAY BUT NEED NOT, CROSS OUT EACH POWER WITHHELD.

INITIAL
_____ (A) Real property transactions.
_____ (B) Tangible personal property transactions.
_____ (C) Stock and bond transactions.
_____ (D) Commodity and option transactions.
_____ (E) Banking and other financial institution transactions.
_____ (F) Business operating transactions.
_____ (G) Insurance and annuity transactions.
_____ (H) Estate, trust, and other beneficiary transaction.
_____ (I) Claims and litigation.
_____ (J) Personal and family maintenance.
_____ (K) Benefits from social security, medicare, medicaid, of other governmental programs, or civil or military service.
_____ (L) Retirement plan transactions.
_____ (M) Tax matters.
_____ (N) ALL OF THE POWERS LISTED ABOVE.
YOU NEED NOT INITIAL ANY OTHER LINES IF YOU INITIAL LINE (N).

SPECIAL INSTRUCTIONS:
ON THE FOLLOWING LINES YOU MAY GIVE SPECIAL INSTRUCTIONS
LIMITING OR EXTENDING THE POWERS GRANTED TO YOUR AGENT.

_____
_____
_____
_____

UNLESS YOU DIRECT OTHERWISE ABOVE, THIS POWER OF ATTORNEY
IS EFFECTIVE IMMEDIATELY AND WILL CONTINUE UNTIL IT IS REVOKED.

This power of attorney will continue to be effective even though I become
incapacitated.

STRIKE THE PRECEDING SENTENCE IF YOU DO NOT WANT THIS
POWER OF ATTORNEY TO CONTINUE IF YOU BECOME INCAPACITATED.
EXERCISE OF POWER OF ATTORNEY WHERE MORE THAN ONE AGENT
DESIGNATED.

If I have designated more than one agent, the agents are to act.

IF YOU APPOINTED MORE THAN ONE AGENT AND YOU WANT EACH
AGENT TO BE ABLE TO ACT ALONE WITHOUT THE OTHER AGENT
JOINING, WRITE THE WORD "SEPARATELY" IN THE BLANK SPACE ABOVE.
IF YOU DO NOT INSERT ANY WORD IN THE BLANK SPACE, OR IF YOU
INSERT THE WORD "JOINTLY", THEN ALL OF YOUR AGENTS MUST ACT
OR SIGN TOGETHER.

I agree that any third party who receives a copy of this document may act under
it. Revocation of the power of attorney is not effective as to a third party until the
third party has actual knowledge of the revocation. I agree to indemnify the third
party for any claims that arise against the third party because of reliance on this
power of attorney.

Signed this _____ day of _____, 20____.

_____
(your signature)

_____
(your social security number)

CERTIFICATE OF ACKNOWLEDGMENT OF NOTARY PUBLIC

STATE OF CALIFORNIA
COUNTY OF _____

On _____, before me, the undersigned notary public, personally appeared _____, personally know to me (or proved to me on the basis of satisfactory evidence) to be the person whose name is subscribed to the within instrument and acknowledged to me that he executed the same in his authorized capacity, and that by his signature on the instrument the person, or the entity upon behalf of which the person acted, executed the instrument.

[Notary Seal, if any]:

_____
(Signature of Notarial Officer)

Notary Public for the State of California

My commission expires: _____

ACKNOWLEDGMENT OF AGENT

BY ACCEPTING OR ACTING UNDER THE APPOINTMENT, THE AGENT ASSUMES THE FIDUCIARY AND OTHER LEGAL RESPONSIBILITIES OF AN AGENT.

_____
[Typed or Printed Name of Agent]
_____
[Signature of Agent]

PREPARATION STATEMENT

This document was prepared by the following individual:

_____
[Typed or Printed Name]
_____
[Signature]

COLORADO STATUTORY POWER OF ATTORNEY FOR PROPERTY

NOTICE: UNLESS YOU LIMIT THE POWER IN THIS DOCUMENT, THIS DOCUMENT GIVES YOUR AGENT THE POWER TO ACT FOR YOU, WITHOUT YOUR CONSENT, IN ANY WAY THAT YOU COULD ACT FOR YOURSELF. THE POWERS GRANTED BY THIS DOCUMENT ARE BROAD AND SWEEPING. THEY ARE EXPLAINED IN THE "UNIFORM STATUTORY FORM POWER OF ATTORNEY ACT", PART 13 OF ARTICLE 1 OF TITLE 15, COLORADO REVISED STATUTES, AND PART 6 OF ARTICLE 14 OF TITLE 15, COLORADO REVISED STATUTES. IF YOU HAVE ANY QUESTIONS ABOUT THESE POWERS, OBTAIN COMPETENT LEGAL ADVICE. THIS DOCUMENT DOES NOT AUTHORIZE ANYONE TO MAKE MEDICAL AND OTHER HEALTH-CARE DECISIONS FOR YOU. YOU MAY REVOKE THIS POWER OF ATTORNEY IF YOU LATER WISH TO DO SO.

THE PURPOSE OF THIS POWER OF ATTORNEY IS TO GIVE THE PERSON YOU DESIGNATE (YOUR "AGENT") BROAD POWERS TO HANDLE YOUR PROPERTY AND AFFAIRS, WHICH MAY INCLUDE POWERS TO PLEDGE, SELL, OR OTHERWISE DISPOSE OF ANY REAL OR PERSONAL PROPERTY WITHOUT ADVANCE NOTICE TO YOU OR APPROVAL BY YOU. THIS FORM DOES NOT IMPOSE A DUTY ON YOUR AGENT TO EXERCISE GRANTED POWERS; BUT WHEN POWERS ARE EXERCISED, YOUR AGENT MUST USE DUE CARE TO ACT FOR YOUR BENEFIT AND IN ACCORDANCE WITH THE PROVISIONS OF THIS FORM AND MUST KEEP A RECORD OF RECEIPTS, DISBURSEMENTS, AND SIGNIFICANT ACTIONS TAKEN AS AGENT. YOU MAY NAME SUCCESSOR AGENTS UNDER THIS FORM BUT NOT CO-AGENTS. UNTIL YOU REVOKE THIS POWER OF ATTORNEY OR A COURT ACTING ON YOUR BEHALF TERMINATES IT, YOUR AGENT MAY EXERCISE THE POWERS GIVEN HERE THROUGHOUT YOUR LIFETIME, EVEN AFTER YOU MAY BECOME DISABLED, UNLESS YOU EXPRESSLY LIMIT THE DURATION OF THIS POWER IN THE MANNER PROVIDED BELOW.

YOU MAY HAVE OTHER RIGHTS OR POWERS UNDER COLORADO LAW NOT SPECIFIED IN THIS FORM.

I, _____,
(insert your full name and address) appoint _____
_____ (insert the full name and address of the person appointed) as my agent (attorney-in-fact) to act for me in any lawful way with respect to the following initialed subjects:

TO GRANT ONE OR MORE OF THE FOLLOWING POWERS, INITIAL THE LINE IN FRONT OF EACH POWER YOU ARE GRANTING. TO WITHHOLD A POWER, DO NOT INITIAL THE LINE IN FRONT OF IT. YOU MAY, BUT NEED NOT, CROSS OUT EACH POWER WITHHELD.

_____ (A) Real estate transactions (when property recorded).
_____ (B) Tangible personal property transactions.
_____ (C) Stock and bond transactions.
_____ (D) Commodity and option transactions.
_____ (E) Banking and other financial institution transactions.
_____ (F) Business operating transactions.
_____ (G) Insurance and annuity transactions.
_____ (H) Estate, trust, and other beneficiary transactions.
_____ (I) Claims and litigation.
_____ (J) Personal and family maintenance.
_____ (K) Benefits from social security, Medicare, Medicaid, or other governmental programs or military service.
_____ (L) Retirement plan transactions.
_____ (M) Tax matters.

UNLESS YOU DIRECT OTHERWISE ABOVE, THIS POWER OF ATTORNEY IS EFFECTIVE IMMEDIATELY AND WILL CONTINUE UNTIL IT IS REVOKED OR TERMINATED AS SPECIFIED BELOW. STRIKE THROUGH AND WRITE YOUR INITIALS TO THE LEFT OF THE FOLLOWING SENTENCE IF YOU DO NOT WANT THIS POWER OF ATTORNEY TO CONTINUE IF YOU BECOME DISABLED, INCAPACITATED, OR INCOMPETENT.

1. (   ) This power of attorney will continue to be effective even though I become disabled, incapacitated, or incompetent.

YOU MAY INCLUDE ADDITIONS TO AND LIMITATIONS ON THE AGENT'S POWERS IN THIS POWER OF ATTORNEY IF THEY ARE SPECIFICALLY DESCRIBED BELOW.

2. The powers granted above shall not include the following powers or shall be modified or limited in the following manner (here you may include any specific limitations you deem appropriate, such as a prohibition of or conditions on the sale of particular stock or real estate or special rules regarding borrowing by the agent):

_____
_____
_____

3. In addition to the powers granted above, I grant my agent the following powers (here you may add any other delegable powers, such as the power to

make gifts, exercise powers of appointment, name or change beneficiaries or joint tenants, or revoke or amend any trust specifically referred to below):

_____
_____
_____

4. SPECIAL INSTRUCTIONS. ON THE FOLLOWING LINES YOU MAY GIVE SPECIAL INSTRUCTIONS TO YOUR AGENT:

_____
_____
_____

YOUR AGENT WILL BE ENTITLED TO REIMBURSEMENT FOR ALL REASONABLE EXPENSES INCURRED IN ACTING UNDER THIS POWER OF ATTORNEY. STRIKE THROUGH AND INITIAL THE NEXT SENTENCE IF YOU DO NOT WANT YOUR AGENT TO ALSO BE ENTITLED TO REASONABLE COMPENSATION FOR SERVICES AS AGENT.

5. (   ) My agent is entitled to reasonable compensation for services rendered as agent under this power of attorney.

THIS POWER OF ATTORNEY MAY BE AMENDED IN ANY MANNER OR REVOKED BY YOU AT ANY TIME. ABSENT AMENDMENT OR REVOCATION, THE AUTHORITY GRANTED IN THIS POWER OF ATTORNEY IS EFFECTIVE WHEN THIS POWER OF ATTORNEY IS SIGNED AND CONTINUES IN EFFECT UNTIL YOUR DEATH, UNLESS YOU MAKE A LIMITATION ON DURATION BY COMPLETING THE FOLLOWING:

6. This power of attorney terminates on _____
_____ (Insert a future date or event, such as court determination of your disability, when you want this power to terminate prior to your death).

BY RETAINING THE FOLLOWING PARAGRAPH, YOU MAY, BUT ARE NOT REQUIRED TO, NAME YOUR AGENT AS GUARDIAN OF YOUR PERSON OR CONSERVATOR OF YOUR PROPERTY, OR BOTH, IF A COURT PROCEEDING IS BEGUN TO APPOINT A GUARDIAN OR CONSERVATOR, OR BOTH, FOR YOU. THE COURT WILL APPOINT YOUR AGENT AS GUARDIAN OR CONSERVATOR, OR BOTH, IF THE COURT FINDS THAT SUCH APPOINTMENT WILL SERVE YOUR BEST INTERESTS AND WELFARE. STRIKE THROUGH AND INITIAL PARAGRAPH 7 IF YOU DO NOT WANT YOUR AGENT TO ACT AS GUARDIAN OR CONSERVATOR, OR BOTH.

7. (   ) If a guardian of my person or a conservator for my property, or both, are to be appointed, I nominate the agent acting under this power of attorney as such guardian or conservator, or both, to serve without bond or security.

IF YOU WISH TO NAME SUCCESSOR AGENTS, INSERT THE NAME AND ADDRESS OF ANY SUCCESSOR AGENT IN THE FOLLOWING PARAGRAPH:

8.   If any agent named by me shall die, become incapacitated, resign, or refuse to accept the office of agent, I name the following each to act alone and successively, in the order named, as successor to such agent:

_____

_____

For purposes of this paragraph 8, a person is considered to be incapacitated if and while the person is a minor or a person adjudicated incapacitated or if the person is unable to give prompt and intelligent consideration to business matters, as certified by a licensed physician.

I agree that any third party who receives a copy of this document may act under it. Revocation of the power of attorney is not effective as to a third party until the third party learns of the revocation. I agree to indemnify the third party for any claims that arise against the third party because of reliance on this power of attorney.

Signed on _____, _____.

IF THERE IS ANYTHING ABOUT THIS FORM THAT YOU DO NOT UNDERSTAND, IT MAY BE IN YOUR BEST INTEREST TO CONSULT A COLORADO LAWYER RATHER THAN SIGN THIS FORM.

_____
(Your signature)

_____
(Your Social Security number)

YOU MAY, BUT ARE NOT REQUIRED TO, REQUEST YOUR AGENT AND SUCCESSOR AGENTS TO PROVIDE SPECIMEN SIGNATURES BELOW. IF YOU INCLUDE SPECIMEN SIGNATURES IN THIS POWER OF ATTORNEY, YOU MUST COMPLETE THE CERTIFICATION OPPOSITE THE SIGNATURES OF THE AGENTS.

NOTICE TO AGENTS: BY EXERCISING POWERS UNDER THIS DOCUMENT, THE AGENT ASSUMES THE FIDUCIARY AND OTHER LEGAL RESPONSIBILITIES OF AN AGENT UNDER COLORADO LAW.

Specimen signatures of agent (and successors)

I certify that the signatures of my agent (and successors) are correct.

_____

Agent

_____

Principal

_____

Successor Agent

_____

Principal

_____

Successor Agent

_____

Principal

STATE OF COLORADO   )

) ss.

COUNTY OF _____)

This document was acknowledged before me on _____ (date) by _____ (name of principal) (who certifies the correctness of the signature(s) of the agent(s).) My commission expires: _____

_____

Notary public

CONNECTICUT STATUTORY SHORT FORM POWER OF ATTORNEY

NOTICE: The powers granted by this document are broad and sweeping. They are defined in Connecticut Statutory Short Form Power of Attorney Act, sections 1-42 through 1-56, inclusive, of the general statutes, as amended by 2006 Public Act 06-195, which expressly permits the use of any other or different form of power of attorney desired by the parties concerned. The grantor of any power of attorney or the attorney-in-fact may make application to a court of probate for an accounting as provided in subsection (b) of Connecticut laws on accounting.

Know all Men by these Presents, which are intended to constitute a GENERAL POWER OF ATTORNEY pursuant to Connecticut Statutory Short Form Power of Attorney Act:

That I, _____(Print your name), of _____ _____(Town), Connecticut, do hereby appoint:

[WRITE IN NAME, TOWN, AND STATE OF ONE OR MORE INDIVIDUALS OR CORPORATIONS TO ACT AS YOUR ATTORNEY-IN-FACT; ADD MORE IF NECESSARY; "x" OUT LINES NOT COMPLETED]

_____, of _____
(Name)   (Town and State)
_____, of _____
(Name)   (Town and State)
_____, of _____
(Name)   (Town and State)

as my attorney(s)-in-fact TO ACT:

CHECK ONE BOX IF APPOINTING MORE THAN ONE ATTORNEY-IN-FACT
    [ ] SEVERALLY (independently
    [ ] JOINTLY (requiring both to consent and sign)

First: in my name, place and stead in any way which I myself could do, if I were personally present, with respect to the following matters as each of them is defined in the Connecticut Statutory Short Form Power of Attorney Act to the extent that I am permitted by law to act through an agent:
(Strike out and initial in the opposite box any one or more of the subdivisions as to which the principal does NOT desire to give the agent authority. Such

elimination of any one or more of subdivisions (A) to (L), inclusive, shall automatically constitute an elimination of subdivision (L).)

NOTE: To strike out any subdivisions the principal must draw a line through the text of that subdivision AND write his or her initials in the box opposite. [If you do not draw a line through and initial, you are giving your agent authority to exercise all of the following powers.]

[ ]   (A) real estate transactions;
[ ]   (B) chattel and goods transactions;
[ ]   (C) bond, share and commodity transactions;
[ ]   (D) banking transactions
[ ]   (E) business operating transactions;
[ ]   (F) insurance transactions;
[ ]   (G) estate transactions;
[ ]   (H) claims and litigation;
[ ]   (I) personal relationships and affairs;
[ ]   (J) benefits from military service;
[ ]   (K) records, reports and statements;
[ ]   (L) all other matters;

[NOTE: You may insert additional powers here]

Second: with full and unqualified authority to delegate any or all the foregoing powers to any person or persons whom my attorneys-in-fact shall select.

Third: hereby ratifying and confirming all that said attorneys or substitutes do or cause to be done.

In Witness Whereof, I have hereunto signed my name and affixed my seal this _____ day of _____, _____.
(date)   (month)   (year)
_____ (L.S.)
(SIGNATURE)

WITNESSES (one of whom may be the notary, attorney, etc. taking the acknowledgment)

Attested and subscribed in the presence of the principal and subsequent to the principal subscribing same:

First Witness signs:_____

Print witness name: _____

Second Witness signs:_____

Print witness name: _____

STATE OF CONNECTICUT   )

) ss:

COUNTY OF _____   )

at _____ on _____ _____, _____

       (Town)   (month)   (day)   (year)

Personally Appeared _____, Signer and Sealer of the foregoing instrument, and acknowledged the same to be his/her free act and deed, before me.

_____

Commissioner of the Superior Court
or Notary Public (if notary) My commission expires:

DISTRICT OF COLUMBIA STATUTORY POWER OF ATTORNEY
(District of Columbia Code 21-2101)

NOTICE: THE POWERS GRANTED BY THIS DOCUMENT ARE BROAD AND SWEEPING. THEY ARE EXPLAINED IN THE UNIFORM STATUTORY FORM POWER OF ATTORNEY ACT OF 1998. IF YOU HAVE ANY QUESTIONS ABOUT THESE POWERS, OBTAIN COMPETENT LEGAL ADVICE. THIS DOCUMENT DOES NOT AUTHORIZE ANYONE TO MAKE MEDICAL AND OTHER HEALTH-CARE DECISIONS FOR YOU. YOU MAY REVOKE THIS POWER OF ATTORNEY IF YOU LATER WISH TO DO SO.

I _____
_____ (insert your name and address)
appoint _____
_____(insert the name and address of the person appointed) as my agent
(attorney-in-fact) to act for me in any lawful way with respect to the following
initialed subjects:

TO GRANT ALL OF THE FOLLOWING POWERS, INITIAL THE LINE IN
FRONT OF (N) AND IGNORE THE LINES IN FRONT OF THE OTHER
POWERS.

TO GRANT ONE OR MORE, BUT FEWER THAN ALL, OF THE FOLLOWING
POWERS, INITIAL THE LINE IN FRONT OF EACH POWER YOU ARE
GRANTING.

TO WITHHOLD A POWER, DO NOT INITIAL THE LINE IN FRONT OF IT. YOU
MAY, BUT NEED NOT, CROSS OUT EACH POWER WITHHELD.

INITIAL

_____ (A) Real property transactions, except transactions subject to D.C.
             Official Code § 42-101.
_____ (B) Tangible personal property transactions.
_____ (C) Stock and bond transactions.
_____ (D) Commodity and option transactions.
_____ (E) Banking and other financial institution transactions.
_____ (F) Business operating transactions.
_____ (G) Insurance and annuity transactions.
_____ (H) Estate, trust, and other beneficiary transactions.

_____ (I) Claims and litigation.
_____ (J) Personal and family maintenance.
_____ (K) Benefits from social security, medicare, medicaid, or other governmental programs, or military service.
_____ (L) Retirement plan transactions.
_____ (M) Tax matters.
_____ (N) ALL OF THE POWERS LISTED ABOVE. YOU NEED NOT INITIAL ANY OTHER LINES IF YOU INITIAL LINE (N).

SPECIAL INSTRUCTIONS:

ON THE FOLLOWING LINES YOU MAY GIVE SPECIAL INSTRUCTIONS LIMITING OR EXTENDING THE POWERS GRANTED TO YOUR AGENT.

_____

_____

_____

UNLESS YOU DIRECT OTHERWISE ABOVE, THIS POWER OF ATTORNEY IS EFFECTIVE IMMEDIATELY AND WILL CONTINUE UNTIL IT IS REVOKED.

This power of attorney will continue to be effective even though I become disabled, incapacitated, or incompetent.

STRIKE THE PRECEDING SENTENCE IF YOU DO NOT WANT THIS POWER OF ATTORNEY TO CONTINUE IF YOU BECOME DISABLED, INCAPACITATED, OR INCOMPETENT.

I agree that any third party who receives a copy of this document may act under it. Revocation of the power of attorney is not effective as to a third party until the third party learns of the revocation. I agree to indemnify the third party for any claims that arise against the third party because of reliance on this power of attorney.

Signed this _____ day of _____, 20____

_____
(Your Signature)

_____
(Your Social Security Number)

The District of Columbia

This document was acknowledged before me on _____ (Date) by
_____ (name of principal)

_____
(Signature of notarial officer)

(Seal, if any) _____
(Title (and Rank))

[My commission expires: _____]

BY ACCEPTING OR ACTING UNDER THE APPOINTMENT, THE AGENT
ASSUMES THE FIDUCIARY AND OTHER LEGAL RESPONSIBILITIES OF AN
AGENT.

GEORGIA POWER OF ATTORNEY

County of _____
State of Georgia

I, _____, (hereinafter 'Principal'), a resident of _____ County, Georgia, do hereby constitute and appoint _____ my true and lawful attorney-in-fact (hereinafter 'Agent') for me and give such person the power(s) specified below to act in my name, place, and stead in any way which I, myself, could do if I were personally present with respect to the following matters:

(Directions: To give the Agent the powers described in paragraphs 1 through 13, place your initials on the blank line at the end of each paragraph. If you DO NOT want to give a power to the Agent, strike through the paragraph or a line within the paragraph and place your initials beside the stricken paragraph or stricken line. The powers described in any paragraph not initialed or which has been struck through will not be conveyed to the Agent. Both the Principal and the Agent must sign their full names at the end of the last paragraph.)

1. Bank and Credit Union Transactions: To make, receive, sign, endorse, execute, acknowledge, deliver, and possess checks, drafts, bills of exchange, letters of credit, notes, stock certificates, withdrawal receipts and deposit instruments relating to accounts or deposits in, or certificates of deposit of banks, savings and loans, credit unions, or other institutions or associations. _____

2. Payment Transactions: To pay all sums of money, at any time or times, that may hereafter be owing by me upon any account, bill or exchange, check, draft, purchase, contract, note, or trade acceptance made, executed, endorsed, accepted, and delivered by me or for me in my name, by my Agent. _____ Note: If you initial paragraph 3 or paragraph 4 which follow, a notarized signature will be required on behalf of the Principal.

3. Real Property Transactions: To lease, sell, mortgage, purchase, exchange, and acquire, and to agree, bargain, and contract for the lease, sale, purchase, exchange, and acquisition of, and to accept, take, receive, and possess any interest in real property whatsoever, on such terms and conditions, and under such covenants, as my Agent shall deem proper; and to maintain, repair, tear down, alter, rebuild, improve, manage, insure, move, rent, lease, sell, convey, subject to liens, mortgages, and security deeds, and in any way or manner deal with all or any part of any interest in real property whatsoever, including specifically, but without limitation,

real property lying and being situate in the State of Georgia, under such terms and conditions, and under such covenants, as my Agent shall deem proper and may for all deferred payments accept purchase money notes payable to me and secured by mortgages or deeds to secure debt, and may from time to time collect and cancel any of said notes, mortgages, security interests, or deeds to secure debt. _____

4.   Personal Property Transactions: To lease, sell, mortgage, purchase, exchange, and acquire, and to agree, bargain, and contract for the lease, sale, purchase, exchange, and acquisition of, and to accept, take, receive, and possess any personal property whatsoever, tangible or intangible, or interest thereto, on such terms and conditions, and under such covenants, as my Agent shall deem proper; and to maintain, repair, improve, manage, insure, rent, lease, sell, convey, subject to liens or mortgages, or to take any other security interests in said property which are recognized under the Uniform Commercial Code as adopted at that   time under the laws of Georgia or any applicable state, or otherwise hypothecate, and in any way or manner deal with all or any part of any real or personal property whatsoever, tangible or intangible, or any interest therein, that I own at the time of execution or may thereafter acquire, under such terms and conditions, and under such covenants, as my Agent shall deem proper. _____

5. Stock and Bond Transactions: To purchase, sell, exchange, surrender, assign, redeem, vote at any meeting, or otherwise transfer any and all shares of stock, bonds, or other securities in any business, association, corporation, partnership, or other legal entity, whether private or public, now or hereafter belonging to me. _____

6. Safe Deposits: To have free access at any time or times to any safe deposit box or vault to which I might have access. _____

7. Borrowing: To borrow from time to time such sums of money as my Agent may deem proper and execute promissory notes, security deeds or agreements, financing statements, or other security instruments in such form as the lender may request and renew said notes and security instruments from time to time in whole or in part. _____

8. Business Operating Transactions: To conduct, engage in, and otherwise transact the affairs of any and all lawful business ventures of whatever nature or kind that I may now or hereafter be involved in. _____

9. Insurance Transactions: To exercise or perform any act, power, duty, right, or obligation, in regard to any contract of life, accident, health, disability, liability, or other type of insurance or any combination of insurance; and to procure new or additional contracts of insurance for me and to designate the beneficiary of same; provided,

however, that my Agent cannot designate himself or herself as beneficiary of any such insurance contracts. _____

10. Disputes and Proceedings: To commence, prosecute, discontinue, or defend all actions or other legal proceedings touching my property, real or personal, or any part thereof, or touching any matter in which I or my property, real or personal, may be in any way concerned. To defend, settle, adjust, make allowances, compound, submit to arbitration, and compromise all accounts, reckonings, claims, and demands whatsoever that now are, or hereafter shall be, pending between me and any person, firm, corporation, or other legal entity, in such manner and in all respects as my Agent shall deem proper. _____

11. Hiring Representatives: To hire accountants, attorneys at law, consultants, clerks, physicians, nurses, agents, servants, workmen, and others and to remove them, and to appoint others in their place, and to pay and allow the persons so employed such salaries, wages, or other remunerations, as my Agent shall deem proper. _____

12. Tax, Social Security, and Unemployment: To prepare, to make elections, to execute and to file all tax, social security, unemployment insurance, and informational returns required by the laws of the United States, or of any state or subdivision thereof, or of any foreign government; to prepare, to execute, and to file all other papers and instruments which the Agent shall think to be desirable or necessary for safeguarding of me against excess or illegal taxation or against penalties imposed for claimed violation of any law or other governmental regulation; and to pay, to compromise, or to contest or to apply for refunds in connection with any taxes or assessments for which I am or may be liable. _____

13. Broad Powers: Without, in any way, limiting the foregoing, generally to do, execute, and perform any other act, deed, matter, or thing whatsoever, that should be done, executed, or performed, including, but not limited to, powers conferred by Code Section 53-12-232 of the Official Code of Georgia Annotated, or that in the opinion of my Agent, should be done, executed, or performed, for my benefit or the benefit of my property, real or personal, and in my name of every nature and kind whatsoever, as fully and effectually as I could do if personally present.

14. Effective Date: This document will become effective upon the date of the Principal's signature unless the Principal indicates that it should become effective at a later date by completing the following, which is optional.

The powers conveyed in this document shall not become effective until the following time or upon the occurrence of the following event or contingency:_____

_____

_____

Note: The Principal may choose to designate one or more persons to determine conclusively that the above-specified event or contingency has occurred. Such person or persons must make a written declaration under penalty of false swearing that such event or contingency has occurred in order to make this document effective. Completion of this provision is optional.

The following person or persons are designated to determine conclusively that the above-specified event or contingency has occurred:

Signed:

_____   _____
Principal   Agent

It is my desire and intention that this power of attorney shall not be affected by my subsequent disability, incapacity, or mental incompetence. Any and all acts done by the Agent pursuant to the powers conveyed herein during any period of my disability or incapacity shall have the same force and effect as if I were competent and not disabled.

I may, at any time, revoke this power of attorney, but it shall be deemed to be in full force and effect as to all persons, institutions, and organizations which shall act in reliance thereon prior to the receipt of written revocation thereof signed by me and prior to receipt of actual notice of my death.

I do hereby ratify and confirm all acts whatsoever which my Agent shall do, or cause to be done, in or about the premises, by virtue of this power of attorney.

All parties dealing in good faith with my Agent may fully rely upon the power of and authority of my Agent to act for me on my behalf and in my name, and may accept and rely on agreements and other instruments entered into or executed by the agent pursuant to this power of attorney.

This instrument shall not be effective as a grant of powers to my Agent until my Agent has executed the Acceptance of Appointment appearing at the end of this instrument. This instrument shall remain effective until revocation by me or my death, whichever occurs first.

Compensation of Agent. (Directions: Initial the line opposite your choice.)

1. My Agent shall receive no compensation for services rendered. _____
2. My Agent shall receive reasonable compensation for services rendered. _____

3. My Agent shall receive $_____ for services rendered. _____

IN WITNESS WHEREOF, I have hereunto set my hand and seal on this _____ day of _____, 20____.

_____
Principal

WITNESSES

_____
_____
Signature and Address

_____
_____
Signature and Address

Note: A notarized signature is not required unless you have initialed paragraph 3 or 4 regarding property transactions.

I, _____, a Notary Public, do hereby certify that _____ personally appeared before me this date and acknowledged the due execution of the foregoing Power of Attorney.

_____
Notary Public

State of Georgia

County of _____

ACCEPTANCE OF APPOINTMENT

I, _____ (print name), have read the foregoing Power of Attorney and am the person identified therein as Agent for _____ (name of grantor of power of attorney), the Principal named therein. I hereby acknowledge the following:

I owe a duty of loyalty and good faith to the Principal, and must use the powers granted to me only for the benefit of the Principal. I must keep the

Principal's funds and other assets separate and apart from my funds and other assets and titled in the name of the Principal. I must not transfer title to any of the Principal's funds or other assets into my name alone. My name must not be added to the title of any funds or other assets of the Principal, unless I am specifically designated as Agent for the Principal in the title.

I must protect and conserve, and exercise prudence and caution in my dealings with, the Principal's funds and other assets. I must keep a full and accurate record of my acts, receipts, and disbursements on behalf of the Principal, and be ready to account to the Principal for such acts, receipts, and disbursements at all times. I must provide an annual accounting to the Principal of my acts, receipts, and disbursements, and must furnish an accounting of such acts, receipts, and disbursements to the personal representative of the Principal's estate within 90 days after the date of death of the Principal.

I have read the Compensation of Agent paragraph in the Power of Attorney and agree to abide by it.

I acknowledge my authority to act on behalf of the Principal ceases at the death of the Principal.

I hereby accept the foregoing appointment as Agent for the Principal with full knowledge of the responsibilities imposed on me, and I will faithfully carry out my duties to the best of my ability.

Dated:_____, 20___.
(Signature)_____
(Address)_____

Note: A notarized signature is not required unless the Principal initialed paragraph 3 or paragraph 4 regarding property transactions.

I, _____, a Notary Public, do hereby certify that _____ personally appeared before me this date and acknowledge the due execution of the foregoing Acceptance of Appointment.

_____
Notary Public

ILLINOIS DURABLE POWER OF ATTORNEY

NOTICE: THE PURPOSE OF THIS POWER OF ATTORNEY IS TO GIVE THE PERSON YOU DESIGNATE (YOUR "AGENT") BROAD POWERS TO HANDLE YOUR PROPERTY, WHICH MAY INCLUDE POWERS TO PLEDGE, SELL OR OTHERWISE DISPOSE OF ANY REAL OR PERSONAL PROPERTY WITHOUT ADVANCE NOTICE TO YOU OR APPROVAL BY YOU. THIS FORM DOES NOT IMPOSE A DUTY ON YOUR AGENT TO EXERCISE GRANTED POWERS; BUT WHEN POWERS ARE EXERCISED, YOUR AGENT WILL HAVE TO USE DUE CARE TO ACT FOR YOUR BENEFIT AND IN ACCORDANCE WITH THIS FORM AND KEEP A RECORD OF RECEIPTS, DISBURSEMENTS AND SIGNIFICANT ACTIONS TAKEN AS AGENT. A COURT CAN TAKE AWAY THE POWERS OF YOUR AGENT IF IT FINDS THE AGENT IS NOT ACTING PROPERLY. YOU MAY NAME SUCCESSOR AGENTS UNDER THIS FORM BUT NOT CO-AGENTS. UNLESS YOU EXPRESSLY LIMIT THE DURATION OF THIS POWER IN THE MANNER PROVIDED BELOW, UNTIL YOU REVOKE THIS POWER OR A COURT ACTING ON YOUR BEHALF TERMINATES IT, YOUR AGENT MAY EXERCISE THE POWERS GIVEN HERE THROUGHOUT YOUR LIFETIME, EVEN AFTER YOU BECOME DISABLED. THE POWERS YOU GIVE YOUR AGENT ARE EXPLAINED MORE FULLY IN SECTION 3-4 OF THE ILLINOIS "STATUTORY SHORT FORM POWER OF ATTORNEY FOR PROPERTY LAW" OF WHICH THIS FORM IS A PART (SEE THE END OF THIS FORM). THAT LAW EXPRESSLY PERMITS THE USE OF ANY DIFFERENT FORM OF POWER OF ATTORNEY YOU MAY DESIRE. IF THERE IS ANYTHING ABOUT THIS FORM THAT YOU DO NOT UNDERSTAND, YOU SHOULD ASK A LAWYER TO EXPLAIN IT TO YOU.

POWER OF ATTORNEY made this _____ day of _____ (month), _____ (year)

1. I, _____, (insert name and address of principal) hereby appoint: _____ _____ (insert name and address of agent) as my attorney-in-fact (my "agent") to act for me and in my name (in any way I could act in person) with respect to the following powers, as defined in Section 3-4 of the "Statutory Short Form Power of Attorney for Property Law" (including all amendments), but subject to any limitations on or additions to the specified powers inserted in paragraph 2 or 3 below:

(YOU MUST STRIKE OUT ANY ONE OR MORE OF THE FOLLOWING CATEGORIES OF POWERS YOU DO NOT WANT YOUR AGENT TO HAVE. FAILURE TO STRIKE THE TITLE OF ANY CATEGORY WILL CAUSE THE POWERS DESCRIBED IN THAT CATEGORY TO BE GRANTED TO THE AGENT. TO STRIKE OUT A CATEGORY YOU MUST DRAW A LINE THROUGH THE TITLE OF THAT CATEGORY.)

1. Real estate transactions.
2. Financial institution transactions.
3. Stock and bond transactions.
4. Tangible personal property transactions.
5. Safe deposit box transactions.
6. Insurance and annuity transactions.
7. Retirement plan transactions.
8. Social Security, employment and military service benefits.
9. Tax matters.
10. Claims and litigation.
11. Commodity and option transactions.
12. Business operations.
13. Borrowing transactions.
14. Estate transactions.
15. All other property powers and transactions.

(LIMITATIONS ON AND ADDITIONS TO THE AGENT'S POWERS MAY BE INCLUDED IN THIS POWER OF ATTORNEY IF THEY ARE SPECIFICALLY DESCRIBED BELOW.)

2. The powers granted above shall not include the following powers or shall be modified or limited in the following particulars (here you may include any specific limitations you deem appropriate, such as a prohibition or conditions on the sale of particular stock or real estate or special rules on borrowing by the agent):

_____
_____
_____

3. In addition to the powers granted above, I grant my agent the following powers (here you may add any other delegable powers including, without limitation, power to make gifts, exercise powers of appointment, name or change beneficiaries or joint tenants or revoke or amend any trust specifically referred to below):

_____
_____
_____

(YOUR AGENT WILL HAVE AUTHORITY TO EMPLOY OTHER PERSONS AS NECESSARY TO ENABLE THE AGENT TO PROPERLY EXERCISE THE POWERS GRANTED IN THIS FORM, BUT YOUR AGENT WILL HAVE TO

MAKE ALL DISCRETIONARY DECISIONS. IF YOU WANT TO GIVE YOUR AGENT THE RIGHT TO DELEGATE DISCRETIONARY DECISION-MAKING POWERS TO OTHERS, YOU SHOULD KEEP THE NEXT SENTENCE, OTHERWISE IT SHOULD BE STRUCK OUT.)

4. My agent shall have the right by written instrument to delegate any or all of the foregoing powers involving discretionary decision-making to any person or persons whom my agent may select, but such delegation may be amended or revoked by any agent (including any successor) named by me who is acting under this power of attorney at the time of reference.

(YOUR AGENT WILL BE ENTITLED TO REIMBURSEMENT FOR ALL REASONABLE EXPENSES INCURRED IN ACTING UNDER THIS POWER OF ATTORNEY. STRIKE OUT THE NEXT SENTENCE IF YOU DO NOT WANT YOUR AGENT TO ALSO BE ENTITLED TO REASONABLE COMPENSATION FOR SERVICES AS AGENT.)

5. My agent shall be entitled to reasonable compensation for services rendered as agent under this power of attorney.

(THIS POWER OF ATTORNEY MAY BE AMENDED OR REVOKED BY YOU AT ANY TIME AND IN ANY MANNER. ABSENT AMENDMENT OR REVOCATION, THE AUTHORITY GRANTED IN THIS POWER OF ATTORNEY WILL BECOME EFFECTIVE AT THE TIME THIS POWER IS SIGNED AND WILL CONTINUE UNTIL YOUR DEATH UNLESS A LIMITATION ON THE BEGINNING DATE OR DURATION IS MADE BY INITIALING AND COMPLETING EITHER (OR BOTH) OF THE FOLLOWING:)

6. ( ) This power of attorney shall become effective on _____ _____ (insert a future date or event during your lifetime, such as court determination of your disability, when you want this power to first take effect)

7. ( ) This power of attorney shall terminate on _____ (insert a future date or event, such as court determination of your disability, when you want this power to terminate prior to your death)

(IF YOU WISH TO NAME SUCCESSOR AGENTS, INSERT THE NAME(S) AND ADDRESS(ES) OF SUCH SUCCESSOR(S) IN THE FOLLOWING PARAGRAPH.)

8. If any agent named by me shall die, become incompetent, resign or refuse

to accept the office of agent, I name the following (each to act alone and successively, in the order named) as successor(s) to such agent:

_____

_____

For purposes of this paragraph 8, a person shall be considered to be incompetent if and while the person is a minor or an adjudicated incompetent or disabled person or the person is unable to give prompt and intelligent consideration to business matters, as certified by a licensed physician. (IF YOU WISH TO NAME YOUR AGENT AS GUARDIAN OF YOUR ESTATE, IN THE EVENT A COURT DECIDES THAT ONE SHOULD BE APPOINTED, YOU MAY, BUT ARE NOT REQUIRED TO, DO SO BY RETAINING THE FOLLOWING PARAGRAPH. THE COURT WILL APPOINT YOUR AGENT IF THE COURT FINDS THAT SUCH APPOINTMENT WILL SERVE YOUR BEST INTERESTS AND WELFARE. STRIKE OUT PARAGRAPH 9 IF YOU DO NOT WANT YOUR AGENT TO ACT AS GUARDIAN.)

9. If a guardian of my estate (my property) is to be appointed, I nominate the agent acting under this power of attorney as such guardian, to serve without bond or security.

10. I am fully informed as to all the contents of this form and understand the full import of this grant of powers to my agent.

Signed _____

              (principal)

(YOU MAY, BUT ARE NOT REQUIRED TO, REQUEST YOUR AGENT AND SUCCESSOR AGENTS TO PROVIDE SPECIMEN SIGNATURES BELOW. IF YOU INCLUDE SPECIMEN SIGNATURES IN THIS POWER OF ATTORNEY, YOU MUST COMPLETE THE CERTIFICATION OPPOSITE THE SIGNATURES OF THE AGENTS.)

Specimen signature of agent (and successors)

_____

(agent)

I certify that the above signature of my agent is correct.

_____

(principal)

Specimen signature of successor agent

_____

(successor agent)

I certify that the above signature of my successor agent is correct.

_____

(principal)

Specimen signature of successor agent

_____

(successor agent)

I certify that the above signature of my successor agent is correct.

_____

(principal)

(THIS POWER OF ATTORNEY WILL NOT BE EFFECTIVE UNLESS IT IS NOTARIZED AND SIGNED BY AT LEAST ONE ADDITIONAL WITNESS, USING THE FORM BELOW.)

State of _____
County of _____

The undersigned, a notary public in and for the above county and state, certifies that _____, known to me to be the same person whose name is subscribed as principal to the foregoing power of attorney, appeared before me and the additional witness in person and acknowledged signing and delivering the instrument as the free and voluntary act of the principal, for the uses and purposes therein set forth(, and certified to the correctness of the signature(s) of the agent(s)).

Dated: _____   (SEAL)

_____

Notary Public

My commission expires _____

The undersigned witness certifies that _____, known to me to be the same person whose name is subscribed as principal to the foregoing power of attorney, appeared before me and the notary public and acknowledged signing and delivering the instrument as the free and voluntary act of the principal, for the uses and purposes therein set forth. I believe him or her to be of sound mind and memory.

Dated: _____ (SEAL)

_____
Witness

(THE NAME AND ADDRESS OF THE PERSON PREPARING THIS FORM SHOULD BE INSERTED IF THE AGENT WILL HAVE POWER TO CONVEY ANY INTEREST IN REAL ESTATE.)

This document was prepared by:

_____

_____

_____

MINNESOTA STATUTORY SHORT FORM POWER OF ATTORNEY

MINNESOTA STATUTES, SECTION 523.23

IMPORTANT NOTICE: The powers granted by this document are broad and sweeping. They are defined in Minnesota Statutes section 523.24. If you have any questions about these powers, obtain competent advice. This power of attorney may be revoked by you if you wish to do so. This power of attorney is automatically terminated if it is to your spouse and proceedings are commenced for dissolution, legal separation or annulment of your marriage. This power of attorney authorizes, but does not require, the attorney-in-fact to act for you.

PRINCIPAL (Name and address of person granting the power)

_____
_____
_____

ATTORNEY(S)-IN-FACT SUCCESSOR ATTORNEY(S)-IN-FACT (Optional)
(Names and Addresses)

_____
_____
_____

To act if any named attorney-in-fact dies, resigns or is otherwise unable to serve. (Name and Address)
First Successor

_____
_____
_____

Second Successor

_____
_____
_____

NOTICE: If more than one attorney-in-fact is designated, make a check or "x" on the line in front of one of the following statements:

_____Each attorney-in-fact may independently exercise the powers granted.

_____All attorneys-in-fact must jointly exercise the powers granted.

EXPIRATION DATE (Optional)_____
Use specific month, day and year only

I (the above named Principal), appoint the above named Attorney(s)-in-fact:

FIRST: To act for me in any way I could act with respect to the following matters, as each of them is defined in Minnesota Statutes, section 523.24:

(To grant the attorney-in fact any of the following powers, make a check or "x" on the line in front of each power being granted. You may, but need not, cross out each power not granted. Failure to make a check or "x" on the line in front of the power will have the effect of deleting the power unless the line in front of the power N is checked or x-ed.)

Check or "x"

_____(A) Real property transactions;
I choose to limit this power to real property in _____County, MN described as follows: (use legal description. Do not use address.)____
_____ (If more space is needed, continue on the back or on an attachment.)

_____(B) Tangible personal property transactions;
_____(C) Bond, share, and commodity transactions;
_____(D) Banking transactions;
_____(E) Business operating transactions;
_____(F) Insurance transactions;
_____(G) Beneficiary transactions;
_____(H) Gift transactions;
_____(I) Fiduciary transactions;
_____(J) Claims and litigations;
_____(K) Family maintenance;
_____(L) Benefits from military service;
_____(M) Records, reports, and statements;
_____(N) All of the powers listed in (A) through (M) above and all other matters.

SECOND: (you must indicate below whether or not this power of attorney will be effective if you become incapacitated or incompetent. Make a check or "x" on the line in front of the statement that expresses you intent.)
_____This power of attorney shall continue to be effective if I become incapacitated or incompetent.
_____This power of attorney **shall not** be effective if I become incapacitated or incompetent.

THIRD: (you must mark below whether or not this power of attorney authorizes the attorney-in-fact to transfer your property to the attorney-in-fact. Make a check or "x" on the line in front of the statement that expresses your intent.)

_____This power of attorney authorizes the attorney-in-fact to transfer my property to the attorney-in-fact.

_____This power of attorney **does not** authorize the attorney-in-fact to transfer my property to the attorney-in-fact.

FOURTH: (you may indicate below whether or not the attorney-in-fact is required to make an accounting.
Make a check or "x" on the line in front of the statement that expresses your intent.)

_____My attorney-in-fact need not render an accounting unless I request it or the accounting is otherwise required by Minnesota Statutes, section 523.21.

_____My attorney-in-fact must render <u>monthly, quarterly, annual (circle one)</u> accounting to me, **or to**_____ (Name and Address) during my lifetime, and a final accounting to the personal representative of my estate, if any is appointed, after my death.

In Witness Whereof I have hereunto signed my name this_____ day of_____ _____ 20_____.

_____
(Signature of Principal)

(Acknowledgment of Principal)

STATE OF MINNESOTA
County of_____
The foregoing instrument was acknowledged before me this _____day of_____20_____ , by_____(Insert name of principal)

_____
Signature of Notary Public

This instrument was drafted by:_____
_____
Specimen signature(s) of Attorney(s)-in-Fact: (Notarization not required)
_____
_____

MONTANA STATUTORY POWER OF ATTORNEY FORM

NOTICE: THE POWERS GRANTED BY THIS DOCUMENT ARE BROAD AND SWEEPING. THEY ARE EXPLAINED IN THIS PART. IF YOU HAVE ANY QUESTIONS ABOUT THESE POWERS, OBTAIN COMPETENT LEGAL ADVICE. THIS DOCUMENT DOES NOT AUTHORIZE ANYONE TO MAKE MEDICAL AND OTHER HEALTH CARE DECISIONS FOR YOU. YOU MAY REVOKE THIS POWER OF ATTORNEY IF YOU LATER WISH TO DO SO.

I _____(insert your name and address) appoint_____(insert the name and address of the person appointed) as my agent (attorney-in-fact) to act for me in any lawful way with respect to the following initialed subjects:

TO GRANT ALL OF THE FOLLOWING POWERS, INITIAL THE LINE IN FRONT OF (N) AND IGNORE THE LINES IN FRONT OF THE OTHER POWERS.

TO GRANT ONE OR MORE, BUT FEWER THAN ALL, OF THE FOLLOWING POWERS, INITIAL THE LINE IN FRONT OF EACH POWER YOU ARE GRANTING.

TO WITHHOLD A POWER, DO NOT INITIAL THE LINE IN FRONT OF IT. YOU MAY, BUT NEED NOT, CROSS OUT EACH POWER WITHHELD.

INITIAL
.... (A) real property transactions;
.... (B) tangible personal property transactions;
.... (C) stock and bond transactions;
.... (D) commodity and option transactions;
.... (E) banking and other financial institution transactions;
.... (F) business operating transactions;
.... (G) insurance and annuity transactions;
.... (H) estate, trust, and other beneficiary transactions;
.... (I) claims and litigation;
.... (J) personal and family maintenance;
.... (K) benefits from social security, medicare, medicaid, or other
        governmental programs or from military service;
.... (L) retirement plan transactions;
.... (M) tax matters;
.... (N) ALL OF THE POWERS LISTED ABOVE. YOU NEED NOT INITIAL
        ANY OTHER LINES IF YOU INITIAL LINE (N).

SPECIAL INSTRUCTIONS: ON THE FOLLOWING LINES, YOU MAY GIVE SPECIAL INSTRUCTIONS LIMITING OR EXTENDING THE POWERS GRANTED TO YOUR AGENT.

_____

_____

UNLESS YOU DIRECT OTHERWISE ABOVE, THIS POWER OF ATTORNEY IS EFFECTIVE IMMEDIATELY AND WILL CONTINUE UNTIL IT IS REVOKED.

This power of attorney revokes all previous powers of attorney signed by me. STRIKE THE PRECEDING SENTENCE IF YOU DO NOT WANT THIS POWER OF ATTORNEY TO REVOKE ALL PREVIOUS POWERS OF ATTORNEY SIGNED BY YOU.

IF YOU DO WANT THIS POWER OF ATTORNEY TO REVOKE ALL PREVIOUS POWERS OF ATTORNEY SIGNED BY YOU, YOU SHOULD READ THOSE POWERS OF ATTORNEY AND SATISFY THEIR PROVISIONS CONCERNING REVOCATION. THIRD PARTIES WHO RECEIVED COPIES OF THOSE POWERS OF ATTORNEY SHOULD BE NOTIFIED.

This power of attorney will continue to be effective if I become disabled, incapacitated, or incompetent. STRIKE THE PRECEDING SENTENCE IF YOU DO NOT WANT THIS POWER OF ATTORNEY TO CONTINUE IF YOU BECOME DISABLED, INCAPACITATED, OR INCOMPETENT.

If it becomes necessary to appoint a conservator of my estate or guardian of my person, I nominate my agent. STRIKE THE PRECEDING SENTENCE IF YOU DO NOT WANT TO NOMINATE YOUR AGENT AS CONSERVATOR OR GUARDIAN.

If any agent named by me dies, becomes incompetent, resigns or refuses to accept the office of agent, I name the following (each to act alone and successively, in the order named) as successor(s) to the agent:

1. _____

2. _____

3. _____

For purposes of this subsection, a person is considered to be incompetent if and while: (1) the person is a minor; (2) the person is an adjudicated incompetent or disabled person; (3) a conservator has been appointed to act for the person; (4)

a guardian has been appointed to act for the person; or (5) the person is unable to give prompt and intelligent consideration to business matters as certified by a licensed physician.

I agree that any third party who receives a copy of this document may act under it. I may revoke this power of attorney by a written document that expressly indicates my intent to revoke. Revocation of the power of attorney is not effective as to a third party until the third party learns of the revocation. I agree to indemnify the third party for any claims that arise against the third party because of reliance on this power of attorney.

Signed this _____ day of _____, 20____

_____
(Your Signature)

_____
(Your Social Security Number)

State of _____
(County) of _____

This document was acknowledged before me on

_____
(Date) by

_____
(Name of Principal)

_____
(Signature of Notarial Officer)

_____
(Seal, if any) (Title) (and Rank)

My commission expires_____

BY ACCEPTING OR ACTING UNDER THE APPOINTMENT, THE AGENT ASSUMES THE FIDUCIARY AND OTHER LEGAL RESPONSIBILITIES OF AN AGENT.

A Montana statutory power of attorney is legally sufficient under this part if the wording of the form substantially complies with subsection (1), the form is properly completed, and the signature of the principal is acknowledged.

If the line in front of (N) of the form under subsection (1) is initialed, an initial on the line in front of any other power does not limit the powers granted by line (N).

NEBRASKA GENERAL DURABLE POWER OF ATTORNEY

THE POWERS YOU GRANT BELOW ARE EFFECTIVE EVEN IF YOU BECOME DISABLED OR INCOMPETENT

NOTICE: THE POWERS GRANTED BY THIS DOCUMENT ARE BROAD AND SWEEPING. THEY ARE EXPLAINED IN THE UNIFORM STATUTORY FORM POWER OF ATTORNEY ACT. IF YOU HAVE ANY QUESTIONS ABOUT THESE POWERS, OBTAIN COMPETENT LEGAL ADVICE. THIS DOCUMENT DOES NOT AUTHORIZE ANYONE TO MAKE MEDICAL AND OTHER HEALTH-CARE DECISIONS FOR YOU. YOU MAY REVOKE THIS POWER OF ATTORNEY IF YOU LATER WISH TO DO SO.

I _____[insert your name and address] appoint _____[insert the name and address of the person appointed] as my Agent (attorney-in-fact) to act for me in any lawful way with respect to the following initialed subjects:

TO GRANT ALL OF THE FOLLOWING POWERS, INITIAL THE LINE IN FRONT OF (N) AND IGNORE THE LINES IN FRONT OF THE OTHER POWERS.

TO GRANT ONE OR MORE, BUT FEWER THAN ALL, OF THE FOLLOWING POWERS, INITIAL THE LINE IN FRONT OF EACH POWER YOU ARE GRANTING.

TO WITHHOLD A POWER, DO NOT INITIAL THE LINE IN FRONT OF IT. YOU MAY, BUT NEED NOT, CROSS OUT EACH POWER WITHHELD.

Note: If you initial Item A or Item B, which follow, a notarized signature will be required on behalf of the Principal.

INITIAL

_____ (A) Real property transactions. To lease, sell, mortgage, purchase, exchange, and acquire, and to agree, bargain, and contract for the lease, sale, purchase, exchange, and acquisition of, and to accept, take, receive, and possess any interest in real property whatsoever, on such terms and conditions, and under such covenants, as my Agent shall deem proper; and to maintain, repair, tear down, alter, rebuild, improve manage, insure, move, rent, lease, sell, convey, subject to liens, mortgages, and security deeds, and in any way or manner deal with all or any part of any interest in real property whatsoever, including specifically, but without limitation, real property lying and being situated in the State of Nebraska, under such terms and conditions, and under such covenants, as my Agent shall deem proper and may for all deferred payments accept purchase money notes payable to me and secured by mortgages or deeds to secure debt, and may from time to time collect and cancel any of said notes, mortgages, security interests, or deeds to secure debt.

_____ (B) Tangible personal property transactions. To lease, sell, mortgage, purchase, exchange, and acquire, and to agree, bargain, and contract for the lease, sale, purchase, exchange, and acquisition of, and to accept, take, receive, and possess any personal property whatsoever, tangible or intangible, or interest thereto, on such terms and conditions, and under such covenants, as my Agent shall deem proper; and to maintain, repair, improve, manage, insure, rent, lease, sell, convey, subject to liens or mortgages, or to take any other security interests in said property which are recognized under the Uniform Commercial Code as adopted at that time under the laws of the State of Nebraska or any applicable state, or otherwise hypothecate (pledge), and in any way or manner deal with all or any part of any real or personal property whatsoever, tangible or intangible, or any interest therein, that I own at the time of execution or may thereafter acquire, under such terms and conditions, and under such covenants, as my Agent shall deem proper.

_____ (C) Stock and bond transactions. To purchase, sell, exchange, surrender, assign, redeem, vote at any meeting, or otherwise transfer any and all shares of stock, bonds, or other securities in any business, association, corporation, partnership, or other legal entity, whether private or public, now or hereafter belonging to me.

_____ (D) Commodity and option transactions. To buy, sell, exchange, assign, convey, settle and exercise commodities futures contracts and call and put options on stocks and stock indices traded on a regulated options exchange and collect and receipt for all proceeds of any such transactions; establish or continue option accounts for the principal with any securities or futures broker; and, in general, exercise all powers with respect to commodities and options which the principal could if present and under no disability.

_____ (E) Banking and other financial institution transactions. To make, receive, sign, endorse, execute, acknowledge, deliver and possess checks, drafts, bills of exchange, letters of credit, notes, stock certificates, withdrawal receipts and deposit instruments relating to accounts or deposits in, or certificates of deposit of banks, savings and loans, credit unions, or other institutions or associations. To pay all sums of money, at any time or times, that may hereafter be owing by me upon any account, bill of exchange, check, draft, purchase, contract, note, or trade acceptance made, executed, endorsed, accepted, and delivered by me or for me in my name, by my Agent. To borrow from time to time such sums of money as my Agent may deem proper and execute promissory notes, security deeds or agreements, financing statements, or other security instruments in such form as the lender may request and renew said notes and security instruments from time to time in whole or in part. To have free access at any time or times to any safe deposit box or vault to which I might have access.

_____ (F) Business operating transactions. To conduct, engage in, and otherwise transact the affairs of any and all lawful business ventures of whatever nature or kind that I may now or hereafter be involved in. To organize or continue and conduct any business which term includes, without limitation, any farming, manufacturing, service, mining, retailing or other type of business operation in any form, whether as a proprietorship, joint venture, partnership, corporation, trust or other legal entity; operate, buy, sell, expand, contract, terminate or liquidate any business; direct, control, supervise, manage or participate in the operation of any business and engage, compensate and discharge business managers, employees, agents, attorneys, accountants and consultants; and, in general, exercise all powers with respect to business interests and operations which the principal could if present and under no disability.

_____ (G) Insurance and annuity transactions. To exercise or perform any act, power, duty, right, or obligation, in regard to any contract of life, accident, health, disability, liability, or other type of insurance or any combination of insurance; and to procure new or additional contracts of insurance for me and to designate the beneficiary of same; provided, however, that my Agent cannot designate himself or herself as beneficiary of any such insurance contracts.

_____ (H) Estate, trust, and other beneficiary transactions. To accept, receipt for, exercise, release, reject, renounce, assign, disclaim, demand, sue for, claim and recover any legacy, bequest, devise, gift or other property interest or payment due or payable to or for the principal; assert any interest in and exercise any power over any trust, estate or property subject to fiduciary control; establish a revocable trust solely for the benefit of the principal that terminates at the death of the principal and is then distributable to the legal representative of the estate of the principal; and, in general, exercise all powers with respect to estates and trusts which the principal could exercise if present and under no disability; provided, however, that the Agent may not make or change a will and may not revoke or amend a trust revocable or amendable by the principal or require the trustee of any trust for the benefit of the principal to pay income or principal to the Agent unless specific authority to that end is given.

_____ (I) Claims and litigation. To commence, prosecute, discontinue, or defend all actions or other legal proceedings touching my property, real or personal, or any part thereof, or touching any matter in which I or my property, real or personal, may be in any way concerned. To defend, settle, adjust, make allowances, compound, submit to arbitration, and compromise all accounts, reckonings, claims, and demands whatsoever that now are, or hereafter shall be, pending between me and any person, firm, corporation, or other legal entity, in such manner and in all respects as my Agent shall deem proper.

_____ (J) Personal and family maintenance. To hire accountants, attorneys at law, consultants, clerks, physicians, nurses, agents, servants, workmen, and others and to remove them, and to appoint others in their place, and to pay and allow the persons so employed such salaries, wages, or other remunerations, as my Agent shall deem proper.

_____ (K) Benefits from Social Security, Medicare, Medicaid, or other governmental programs, or military service. To prepare, sign and file any claim or application for Social Security, unemployment or military service benefits; sue for, settle or abandon any claims to any benefit or assistance under any federal, state, local or foreign statute or regulation; control, deposit to any account, collect, receipt for, and take title to and hold all benefits under any Social Security, unemployment, military service or other state, federal, local or foreign statute or regulation; and, in general, exercise all powers with respect to Social Security, unemployment, military service, and governmental benefits, including but not limited to Medicare and Medicaid, which the principal could exercise if present and under no disability.

_____ (L) Retirement plan transactions. To contribute to, withdraw from and deposit funds in any type of retirement plan (which term includes, without limitation, any tax qualified or nonqualified pension, profit sharing, stock bonus, employee savings and other retirement plan, individual retirement account, deferred compensation plan and any other type of employee benefit plan); select and change payment options for the principal under any retirement plan; make rollover contributions from any retirement plan to other retirement plans or individual retirement accounts; exercise all investment powers available under any type of self-directed retirement plan; and, in general, exercise all powers with respect to retirement plans and retirement plan account balances which the principal could if present and under no disability.

_____ (M) Tax matters. To prepare, to make elections, to execute and to file all tax, social security, unemployment insurance, and informational returns required by the laws of the United States, or of any state or subdivision thereof, or of any foreign government; to prepare, to execute, and to file all other papers and instruments which the Agent shall think to be desirable or necessary for safeguarding of me against excess or illegal taxation or against penalties imposed for claimed violation of any law or other governmental regulation; and to pay, to compromise, or to contest or to apply for refunds in connection with any taxes or assessments for which I am or may be liable.

_____ (N) ALL OF THE POWERS LISTED ABOVE. YOU NEED NOT INITIAL ANY OTHER LINES IF YOU INITIAL LINE (N).

SPECIAL INSTRUCTIONS:

ON THE FOLLOWING LINES YOU MAY GIVE SPECIAL INSTRUCTIONS LIMITING OR EXTENDING THE POWERS GRANTED TO YOUR AGENT.

_____

_____

_____

THIS POWER OF ATTORNEY IS EFFECTIVE IMMEDIATELY AND WILL CONTINUE UNTIL IT IS REVOKED.

THIS POWER OF ATTORNEY SHALL BE CONSTRUED AS A GENERAL DURABLE POWER OF ATTORNEY AND SHALL CONTINUE TO BE EFFECTIVE EVEN IF I BECOME DISABLED, INCAPACITATED, OR INCOMPETENT.

(YOUR AGENT WILL HAVE AUTHORITY TO EMPLOY OTHER PERSONS AS NECESSARY TO ENABLE THE AGENT TO PROPERLY EXERCISE THE POWERS GRANTED IN THIS FORM, BUT YOUR AGENT WILL HAVE TO MAKE ALL DISCRETIONARY DECISIONS. IF YOU WANT TO GIVE YOUR AGENT THE RIGHT TO DELEGATE DISCRETIONARY DECISION-MAKING POWERS TO OTHERS, YOU SHOULD KEEP THE NEXT SENTENCE, OTHERWISE IT SHOULD BE STRICKEN.)

Authority to Delegate. My Agent shall have the right by written instrument to delegate any or all of the foregoing powers involving discretionary decision-making to any person or persons whom my Agent may select, but such delegation may be amended or revoked by any agent (including any successor) named by me who is acting under this power of attorney at the time of reference.

(YOUR AGENT WILL BE ENTITLED TO REIMBURSEMENT FOR ALL REASONABLE EXPENSES INCURRED IN ACTING UNDER THIS POWER

OF ATTORNEY. STRIKE OUT THE NEXT SENTENCE IF YOU DO NOT WANT YOUR AGENT TO ALSO BE ENTITLED TO REASONABLE COMPENSATION FOR SERVICES AS AGENT.)

Right to Compensation. My Agent shall be entitled to reasonable compensation for services rendered as agent under this power of attorney.

(IF YOU WISH TO NAME SUCCESSOR AGENTS, INSERT THE NAME(S) AND ADDRESS(ES) OF SUCH SUCCESSOR(S) IN THE FOLLOWING PARAGRAPH.)

Successor Agent. If any Agent named by me shall die, become incompetent, resign or refuse to accept the office of Agent, I name the following (each to act alone and successively, in the order named) as successor(s) to such Agent:
_____
_____

Choice of Law. THIS POWER OF ATTORNEY WILL BE GOVERNED BY THE LAWS OF THE STATE OF NEBRASKA WITHOUT REGARD FOR CONFLICTS OF LAWS PRINCIPLES. IT WAS EXECUTED IN THE STATE OF NEBRASKA AND IS INTENDED TO BE VALID IN ALL JURISDICTIONS OF THE UNITED STATES OF AMERICA AND ALL FOREIGN NATIONS.

I am fully informed as to all the contents of this form and understand the full import of this grant of powers to my Agent.

I agree that any third party who receives a copy of this document may act under it. Revocation of the power of attorney is not effective as to a third party until the third party learns of the revocation. I agree to indemnify the third party for any claims that arise against the third party because of reliance on this power of attorney.

Signed this _____ day of _____, 20____
_____
[Your Signature]

CERTIFICATE OF ACKNOWLEDGMENT OF NOTARY PUBLIC

STATE OF NEBRASKA
COUNTY OF _____

This document was acknowledged before me on _____ [Date] by
_____ [name of principal].

[Notary Seal, if any]:
_____
(Signature of Notarial Officer)

Notary Public for the State of Nebraska

My commission expires: _____

ACKNOWLEDGMENT OF AGENT

BY ACCEPTING OR ACTING UNDER THE APPOINTMENT, THE AGENT
ASSUMES THE FIDUCIARY AND OTHER LEGAL RESPONSIBILITIES OF AN
AGENT.

_____
[Typed or Printed Name of Agent]

_____
[Signature of Agent]

PREPARATION STATEMENT

This document was prepared by the following individual:

_____
[Typed or Printed Name]
_____
[Signature]

NEW HAMPSHIRE GENERAL DURABLE POWER OF ATTORNEY

THE POWERS YOU GRANT BELOW ARE EFFECTIVE EVEN IF YOU
BECOME DISABLED OR INCOMPETENT

**NOTICE: THE POWERS GRANTED BY THIS DOCUMENT ARE BROAD
AND SWEEPING. THEY ARE EXPLAINED IN THE UNIFORM STATUTORY
FORM POWER OF ATTORNEY ACT. IF YOU HAVE ANY QUESTIONS
ABOUT THESE POWERS, OBTAIN COMPETENT LEGAL ADVICE. THIS
DOCUMENT DOES NOT AUTHORIZE ANYONE TO MAKE MEDICAL AND
OTHER HEALTH-CARE DECISIONS FOR YOU. YOU MAY REVOKE THIS
POWER OF ATTORNEY IF YOU LATER WISH TO DO SO.**

I _____

_____ [insert your name and address] appoint _____

_____ [insert the name and
address of the person appointed] as my Agent (attorney-in-fact) to act for me in
any lawful way with respect to the following initialed subjects:

TO GRANT ALL OF THE FOLLOWING POWERS, INITIAL THE LINE IN FRONT
OF (N) AND IGNORE THE LINES IN FRONT OF THE OTHER POWERS.

TO GRANT ONE OR MORE, BUT FEWER THAN ALL, OF THE FOLLOWING
POWERS, INITIAL THE LINE IN FRONT OF EACH POWER YOU ARE
GRANTING.

TO WITHHOLD A POWER, DO NOT INITIAL THE LINE IN FRONT OF IT. YOU
MAY, BUT NEED NOT, CROSS OUT EACH POWER WITHHELD.

Note: If you initial Item A or Item B, which follow, a notarized signature will be
required on behalf of the Principal.

INITIAL

_____ (A) Real property transactions. To lease, sell, mortgage, purchase,
exchange, and acquire, and to agree, bargain, and contract for the lease, sale,
purchase, exchange, and acquisition of, and to accept, take, receive, and
possess any interest in real property whatsoever, on such terms and conditions,
and under such covenants, as my Agent shall deem proper; and to maintain,
repair, tear down, alter, rebuild, improve manage, insure, move, rent, lease,
sell, convey, subject to liens, mortgages, and security deeds, and in any way

or manner deal with all or any part of any interest in real property whatsoever, including specifically, but without limitation, real property lying and being situated in the State of New Hampshire, under such terms and conditions, and under such covenants, as my Agent shall deem proper and may for all deferred payments accept purchase money notes payable to me and secured by mortgages or deeds to secure debt, and may from time to time collect and cancel any of said notes, mortgages, security interests, or deeds to secure debt.

_____ (B) Tangible personal property transactions. To lease, sell, mortgage, purchase, exchange, and acquire, and to agree, bargain, and contract for the lease, sale, purchase, exchange, and acquisition of, and to accept, take, receive, and possess any personal property whatsoever, tangible or intangible, or interest thereto, on such terms and conditions, and under such covenants, as my Agent shall deem proper; and to maintain, repair, improve, manage, insure, rent, lease, sell, convey, subject to liens or mortgages, or to take any other security interests in said property which are recognized under the Uniform Commercial Code as adopted at that time under the laws of the State of New Hampshire or any applicable state, or otherwise hypothecate (pledge), and in any way or manner deal with all or any part of any real or personal property whatsoever, tangible or intangible, or any interest therein, that I own at the time of execution or may thereafter acquire, under such terms and conditions, and under such covenants, as my Agent shall deem proper.

_____ (C) Stock and bond transactions. To purchase, sell, exchange, surrender, assign, redeem, vote at any meeting, or otherwise transfer any and all shares of stock, bonds, or other securities in any business, association, corporation, partnership, or other legal entity, whether private or public, now or hereafter belonging to me.

_____ (D) Commodity and option transactions. To buy, sell, exchange, assign, convey, settle and exercise commodities futures contracts and call and put options on stocks and stock indices traded on a regulated options exchange and collect and receipt for all proceeds of any such transactions; establish or continue option accounts for the principal with any securities or futures broker; and, in general, exercise all powers with respect to commodities and options which the principal could if present and under no disability.

_____ (E) Banking and other financial institution transactions. To make, receive, sign, endorse, execute, acknowledge, deliver and possess checks, drafts, bills of exchange, letters of credit, notes, stock certificates, withdrawal receipts and deposit instruments relating to accounts or deposits in, or certificates of deposit of banks, savings and loans, credit unions, or other institutions or associations. To pay all sums of money, at any time or times, that may hereafter be owing by me upon any account, bill of exchange, check, draft, purchase, contract, note, or trade acceptance made, executed, endorsed, accepted, and delivered by me or for me in my name, by my Agent. To borrow from time to time such sums of money as my Agent may deem proper and execute promissory notes, security deeds or agreements, financing statements, or other security instruments in such form as the lender may request and renew said notes and security instruments from time to time in whole or in part. To have free access at any time or times to any safe deposit box or vault to which I might have access.

_____ (F) Business operating transactions. To conduct, engage in, and otherwise transact the affairs of any and all lawful business ventures of whatever nature or kind that I may now or hereafter be involved in. To organize or continue and conduct any business which term includes, without limitation, any farming, manufacturing, service, mining, retailing or other type of business operation in any form, whether as a proprietorship, joint venture, partnership, corporation, trust or other legal entity; operate, buy, sell, expand, contract, terminate or liquidate any business; direct, control, supervise, manage or participate in the operation of any business and engage, compensate and discharge business managers, employees, agents, attorneys, accountants and consultants; and, in general, exercise all powers with respect to business interests and operations which the principal could if present and under no disability.

_____ (G) Insurance and annuity transactions. To exercise or perform any act, power, duty, right, or obligation, in regard to any contract of life, accident, health, disability, liability, or other type of insurance or any combination of insurance; and to procure new or additional contracts of insurance for me and to designate the beneficiary of same; provided, however, that my Agent cannot designate himself or herself as beneficiary of any such insurance contracts.

_____ (H) Estate, trust, and other beneficiary transactions. To accept, receipt for, exercise, release, reject, renounce, assign, disclaim, demand, sue for, claim and recover any legacy, bequest, devise, gift or other property interest or payment due or payable to or for the principal; assert any interest in and exercise any power over any trust, estate or property subject to fiduciary control; establish a revocable trust solely for the benefit of the principal that terminates at the death of the principal and is then distributable to the legal representative of the estate of the principal; and, in general, exercise all powers with respect to estates and trusts which the principal could exercise if present and under no disability; provided, however, that the Agent may not make or change a will and may not revoke or amend a trust revocable or amendable by the principal or require the trustee of any trust for the benefit of the principal to pay income or principal to the Agent unless specific authority to that end is given.

_____ (I) Claims and litigation. To commence, prosecute, discontinue, or defend all actions or other legal proceedings touching my property, real or personal, or any part thereof, or touching any matter in which I or my property, real or personal, may be in any way concerned. To defend, settle, adjust, make allowances, compound, submit to arbitration, and compromise all accounts, reckonings, claims, and demands whatsoever that now are, or hereafter shall be, pending between me and any person, firm, corporation, or other legal entity, in such manner and in all respects as my Agent shall deem proper.

_____ (J) Personal and family maintenance. To hire accountants, attorneys at law, consultants, clerks, physicians, nurses, agents, servants, workmen, and others and to remove them, and to appoint others in their place, and to pay and allow the persons so employed such salaries, wages, or other remunerations, as my Agent shall deem proper.

_____ (K) Benefits from Social Security, Medicare, Medicaid, or other governmental programs, or military service. To prepare, sign and file any claim or application for Social Security, unemployment or military service benefits; sue for, settle or abandon any claims to any benefit or assistance under any federal, state, local or foreign statute or regulation; control, deposit to any account, collect, receipt for, and take title to and hold all benefits under any Social Security, unemployment, military service or other state, federal, local or foreign statute or regulation; and, in general, exercise all powers with respect to Social Security, unemployment, military service, and governmental benefits, including but not limited to Medicare and Medicaid, which the principal could exercise if present and under no disability.

_____ (L) Retirement plan transactions. To contribute to, withdraw from and deposit funds in any type of retirement plan (which term includes, without limitation, any tax qualified or nonqualified pension, profit sharing, stock bonus, employee savings and other retirement plan, individual retirement account, deferred compensation plan and any other type of employee benefit plan); select and change payment options for the principal under any retirement plan; make rollover contributions from any retirement plan to other retirement plans or individual retirement accounts; exercise all investment powers available under any type of self-directed retirement plan; and, in general, exercise all powers with respect to retirement plans and retirement plan account balances which the principal could if present and under no disability.

_____ (M) Tax matters. To prepare, to make elections, to execute and to file all tax, social security, unemployment insurance, and informational returns required by the laws of the United States, or of any state or subdivision thereof, or of any foreign government; to prepare, to execute, and to file all other papers and instruments which the Agent shall think to be desirable or necessary for safeguarding of me against excess or illegal taxation or against penalties imposed for claimed violation of any law or other governmental regulation; and to pay, to compromise, or to contest or to apply for refunds in connection with any taxes or assessments for which I am or may be liable.

_____ (N) ALL OF THE POWERS LISTED ABOVE. YOU NEED NOT INITIAL ANY OTHER LINES IF YOU INITIAL LINE (N).

SPECIAL INSTRUCTIONS:

ON THE FOLLOWING LINES YOU MAY GIVE SPECIAL INSTRUCTIONS LIMITING OR EXTENDING THE POWERS GRANTED TO YOUR AGENT.

_____

_____

_____

_____

THIS POWER OF ATTORNEY IS EFFECTIVE IMMEDIATELY AND WILL CONTINUE UNTIL IT IS REVOKED.

THIS POWER OF ATTORNEY SHALL BE CONSTRUED AS A GENERAL DURABLE POWER OF ATTORNEY AND SHALL CONTINUE TO BE EFFECTIVE EVEN IF I BECOME DISABLED, INCAPACITATED, OR INCOMPETENT.

(YOUR AGENT WILL HAVE AUTHORITY TO EMPLOY OTHER PERSONS AS NECESSARY TO ENABLE THE AGENT TO PROPERLY EXERCISE THE POWERS GRANTED IN THIS FORM, BUT YOUR AGENT WILL HAVE TO MAKE ALL DISCRETIONARY DECISIONS. IF YOU WANT TO GIVE YOUR AGENT THE RIGHT TO DELEGATE DISCRETIONARY DECISION-MAKING POWERS TO OTHERS, YOU SHOULD KEEP THE NEXT SENTENCE, OTHERWISE IT SHOULD BE STRICKEN.)

Authority to Delegate. My Agent shall have the right by written instrument to delegate any or all of the foregoing powers involving discretionary decision-making to any person or persons whom my Agent may select, but such delegation may be amended or revoked by any agent (including any successor) named by me who is acting under this power of attorney at the time of reference.

(YOUR AGENT WILL BE ENTITLED TO REIMBURSEMENT FOR ALL REASONABLE EXPENSES INCURRED IN ACTING UNDER THIS POWER OF ATTORNEY. STRIKE OUT THE NEXT SENTENCE IF YOU DO NOT WANT YOUR AGENT TO ALSO BE ENTITLED TO REASONABLE COMPENSATION FOR SERVICES AS AGENT.)

Right to Compensation. My Agent shall be entitled to reasonable compensation for services rendered as agent under this power of attorney.

(IF YOU WISH TO NAME SUCCESSOR AGENTS, INSERT THE NAME(S) AND ADDRESS(ES) OF SUCH SUCCESSOR(S) IN THE FOLLOWING PARAGRAPH.)

Successor Agent. If any Agent named by me shall die, become incompetent, resign or refuse to accept the office of Agent, I name the following (each to act alone and successively, in the order named) as successor(s) to such Agent:

_____

_____

Choice of Law. THIS POWER OF ATTORNEY WILL BE GOVERNED BY THE LAWS OF THE STATE OF NEW HAMPSHIRE WITHOUT REGARD FOR CONFLICTS OF LAWS PRINCIPLES. IT WAS EXECUTED IN THE STATE OF NEW HAMPSHIRE AND IS INTENDED TO BE VALID IN ALL JURISDICTIONS OF THE UNITED STATES OF AMERICA AND ALL FOREIGN NATIONS.

I am fully informed as to all the contents of this form and understand the full import of this grant of powers to my Agent.

I agree that any third party who receives a copy of this document may act under it. Revocation of the power of attorney is not effective as to a third party until the third party learns of the revocation. I agree to indemnify the third party for any claims that arise against the third party because of reliance on this power of attorney.

Signed this _____ day of _____, 20____

_____
[Your Signature]

CERTIFICATE OF ACKNOWLEDGMENT OF NOTARY PUBLIC

STATE OF NEW HAMPSHIRE
COUNTY OF _____

This document was acknowledged before me on _____ [Date]
by _____ [name of
principal].

[Notary Seal, if any]:

_____
(Signature of Notarial Officer)

Notary Public for the State of New Hampshire

My commission expires: _____

ACKNOWLEDGMENT OF AGENT

BY ACCEPTING OR ACTING UNDER THE APPOINTMENT, THE AGENT
ASSUMES THE FIDUCIARY AND OTHER LEGAL RESPONSIBILITIES OF AN
AGENT.

_____
[Typed or Printed Name of Agent]

_____
[Signature of Agent]

PREPARATION STATEMENT

This document was prepared by the following individual:

_____
[Typed or Printed Name]

_____
[Signature]

NEW MEXICO STATUTORY FORM POWER OF ATTORNEY

IMPORTANT INFORMATION

This power of attorney authorizes another person (your agent) to make decisions concerning your property for you (the principal). Your agent will be able to make decisions and act with respect to your property (including your money) whether or not you are able to act for yourself. The meaning of authority over subjects listed on this form is explained in the Uniform Power of Attorney Act.

This power of attorney does not authorize the agent to make health care decisions for you.

You should select someone you trust to serve as your agent. Unless you specify otherwise, generally the agent's authority will continue until you die or revoke the power of attorney or the agent resigns or is unable to act for you.

Your agent is entitled to reasonable compensation unless you state otherwise in the Special Instructions.

This form provides for designation of one agent. If you wish to name more than one agent, you may name a co-agent in the Special Instructions. Co-agents are not required to act together unless you include that requirement in the Special Instructions.

If your agent is unable or unwilling to act for you, your power of attorney will end unless you have named a successor agent. You may also name a second successor agent. This power of attorney becomes effective immediately unless you state otherwise in the Special Instructions.

If you have questions about the power of attorney or the authority you are granting to your agent, you should seek legal advice before signing this form.

DESIGNATION OF AGENT

I,_____
   (Your Name)
name the following person as my agent:
Name of Agent: _____
Agent's Address: _____
Agent's Telephone Number: _____
DESIGNATION OF SUCCESSOR AGENT(S) (OPTIONAL)

If my agent is unable or unwilling to act for me, I name as my successor agent:

Name of Successor Agent: _____

Successor Agent's Address: _____

Successor Agent's Telephone Number: _____

If my successor agent is unable or unwilling to act for me, I name as my second successor agent:

Name of Second Successor Agent: _____

Second Successor Agent's Address: _____

Second Successor Agent's Telephone Number: _____

GRANT OF GENERAL AUTHORITY

I grant my agent and any successor agent general authority to act for me with respect to the following subjects as defined in the Uniform Power of Attorney Act:

(INITIAL each subject you want to include in the agent's general authority. If you wish to grant general authority over all of the subjects, you may initial "All Preceding Subjects" instead of initialing each subject.)

(_____) Real Property

(_____) Tangible Personal Property

(_____) Stocks and Bonds

(_____) Commodities and Options

(_____) Banks and Other Financial Institutions

(_____) Operation of Entity or Business

(_____) Insurance and Annuities

(_____) Estates, Trusts and Other Beneficial Interests

(_____) Claims and Litigation

(_____) Personal and Family Maintenance

(_____) Benefits from Governmental Programs or Civil or Military Service

(_____) Retirement Plans

(_____) Taxes

(_____) All Preceding Subjects

GRANT OF SPECIFIC AUTHORITY (OPTIONAL)

My agent MAY NOT do any of the following specific acts for me UNLESS I have INITIALED the specific authority listed below:

(CAUTION: Granting any of the following will give your agent the authority to take actions that could significantly reduce your property or change how your property is distributed at your death. INITIAL ONLY the specific authority you WANT to give your agent.)

(_____) Create, amend, revoke or terminate an inter vivos trust
(_____) Make a gift, subject to the limitations of Section 217 of the Uniform Power of Attorney Act and any special instructions in this power of attorney
(_____) Create or change rights of survivorship
(_____) Create or change a beneficiary designation
(_____) Authorize another person to exercise the authority granted under this power of attorney
(_____) Waive the principal's right to be a beneficiary of a joint and survivor annuity, including a survivor benefit under a retirement plan
(_____) Exercise fiduciary powers that the principal has authority to delegate
(_____) Disclaim or refuse an interest in property, including a power of appointment

LIMITATION ON AGENT'S AUTHORITY

An agent that is not my ancestor, spouse or descendant MAY NOT use my property to benefit the agent or a person to whom the agent owes an obligation of support unless I have included that authority in the Special Instructions.

SPECIAL INSTRUCTIONS (OPTIONAL)

You may give special instructions on the following lines: _____
_____
_____

EFFECTIVE DATE

This power of attorney is effective immediately unless I have stated otherwise in the Special Instructions.

NOMINATION OF CONSERVATOR OR GUARDIAN (OPTIONAL)

If it becomes necessary for a court to appoint a conservator or guardian of my estate or guardian of my person, I nominate the following person(s) for appointment:

Name of Nominee for conservator of my estate: _____

Nominee's Address: _____
Nominee's Telephone Number: _____
Name of Nominee for guardian of my person: _____
Nominee's Address: _____
Nominee's Telephone Number: _____

RELIANCE ON THIS POWER OF ATTORNEY

Any person, including my agent, may rely upon the validity of this power of attorney or a copy of it unless that person knows it has terminated or is invalid.

SIGNATURE AND ACKNOWLEDGMENT

Your Signature: _____   Date: _____
Your Name Printed: _____
Your Address: _____
Your Telephone Number: _____

State of _____
(County) of _____

This instrument was acknowledged before me on _____(Date)
by_____ (Name of Principal).

(Seal, if any)

Signature of notarial officer: _____
My commission expires: _____

IMPORTANT INFORMATION FOR AGENT

Agent's Duties
When you accept the authority granted under this power of attorney, a special legal relationship is created between you and the principal. This relationship imposes upon you legal duties that continue until you resign or the power of attorney is terminated or revoked. You must:
1. do what you know the principal reasonably expects you to do with the principal's property or, if you do not know the principal's expectations, act in the principal's best interest;
2. act in good faith;
3. do nothing beyond the authority granted in this power of attorney; and

4. disclose your identity as an agent whenever you act for the principal by writing or printing the name of the principal and signing your own name as "agent" in the following manner:

_____by _____ as Agent
(Principal's Name)   (Your Signature)

Unless the Special Instructions in this power of attorney state otherwise, you must also:
1. act loyally for the principal's benefit;
2. avoid conflicts that would impair your ability to act in the principal's best interest;
3. act with care, competence and diligence;
4. keep a record of all receipts, disbursements and transactions made on behalf of the principal;
5. cooperate with any person that has authority to make health care decisions for the principal to do what you know the principal reasonably expects or, if you do not know the principal's expectations, to act in the principal's best interest; and
6. attempt to preserve the principal's estate plan if you know the plan and preserving the plan is consistent with the principal's best interest.

Termination of Agent's Authority
You must stop acting on behalf of the principal if you learn of any event that terminates this power of attorney or your authority under this power of attorney. Events that terminate a power of attorney or your authority to act under a power of attorney include:

1. death of the principal;
2. the principal's revocation of the power of attorney or your authority;
3. the occurrence of a termination event stated in the power of attorney;
4. the purpose of the power of attorney is fully accomplished; or
5. if you are married to the principal, a legal action is filed with a court to end your marriage, or for your legal separation, unless the Special Instructions in this power of attorney state that such an action will not terminate your authority.

Liability of Agent
The meaning of the authority granted to you is defined in the Uniform Power of Attorney Act. If you violate the Uniform Power of Attorney Act or act outside the authority granted, you may be liable for any damages caused by your violation.

If there is anything about this document or your duties that you do not understand, you should seek legal advice.

Note: This document has recently been updated to ensure compliance with N.Y. General Obligations Law, Article 5, Title 15: § 5-1513, which became effective March 1, 2009.

POWER OF ATTORNEY NEW YORK STATUTORY SHORT FORM

(a) CAUTION TO THE PRINCIPAL: Your Power of Attorney is an important document. As the "principal," you give the person whom you choose (your "agent") authority to spend your money and sell or dispose of your property during your lifetime without telling you. You do not lose your authority to act even though you have given your agent similar authority.

When your agent exercises this authority, he or she must act according to any instructions you have provided or, where there are no specific instructions, in your best interest. "Important Information for the Agent" at the end of this document describes your agent's responsibilities.

Your agent can act on your behalf only after signing the Power of Attorney before a notary public.

You can request information from your agent at any time. If you are revoking a prior Power of Attorney by executing this Power of Attorney, you should provide written notice of the revocation to your prior agent(s) and to the financial institutions where your accounts are located.

You can revoke or terminate your Power of Attorney at any time for any reason as long as you are of sound mind. If you are no longer of sound mind, a court can remove an agent for acting improperly.

Your agent cannot make health care decisions for you. You may execute a "Health Care Proxy" to do this.

The law governing Powers of Attorney is contained in the New York General Obligations Law, Article 5, Title 15. This law is available at a law library, or online through the New York State Senate or Assembly websites, www.senate.state.ny.us or www.assembly.state.ny.us.

If there is anything about this document that you do not understand, you should ask a lawyer of your own choosing to explain it to you.

(b) DESIGNATION OF AGENT(S): I, _____

_____[name and address of principal], hereby

appoint: **_____**

_____[name(s) and address(es) of agent(s)] as my agent(s).

If you designate more than one agent above, they must act together unless you initial the statement below.

(_____) My agents may act SEPARATELY.

(c) DESIGNATION OF SUCCESSOR AGENT(S): (OPTIONAL)
If every agent designated above is unable or unwilling to serve, I appoint as my successor agent(s):

_____
[name(s) and address(es) of successor agent(s)]

Successor agents designated above must act together unless you initial the statement below.

(_____) My successor agents may act SEPARATELY.

(d) This POWER OF ATTORNEY shall not be affected by my subsequent incapacity unless I have stated otherwise below, under "Modifications".

(e) This POWER OF ATTORNEY REVOKES any and all prior Powers of Attorney executed by me unless I have stated otherwise below, under "Modifications."

If you are NOT revoking your prior Powers of Attorney, and if you are granting the same authority in two or more Powers of Attorney, you must also indicate under "Modifications" whether the agents given these powers are to act together or separately.

(f) GRANT OF AUTHORITY:
To grant your agent some or all of the authority below, either
(1) Initial the bracket at each authority you grant, or
(2) Write or type the letters for each authority you grant on the blank line at (P), and initial the bracket at (P). If you initial (P), you do not need to initial the other lines.

I grant authority to my agent(s) with respect to the following subjects as defined in sections 5-1502A through 5-1502N of the New York General Obligations Law:

(_____)   (A)   real estate transactions;
(_____)   (B)   chattel and goods transactions;

(_____)   (C)   bond, share, and commodity transactions;
(_____)   (D)   banking transactions;
(_____)   (E)   business operating transactions;
(_____)   (F)   insurance transactions;
(_____)   (G)   estate transactions;
(_____)   (H)   claims and litigation;
(_____)   (I)   personal and family maintenance;
(_____)   (J)   benefits from governmental programs or civil or military service;
(_____)   (K)   health care billing and payment matters; records, reports, and statements;
(_____)   (L)   retirement benefit transactions;
(_____)   (M)   tax matters;
(_____)   (N)   all other matters;
(_____)   (O)   full and unqualified authority to my agent(s) to delegate any or all of the foregoing powers to any person or persons whom my agent(s) select;
(_____)   (P)   EACH of the matters identified by the following letters _____.

You need not initial the other lines if you initial line (P).

(g) MODIFICATIONS: (OPTIONAL)
In this section, you may make additional provisions, including language to limit or supplement authority granted to your agent. However, you cannot use this Modifications section to grant your agent authority to make major gifts or changes to interests in your property. If you wish to grant your agent such authority, you MUST complete the Statutory Major Gifts Rider.

_____

_____

(h) MAJOR GIFTS AND OTHER TRANSFERS: STATUTORY MAJOR GIFTS RIDER (OPTIONAL) In order to authorize your agent to make major gifts and other transfers of your property, you must initial the statement below and execute a Statutory Major Gifts Rider at the same time as this instrument. Initialing the statement below by itself does not authorize your agent to make major gifts and other transfers. The preparation of the Statutory Major Gifts Rider should be supervised by a lawyer.

(_____) (SMGR) I grant my agent authority to make major gifts and other transfers of my property, in accordance with the terms and conditions of the Statutory Major Gifts Rider that supplements this Power of Attorney.

(i) DESIGNATION OF MONITOR(S): (OPTIONAL)
I wish to designate _____, whose address(es) is (are) __
_____
_____
_____,
as monitor(s).
Upon the request of the monitor(s), my agent(s) must provide the monitor(s)
with a copy of the power of attorney and a record of all transactions done or
made on my behalf. Third parties holding records of such transactions shall
provide the records to the monitor(s) upon request.

(j) COMPENSATION OF AGENT(S): (OPTIONAL)
Your agent is entitled to be reimbursed from your assets for reasonable
expenses incurred on your behalf. If you ALSO wish your agent(s) to be
compensated from your assets for services rendered on your behalf, initial the
statement below. If you wish to define "reasonable compensation", you may do
so above, under "Modifications".

(_____) My agent(s) shall be entitled to reasonable compensation for services
rendered.

(k) ACCEPTANCE BY THIRD PARTIES: I agree to indemnify the third party for
any claims that may arise against the third party because of reliance on this
Power of Attorney. I understand that any termination of this Power of Attorney,
whether the result of my revocation of the Power of Attorney or otherwise,
is not effective as to a third party until the third party has actual notice or
knowledge of the termination.

(l) TERMINATION: This Power of Attorney continues until I revoke it or it is
terminated by my death or other event described in section 5-1511 of the
General Obligations Law. Section 5-1511 of the General Obligations Law
describes the manner in which you may revoke your Power of Attorney, and the
events which terminate the Power of Attorney.

(m) SIGNATURE AND ACKNOWLEDGMENT:
In Witness Whereof I have hereunto signed my name on _____,20___.

PRINCIPAL signs here: ==> _____

ACKNOWLEDGEMENT

STATE OF NEW YORK
COUNTY OF _____

On this _____ day of _____, 20_____ before me the
undersigned, personally appeared _____, personally known to be or
proved to me on the basis of satisfactory evidence to be the individual whose
name is subscribed to the within instrument and acknowledged to me that he
executed the same in his capacity, and that by his signature on the instrument,
the individual, or the person who acted on behalf of the individual, executed
the instrument and that such individual made such appearance before the
undersigned in the City of _____, County of _____,
State of New York.

_____
Notary

(n) IMPORTANT INFORMATION FOR THE AGENT:

When you accept the authority granted under this Power of Attorney, a special legal
relationship is created between you and the principal.

This relationship imposes on you legal responsibilities that continue until you resign or
the Power of Attorney is terminated or revoked.

You must:

(1) act according to any instructions from the principal, or, where there are no
instructions, in the principal's best interest;
(2) avoid conflicts that would impair your ability to act in the principal's best interest;
(3) keep the principal's property separate and distinct from any assets you own or
control, unless otherwise permitted by law;
(4) keep a record or all receipts, payments, and transactions conducted for the principal;
and
(5) disclose your identity as an agent whenever you act for the principal by writing or
printing the principal's name and signing your own name as "agent" in either of the
following manner: (Principal's Name) by (Your Signature) as Agent, or (your signature)
as Agent for (Principal's Name).

You may not use the principal's assets to benefit yourself or give major gifts to yourself
or anyone else unless the principal has specifically granted you that authority in this
Power of Attorney or in a Statutory Major Gifts Rider attached to this Power of Attorney.
If you have that authority, you must act according to any instructions of the principal or,
where there are no such instructions, in the principal's best interest. You may resign

by giving written notice to the principal and to any co-agent, successor agent, monitor if one has been named in this document, or the principal's guardian if one has been appointed. If there is anything about this document or your responsibilities that you do not understand, you should seek legal advice.

Liability of agent:

The meaning of the authority given to you is defined in New York's General Obligations Law, Article 5, Title 15. If it is found that you have violated the law or acted outside the authority granted to you in the Power of Attorney, you may be liable under the law for your violation.

(o) AGENT'S SIGNATURE AND ACKNOWLEDGMENT OF APPOINTMENT:
It is not required that the principal and the agent(s) sign at the same time, nor that multiple agents sign at the same time.

I/we, _____, have read the foregoing Power of Attorney. I am/we are the person(s) identified therein as agent(s) for the principal named therein.

I/we acknowledge my/our legal responsibilities.

Agent(s) sign(s) here: ==> _____

ACKNOWLEDGEMENT

STATE OF NEW YORK
COUNTY OF _____

On this _____ day of _____, 20_____ before me the undersigned, personally appeared _____,
personally known to be or proved to me on the basis of satisfactory evidence to be the individual whose name is subscribed to the within instrument and acknowledged to me that he executed the same in his capacity, and that by his signature on the instrument, the individual, or the person who acted on behalf of the individual, executed the instrument and that such individual made such appearance before the undersigned in the City of _____, County of _____, State of New York.

_____

NORTH CAROLINA STATUTORY SHORT FORM OF GENERAL POWER OF ATTORNEY

NOTICE
THE POWERS GRANTED BY THIS DOCUMENT ARE BROAD AND SWEEPING. THEY ARE DEFINED IN CHAPTER 32A OF THE NORTH CAROLINA GENERAL STATUTES WHICH EXPRESSLY PERMITS THE USE OF ANY OTHER OR DIFFERENT FORM OF POWER OF ATTORNEY DESIRED BY THE PARTIES CONCERNED.

State of _____
County of _____

I _____, appoint _____ to be my attorney in fact, to act in my name in any way which I could act for myself, with respect to the following matters as each of them is defined in Chapter 32A of the North Carolina General Statutes. (DIRECTIONS: Initial the line opposite any one or more of the subdivisions as to which the principal desires to give the attorney in fact authority.)

_____ (1) Real property transactions
_____ (2) Personal property transactions
_____ (3) Bond, share, stock, securities and commodity transactions
_____ (4) Banking transactions
_____ (5) Safe deposits
_____ (6) Business operating transactions
_____ (7) Insurance transactions
_____ (8) Estate transactions
_____ (9) Personal relationships and affairs
_____ (10) Social security and unemployment
_____ (11) Benefits from military service
_____ (12) Tax matters
_____ (13) Employment of agents
_____ (14) Gifts to charities, and to individuals other than the attorney in fact
_____ (15) Gifts to the named attorney in fact

(If power of substitution and revocation is to be given, add: 'I also give to such person full power to appoint another to act as my attorney in fact and full power to revoke such appointment.')

(If period of power of attorney is to be limited, add: 'This power terminates_____ _____, _____')

(If power of attorney is to be a durable power of attorney under the provision of Article 2 of Chapter 32A and is to continue in effect after the incapacity or mental incompetence of the principal, add: 'This power of attorney shall not be affected by my subsequent incapacity or mental incompetence.')

(If power of attorney is to take effect only after the incapacity or mental incompetence of the principal, add: 'This power of attorney shall become effective after I become incapacitated or mentally incompetent.')

(If power of attorney is to be effective to terminate or direct the administration of a custodial trust created under the Uniform Custodial Trust Act, add: 'In the event of my subsequent incapacity or mental incompetence, the attorney in fact of this power of attorney shall have the power to terminate or to direct the administration of any custodial trust of which I am the beneficiary.')

(If power of attorney is to be effective to determine whether a beneficiary under the Uniform Custodial Trust Act is incapacitated or ceases to be incapacitated, add: 'The attorney in fact of this power of attorney shall have the power to determine whether I am incapacitated or whether my incapacity has ceased for the purposes of any custodial trust of which I am the beneficiary.')

Dated_____, _____.

　　　　(Seal)

Signature _____

STATE OF _____ COUNTY OF _____

On this _____ day of_____, _____, personally appeared before me, the said named _____ to me known and known to me to be the person described in and who executed the foregoing instrument and he (or she) acknowledged that he (or she) executed the same and being duly sworn by me, made oath that the statements in the foregoing instrument are true.

My Commission Expires _____.
_____ (Signature of Notary Public)

Notary Public (Official Seal)

OKLAHOMA STATUTORY FORM FOR POWER OF ATTORNEY

NOTICE: THE POWERS GRANTED BY THIS DOCUMENT ARE BROAD AND SWEEPING. THEY ARE EXPLAINED IN THE UNIFORM STATUTORY FORM POWER OF ATTORNEY ACT. IF YOU HAVE ANY QUESTIONS ABOUT THESE POWERS, OBTAIN COMPETENT LEGAL ADVICE. THIS DOCUMENT DOES NOT AUTHORIZE ANYONE TO MAKE MEDICAL AND OTHER HEALTH-CARE DECISIONS FOR YOU. YOU MAY REVOKE THIS POWER OF ATTORNEY IF YOU LATER WISH TO DO SO.

I _____ (insert your name and address) appoint _____ (insert the name and address of the person appointed) as my agent (attorney-in-fact) to act for me in any lawful way with respect to the following initialed subjects:

TO GRANT ALL OF THE FOLLOWING POWERS, INITIAL THE LINE IN FRONT OF (N) AND IGNORE THE LINES IN FRONT OF THE OTHER POWERS.

TO GRANT ONE OR MORE, BUT FEWER THAN ALL, OF THE FOLLOWING POWERS, INITIAL THE LINE IN FRONT OF EACH POWER YOU ARE GRANTING.

TO WITHHOLD A POWER, DO NOT INITIAL THE LINE IN FRONT OF IT. YOU MAY, BUT NEED NOT, CROSS OUT EACH POWER WITHHELD.

INITIAL

_____ (A) Real property transactions.
_____ (B) Tangible personal property transactions.
_____ (C) Stock and bond transactions.
_____ (D) Commodity and option transactions.
_____ (E) Banking and other financial institution transactions.
_____ (F) Business operating transactions.
_____ (G) Insurance and annuity transactions.
_____ (H) Estate, trust, and other beneficiary transactions.
_____ (I) Claims and litigation.
_____ (J) Personal and family maintenance.
_____ (K) Benefits from Social Security, Medicare, Medicaid, or other governmental programs, or military service.
_____ (L) Retirement plan transactions.
_____ (M) Tax matters.
_____ (N) ALL OF THE POWERS LISTED ABOVE. YOU NEED NOT INITIAL ANY OTHER LINES IF YOU INITIAL LINE (N).

SPECIAL INSTRUCTIONS:

ON THE FOLLOWING LINES YOU MAY GIVE SPECIAL INSTRUCTIONS
LIMITING OR EXTENDING THE POWERS GRANTED TO YOUR AGENT.

_____

_____

(Attach additional pages if needed.)

UNLESS YOU DIRECT OTHERWISE ABOVE, THIS POWER OF ATTORNEY IS
EFFECTIVE IMMEDIATELY AND WILL CONTINUE UNTIL IT IS REVOKED.

This power of attorney will continue to be effective even though I become disabled,
incapacitated, or incompetent.

STRIKE THE PRECEDING SENTENCE IF YOU DO NOT WANT THIS POWER OF
ATTORNEY TO CONTINUE IF YOU BECOME DISABLED, INCAPACITATED, OR
INCOMPETENT.

I agree that any third party who receives a copy of this document may act under it.
Revocation of the power of attorney is not effective as to a third party until the third party
learns of the revocation. I agree to indemnify the third party for any claims that arise
against the third party because of reliance on this power of attorney.

Signed this _____ day of _____, 20___

_____
(Your Signature)

_____
(Your Social Security Number)

State of _____
(County) of_____

This document was acknowledged before me on _____(Date)
by_____
(Name of principal)

_____
(Signature of notarial officer)

_____
(Title and Rank)
(Seal, if any)

My commission expires: _____BY ACCEPTING OR ACTING UNDER
THE APPOINTMENT, THE AGENT ASSUMES THE FIDUCIARY AND OTHER
LEGAL RESPONSIBILITIES OF AN AGENT.

PENNSYLVANIA GENERAL DURABLE POWER OF ATTORNEY

THE POWERS YOU GRANT BELOW ARE EFFECTIVE EVEN IF YOU BECOME DISABLED OR INCOMPETENT

NOTICE: THE PURPOSE OF THIS POWER OF ATTORNEY IS TO GIVE THE PERSON YOU DESIGNATE (YOUR "AGENT") BROAD POWERS TO HANDLE YOUR PROPERTY, WHICH MAY INCLUDE POWERS TO SELL OR OTHERWISE DISPOSE OF ANY REAL OR PERSONAL PROPERTY WITHOUT ADVANCE NOTICE TO YOU OR APPROVAL BY YOU.

THIS POWER OF ATTORNEY DOES NOT IMPOSE A DUTY ON YOUR AGENT TO EXERCISE GRANTED POWERS, BUT WHEN POWERS ARE EXERCISED, YOUR AGENT MUST USE DUE CARE TO ACT FOR YOUR BENEFIT AND IN ACCORDANCE WITH THIS POWER OF ATTORNEY.

YOUR AGENT MAY EXERCISE THE POWERS GIVEN HERE THROUGHOUT YOUR LIFETIME, EVEN AFTER YOU BECOME INCAPACITATED, UNLESS YOU EXPRESSLY LIMIT THE DURATION OF THESE POWERS OR YOU REVOKE THESE POWERS OR A COURT ACTING ON YOUR BEHALF TERMINATES YOUR AGENT'S AUTHORITY.

YOUR AGENT MUST KEEP YOUR FUNDS SEPARATE FROM YOUR AGENT'S FUNDS.

A COURT CAN TAKE AWAY THE POWERS OF YOUR AGENT IF IT FINDS YOUR AGENT IS NOT ACTING PROPERLY.

THE POWERS AND DUTIES OF AN AGENT UNDER A POWER OF ATTORNEY ARE EXPLAINED MORE FULLY IN 20 PA.C.S. CH. 56.

IF THERE IS ANYTHING ABOUT THIS FORM THAT YOU DO NOT UNDERSTAND, YOU SHOULD ASK A LAWYER OF YOUR OWN CHOOSING TO EXPLAIN IT TO YOU.

I HAVE READ OR HAD EXPLAINED TO ME THIS NOTICE AND I UNDERSTAND ITS CONTENTS.

DATE:

_____
(SIGNATURE OF PRINCIPAL)

_____
(PRINT NAME OF PRINCIPAL)

PENNSYLVANIA GENERAL DURABLE POWER OF ATTORNEY

THE POWERS YOU GRANT BELOW ARE EFFECTIVE EVEN IF YOU BECOME DISABLED OR INCOMPETENT

NOTICE: THE POWERS GRANTED BY THIS DOCUMENT ARE BROAD AND SWEEPING. THEY ARE EXPLAINED IN THE UNIFORM STATUTORY FORM POWER OF ATTORNEY ACT. IF YOU HAVE ANY QUESTIONS ABOUT THESE POWERS, OBTAIN COMPETENT LEGAL ADVICE. THIS DOCUMENT DOES NOT AUTHORIZE ANYONE TO MAKE MEDICAL AND OTHER HEALTH-CARE DECISIONS FOR YOU. YOU MAY REVOKE THIS POWER OF ATTORNEY IF YOU LATER WISH TO DO SO.

I _____[insert your name and address] appoint _____ [insert the name and address of the person appointed] as my Agent (attorney-in-fact) to act for me in any lawful way with respect to the following initialed subjects:

TO GRANT ALL OF THE FOLLOWING POWERS, INITIAL THE LINE IN FRONT OF (N) AND IGNORE THE LINES IN FRONT OF THE OTHER POWERS.

TO GRANT ONE OR MORE, BUT FEWER THAN ALL, OF THE FOLLOWING POWERS, INITIAL THE LINE IN FRONT OF EACH POWER YOU ARE GRANTING.

TO WITHHOLD A POWER, DO NOT INITIAL THE LINE IN FRONT OF IT. YOU MAY, BUT NEED NOT, CROSS OUT EACH POWER WITHHELD.

Note: If you initial Item A or Item B, which follow, a notarized signature will be required on behalf of the Principal.

INITIAL

_____ (A) Real property transactions. To lease, sell, mortgage, purchase, exchange, and acquire, and to agree, bargain, and contract for the lease, sale, purchase, exchange, and acquisition of, and to accept, take, receive, and possess any interest in real property whatsoever, on such terms and conditions, and under such covenants, as my Agent shall deem proper; and to maintain, repair, tear down, alter, rebuild, improve manage, insure, move, rent, lease, sell, convey, subject to liens, mortgages, and security deeds, and in any way or manner deal with all or any part of any interest in real property whatsoever, including specifically, but without limitation, real property lying and being situated in the Commonwealth of Pennsylvania, under such terms and conditions, and under such covenants, as my Agent shall deem proper and may for all deferred payments accept purchase money notes payable to me and secured by mortgages or deeds to secure debt, and may from time to time collect and cancel any of said notes, mortgages, security interests, or deeds to secure debt.

_____ (B) Tangible personal property transactions. To lease, sell, mortgage, purchase, exchange, and acquire, and to agree, bargain, and contract for the lease, sale, purchase, exchange, and acquisition of, and to accept, take, receive, and possess any personal property whatsoever, tangible or intangible, or interest thereto, on such terms and conditions, and under such covenants, as my Agent shall deem proper; and to maintain, repair, improve, manage, insure, rent, lease, sell, convey, subject to liens or mortgages, or to take any other security interests in said property which are recognized under the Uniform Commercial Code as adopted at that time under the laws of the Commonwealth of Pennsylvania or any applicable state, or otherwise hypothecate (pledge), and in any way or manner deal with all or any part of any real or personal property whatsoever, tangible or intangible, or any interest therein, that I own at the time of execution or may thereafter acquire, under such terms and conditions, and under such covenants, as my Agent shall deem proper.

_____ (C) Stock and bond transactions. To purchase, sell, exchange, surrender, assign, redeem, vote at any meeting, or otherwise transfer any and all shares of stock, bonds, or other securities in any business, association, corporation, partnership, or other legal entity, whether private or public, now or hereafter belonging to me.

_____ (D) Commodity and option transactions. To buy, sell, exchange, assign, convey, settle and exercise commodities futures contracts and call and put options on stocks and stock indices traded on a regulated options exchange and collect and receipt for all proceeds of any such transactions; establish or continue option accounts for the principal with any securities or futures broker; and, in general, exercise all powers with respect to commodities and options which the principal could if present and under no disability.

_____ (E) Banking and other financial institution transactions. To make, receive, sign, endorse, execute, acknowledge, deliver and possess checks, drafts, bills of exchange, letters of credit, notes, stock certificates, withdrawal receipts and deposit instruments relating to accounts or deposits in, or certificates of deposit of banks, savings and loans, credit unions, or other institutions or associations. To pay all sums of money, at any time or times, that may hereafter be owing by me upon any account, bill of exchange, check, draft, purchase, contract, note, or trade acceptance made, executed, endorsed, accepted, and delivered by me or for me in my name, by my Agent. To borrow from time to time such sums of money as my Agent may deem proper and execute promissory notes, security deeds or agreements, financing statements, or other security instruments in such form as the lender may request and renew said notes and security instruments from time to time in whole or in part. To have free access at any time or times to any safe deposit box or vault to which I might have access.

_____ (F) Business operating transactions. To conduct, engage in, and otherwise transact the affairs of any and all lawful business ventures of whatever nature or kind that I may now or hereafter be involved in. To organize or continue and conduct any business which term includes, without limitation, any farming, manufacturing, service, mining, retailing or other type of business operation in any form, whether as a proprietorship, joint venture, partnership, corporation, trust or other legal entity; operate, buy, sell, expand, contract, terminate or liquidate any business; direct, control, supervise, manage or participate in the operation of any business and engage, compensate and discharge business managers, employees, agents, attorneys, accountants and consultants; and, in general, exercise all powers with respect to business interests and operations which the principal could if present and under no disability.

_____ (G) Insurance and annuity transactions. To exercise or perform any act, power, duty, right, or obligation, in regard to any contract of life, accident, health, disability, liability, or other type of insurance or any combination of insurance; and to procure new or additional contracts of insurance for me and to designate the beneficiary of same; provided, however, that my Agent cannot designate himself or herself as beneficiary of any such insurance contracts.

_____ (H) Estate, trust, and other beneficiary transactions. To accept, receipt for, exercise, release, reject, renounce, assign, disclaim, demand, sue for, claim and recover any legacy, bequest, devise, gift or other property interest or payment due or payable to or for the principal; assert any interest in and exercise any power over any trust, estate or property subject to fiduciary control; establish a revocable trust solely for the benefit of the principal that terminates at the death of the principal and is then distributable to the legal representative of the estate of the principal; and, in general, exercise all powers with respect to estates and trusts which the principal could exercise if present and under no disability; provided, however, that the Agent may not make or change a will and may not revoke or amend a trust revocable or amendable by the principal or require the trustee of any trust for the benefit of the principal to pay income or principal to the Agent unless specific authority to that end is given.

_____ (I) Claims and litigation. To commence, prosecute, discontinue, or defend all actions or other legal proceedings touching my property, real or personal, or any part thereof, or touching any matter in which I or my property, real or personal, may be in any way concerned. To defend, settle, adjust, make allowances, compound, submit to arbitration, and compromise all accounts, reckonings, claims, and demands whatsoever that now are, or hereafter shall be, pending between me and any person, firm, corporation, or other legal entity, in such manner and in all respects as my Agent shall deem proper.

_____ (J) Personal and family maintenance. To hire accountants, attorneys at law, consultants, clerks, physicians, nurses, agents, servants, workmen, and others and to remove them, and to appoint others in their place, and to pay and allow the persons so employed such salaries, wages, or other remunerations, as my Agent shall deem proper.

_____ (K) Benefits from Social Security, Medicare, Medicaid, or other governmental programs, or military service. To prepare, sign and file any claim or application for Social Security, unemployment or military service benefits; sue for, settle or abandon any claims to any benefit or assistance under any federal, state, local or foreign statute or regulation; control, deposit to any account, collect, receipt for, and take title to and hold all benefits under any Social Security, unemployment, military service or other state, federal, local or foreign statute or regulation; and, in general, exercise all powers with respect to Social Security, unemployment, military service, and governmental benefits, including but not limited to Medicare and Medicaid, which the principal could exercise if present and under no disability.

_____ (L) Retirement plan transactions. To contribute to, withdraw from and deposit funds in any type of retirement plan (which term includes, without limitation, any tax qualified or nonqualified pension, profit sharing, stock bonus, employee savings and other retirement plan, individual retirement account, deferred compensation plan and any other type of employee benefit plan); select and change payment options for the principal under any retirement plan; make rollover contributions from any retirement plan to other retirement plans or individual retirement accounts; exercise all investment powers available under any type of self-directed retirement plan; and, in general, exercise all powers with respect to retirement plans and retirement plan account balances which the principal could if present and under no disability.

_____ (M) Tax matters. To prepare, to make elections, to execute and to file all tax, social security, unemployment insurance, and informational returns required by the laws of the United States, or of any state or subdivision thereof, or of any foreign government; to prepare, to execute, and to file all other papers and instruments which the Agent shall think to be desirable or necessary for safeguarding of me against excess or illegal taxation or against penalties imposed for claimed violation of any law or other governmental regulation; and to pay, to compromise, or to contest or to apply for refunds in connection with any taxes or assessments for which I am or may be liable.

_____ (N) ALL OF THE POWERS LISTED ABOVE. YOU NEED NOT INITIAL ANY OTHER LINES IF YOU INITIAL LINE (N).

SPECIAL INSTRUCTIONS:

ON THE FOLLOWING LINES YOU MAY GIVE SPECIAL INSTRUCTIONS LIMITING OR EXTENDING THE POWERS GRANTED TO YOUR AGENT.

_____

_____

THIS POWER OF ATTORNEY IS EFFECTIVE IMMEDIATELY AND WILL CONTINUE UNTIL IT IS REVOKED.

THIS POWER OF ATTORNEY SHALL BE CONSTRUED AS A GENERAL DURABLE POWER OF ATTORNEY AND SHALL CONTINUE TO BE EFFECTIVE EVEN IF I BECOME DISABLED, INCAPACITATED, OR INCOMPETENT.

(YOUR AGENT WILL HAVE AUTHORITY TO EMPLOY OTHER PERSONS AS NECESSARY TO ENABLE THE AGENT TO PROPERLY EXERCISE THE POWERS GRANTED IN THIS FORM, BUT YOUR AGENT WILL HAVE TO MAKE ALL DISCRETIONARY DECISIONS. IF YOU WANT TO GIVE YOUR AGENT THE RIGHT TO DELEGATE DISCRETIONARY DECISION-MAKING POWERS TO OTHERS, YOU SHOULD KEEP THE NEXT SENTENCE, OTHERWISE IT SHOULD BE STRICKEN.)

Authority to Delegate. My Agent shall have the right by written instrument to delegate any or all of the foregoing powers involving discretionary decision-making to any person or persons whom my Agent may select, but such delegation may be amended or revoked by any agent (including any successor) named by me who is acting under this power of attorney at the time of reference.

(YOUR AGENT WILL BE ENTITLED TO REIMBURSEMENT FOR ALL REASONABLE EXPENSES INCURRED IN ACTING UNDER THIS POWER

OF ATTORNEY. STRIKE OUT THE NEXT SENTENCE IF YOU DO NOT WANT YOUR AGENT TO ALSO BE ENTITLED TO REASONABLE COMPENSATION FOR SERVICES AS AGENT.)

Right to Compensation. My Agent shall be entitled to reasonable compensation for services rendered as agent under this power of attorney.

(IF YOU WISH TO NAME SUCCESSOR AGENTS, INSERT THE NAME(S) AND ADDRESS(ES) OF SUCH SUCCESSOR(S) IN THE FOLLOWING PARAGRAPH.)

Successor Agent. If any Agent named by me shall die, become incompetent, resign or refuse to accept the office of Agent, I name the following (each to act alone and successively, in the order named) as successor(s) to such Agent:

_____

_____

Choice of Law. THIS POWER OF ATTORNEY WILL BE GOVERNED BY THE LAWS OF THE COMMONWEALTH OF PENNSYLVANIA WITHOUT REGARD FOR CONFLICTS OF LAWS PRINCIPLES. IT WAS EXECUTED IN THE COMMONWEALTH OF PENNSYLVANIA AND IS INTENDED TO BE VALID IN ALL JURISDICTIONS OF THE UNITED STATES OF AMERICA AND ALL FOREIGN NATIONS.

I am fully informed as to all the contents of this form and understand the full import of this grant of powers to my Agent.

I agree that any third party who receives a copy of this document may act under it. Revocation of the power of attorney is not effective as to a third party until the third party learns of the revocation. I agree to indemnify the third party for any claims that arise against the third party because of reliance on this power of attorney.

Signed this _____ day of _____, 20_____

_____
[Your Signature]

STATEMENT OF WITNESS
On the date written above, the principal declared to me in my presence that this instrument is his general durable power of attorney and that he or she had willingly signed or directed another to sign for him or her, and that he or

she executed it as his or her free and voluntary act for the purposes therein expressed.

_____ [Signature of Witness #1]
_____ [Printed or typed name of Witness #1]
_____ [Address of Witness #1, Line 1]
_____ [Address of Witness #1, Line 2]

_____ [Signature of Witness #2]
_____ [Printed or typed name of Witness #2]
_____ [Address of Witness #2, Line 1]
_____ [Address of Witness #2, Line 2]

A Note About Selecting Witnesses: The agent (attorney-in-fact) may not also serve as a witness. Each witness must be present at the time that principal signs the Power of Attorney in front of the notary. Each witness must be a mentally competent adult. Witnesses should ideally reside close by, so that they will be easily accessible in the event they are one day needed to affirm this document's validity.

CERTIFICATE OF ACKNOWLEDGMENT OF NOTARY PUBLIC
COMMONWEALTH OF PENNSYLVANIA
COUNTY OF _____

On this, the _____ day of _____, 20____, before me _____
_____, the undersigned officer, personally appeared _____,
known to me (or satisfactorily proven) to be the person(s) whose name(s) is/are subscribed to the within instrument, and acknowledged that _____ executed the same for the purposes therein contained.
In witness whereof, I hereunto set my hand and official seals.

[Notary Seal, if any]:

_____
(Signature of Notarial Officer)

Notary Public for the Commonwealth of Pennsylvania
My commission expires: _____
ACKNOWLEDGMENT EXECUTED BY AGENT

I, _____ [name of agent], have read the attached power of attorney and am the person identified as the agent for the principal. I hereby acknowledge that in the absence of a specific provision to the contrary in the power of attorney or in 20 Pa.C.S. when I act as agent:

I shall exercise the powers for the benefit of the principal.

I shall keep the assets of the principal separate from my assets.

I shall exercise reasonable caution and prudence.

I shall keep a full and accurate record of all actions, receipts and disbursements on behalf of the principal.

_____

Agent's Signature

_____

Agent's Printed Name

_____

Date

PREPARATION STATEMENT

This document was prepared by the following individual:

_____

[Typed or Printed Name]

_____

[Signature]

RHODE ISLAND SHORT FORM POWER OF ATTORNEY

WARNING TO PERSON EXECUTING THIS DOCUMENT

This is an important legal document which is authorized by the general laws of this state. The powers granted by this document are broad and sweeping. They are defined in §§ 18-16-1 to 18-16-12, both inclusive, of the Rhode Island general laws in chapter 18-16 entitled "Rhode Island Short Form Power of Attorney Act."

The use of the short form power of attorney is strictly voluntary, and chapter 18-16 specifically authorizes the use of any other or different form of power of attorney upon mutual agreement of the parties concerned.

Known All Men by These Presents, which are intended to constitute a GENERAL POWER OF ATTORNEY pursuant to the Rhode Island Short Form Power of Attorney Act:

That I _____ (insert name and address of the principal) do hereby appoint _____ (insert name and address of the agent, or each agent, if more than one is designated) my attorney(s)-in-fact TO ACT _____ .

(If more than one agent is designated and the principal wishes each agent alone to be able to exercise the power conferred, insert in this blank the word "severally". Failure to make any insertion or the insertion of the word "jointly" shall require the agents to act jointly.)

First: In my name, place and stead in any way which I myself could do, if I were personally present, with respect to the following matters as each of them is defined in the Rhode Island Statutory Short Form Power of Attorney Act to the extent that I am permitted by law to act through an agent:

(STRIKE OUT AND INITIAL ON THE OPPOSITE LINE ANY ONE OR MORE OF THE SUBDIVISIONS AS TO WHICH THE PRINCIPAL DOES NOT DESIRE TO GIVE THE AGENT AUTHORITY. THIS ELIMINATION OF ANY ONE OR MORE OF SUBDIVISIONS (A) TO (I), INCLUSIVE, SHALL AUTOMATICALLY CONSTITUTE AN ELIMINATION ALSO OF SUBDIVISION (J).

To strike out any subdivision the principal must draw a line through the text of that subdivision AND write his initials in the line opposite.

INITIAL HERE

_____ (A) real state transactions;
_____ (B) chattel and goods transactions;
_____ (C) bond, share and commodity transactions;
_____ (D) banking transactions;
_____ (E) business operating transactions;
_____ (F) insurance transactions;
_____ (G) claims and litigations;
_____ (H) benefits from military service;
_____ (I) records, reports and statements;
_____ (J) all other matters;

(Special provisions and limitations may be included in the statutory short form power of attorney only if they conform to the requirements of the Rhode Island Statutory Short Form Power of Attorney Act.)

Second: This power of attorney shall:

(A) be of indefinite duration or

(B) terminate on the following date, _____, unless otherwise terminated by revocation, destruction or other affirmative action.

Third: Hereby ratifying and confirming all that said attorney(s) or substitute(s) do or cause to be done.

In witness whereof I have hereunto signed my name and affixed my seal this _____ day of _____, 20____.

_____ (Signature of Principal) (Seal)

(ACKNOWLEDGEMENT)

This power of attorney shall not be affected by the subsequent incompetency of the donor.

In witness whereof I have hereunto signed my name and affixed my seal this _____ day of _____ 20____.

_____ (Signature of Principal) (Seal)

(ACKNOWLEDGEMENT)

The execution of this statutory short form power of attorney shall be duly acknowledged by the principal in the manner prescribed for the acknowledgement of a conveyance of real property. This means having this document recorded or filed by the town clerk or recorder of deeds.

If more than one agent is designated by the principal, such agents, in the exercise of the powers conferred, shall act jointly unless the principal specifically provides in such statutory short form power of attorney that they are to act severally.

TEXAS STATUTORY DURABLE POWER OF ATTORNEY

NOTICE: THE POWERS GRANTED BY THIS DOCUMENT ARE BROAD AND SWEEPING. THEY ARE EXPLAINED IN THE DURABLE POWER OF ATTORNEY ACT, CHAPTER XII, TEXAS PROBATE CODE. IF YOU HAVE ANY QUESTIONS ABOUT THESE POWERS, OBTAIN COMPETENT LEGAL ADVICE. THIS DOCUMENT DOES NOT AUTHORIZE ANYONE TO MAKE MEDICAL AND OTHER HEALTH-CARE DECISIONS FOR YOU. YOU MAY REVOKE THIS POWER OF ATTORNEY IF YOU LATER WISH TO DO SO.

I, _____ (insert your name and address), appoint _____(insert the name and address of the person appointed) as my agent (attorney-in-fact) to act for me in any lawful way with respect to all of the following powers except for a power that I have crossed out below.

TO WITHHOLD A POWER, YOU MUST CROSS OUT EACH POWER WITHHELD.

Real property transactions;
Tangible personal property transactions;
Stock and bond transactions;
Commodity and option transactions;
Banking and other financial institution transactions;
Business operating transactions;
Insurance and annuity transactions;
Estate, trust, and other beneficiary transactions;
Claims and litigation;
Personal and family maintenance;
Benefits from social security, Medicare, Medicaid, or other governmental programs or civil or military service;
Retirement plan transactions;
Tax matters.

IF NO POWER LISTED ABOVE IS CROSSED OUT, THIS DOCUMENT SHALL BE CONSTRUED AND INTERPRETED AS A GENERAL POWER OF ATTORNEY AND MY AGENT (ATTORNEY IN FACT) SHALL HAVE THE POWER AND AUTHORITY TO PERFORM OR UNDERTAKE ANY ACTION I COULD PERFORM OR UNDERTAKE IF I WERE PERSONALLY PRESENT.

SPECIAL INSTRUCTIONS:

Special instructions applicable to gifts (initial in front of the following sentence to have it apply):

I grant my agent (attorney in fact) the power to apply my property to make gifts, except that the amount of a gift to an individual may not exceed the amount of annual exclusions allowed from the federal gift tax for the calendar year of the gift.

ON THE FOLLOWING LINES YOU MAY GIVE SPECIAL INSTRUCTIONS LIMITING OR EXTENDING THE POWERS GRANTED TO YOUR AGENT.

_____

_____

UNLESS YOU DIRECT OTHERWISE ABOVE, THIS POWER OF ATTORNEY IS EFFECTIVE IMMEDIATELY AND WILL CONTINUE UNTIL IT IS REVOKED.

CHOOSE ONE OF THE FOLLOWING ALTERNATIVES BY CROSSING OUT THE ALTERNATIVE NOT CHOSEN:

(A) This power of attorney is not affected by my subsequent disability or incapacity.

(B) This power of attorney becomes effective upon my disability or incapacity.

YOU SHOULD CHOOSE ALTERNATIVE (A) IF THIS POWER OF ATTORNEY IS TO BECOME EFFECTIVE ON THE DATE IT IS EXECUTED.

IF NEITHER (A) NOR (B) IS CROSSED OUT, IT WILL BE ASSUMED THAT YOU CHOSE ALTERNATIVE (A).

If Alternative (B) is chosen and a definition of my disability or incapacity is not contained in this power of attorney, I shall be considered disabled or incapacitated for purposes of this power of attorney if a physician certifies in writing at a date later than the date this power of attorney is executed that, based on the physician's medical examination of me, I am mentally incapable of managing my financial affairs. I authorize the physician who examines me for this purpose to disclose my physical or mental condition to another person for purposes of this power of attorney. A third party who accepts this power of attorney is fully protected from any action taken under this power of attorney that is based on the determination made by a physician of my disability or incapacity.

I agree that any third party who receives a copy of this document may act under it. Revocation of the durable power of attorney is not effective as to a third party until the third party receives actual notice of the revocation. I agree to indemnify the third party for any claims that arise against the third party because of reliance on this power of attorney.

If any agent named by me dies, becomes legally disabled, resigns, or refuses to act, I name the following (each to act alone and successively, in the order named) as successor(s) to that agent: _____.

Signed this _____ day of _____, 19___.

_____
(your signature)

State of _____

County of _____

This document was acknowledged before me on _____(date) by _____ (name of principal).

_____
(signature of notarial officer)

(Seal, if any, of notary)

_____
(printed name)

My commission expires: _____

THE ATTORNEY IN FACT OR AGENT, BY ACCEPTING OR ACTING UNDER THE APPOINTMENT, ASSUMES THE FIDUCIARY AND OTHER LEGAL RESPONSIBILITIES OF AN AGENT.

WISCONSIN BASIC POWER OF ATTORNEY FOR FINANCES AND PROPERTY

NOTICE: THIS IS AN IMPORTANT DOCUMENT. BEFORE SIGNING THIS DOCUMENT, YOU SHOULD KNOW THESE IMPORTANT FACTS. BY SIGNING THIS DOCUMENT, YOU ARE NOT GIVING UP ANY POWERS OR RIGHTS TO CONTROL YOUR FINANCES AND PROPERTY YOURSELF. IN ADDITION TO YOUR OWN POWERS AND RIGHTS, YOU ARE GIVING ANOTHER PERSON, YOUR AGENT, BROAD POWERS TO HANDLE YOUR FINANCES AND PROPERTY. THIS BASIC POWER OF ATTORNEY FOR FINANCES AND PROPERTY MAY GIVE THE PERSON WHOM YOU DESIGNATE (YOUR "AGENT") BROAD POWERS TO HANDLE YOUR FINANCES AND PROPERTY, WHICH MAY INCLUDE POWERS TO ENCUMBER, SELL OR OTHERWISE DISPOSE OF ANY REAL OR PERSONAL PROPERTY WITHOUT ADVANCE NOTICE TO YOU OR APPROVAL BY YOU. THE POWERS WILL EXIST AFTER YOU BECOME DISABLED, OR INCAPACITATED, IF YOU CHOOSE THAT PROVISION. THIS DOCUMENT DOES NOT AUTHORIZE ANYONE TO MAKE MEDICAL OR OTHER HEALTH CARE DECISIONS FOR YOU. IF YOU OWN COMPLEX OR SPECIAL ASSETS SUCH AS A BUSINESS, OR IF THERE IS ANYTHING ABOUT THIS FORM THAT YOU DO NOT UNDERSTAND, YOU SHOULD ASK A LAWYER TO EXPLAIN THIS FORM TO YOU BEFORE YOU SIGN IT.

IF YOU WISH TO CHANGE YOUR BASIC POWER OF ATTORNEY FOR FINANCES AND PROPERTY, YOU MUST COMPLETE A NEW DOCUMENT AND REVOKE THIS ONE. YOU MAY REVOKE THIS DOCUMENT AT ANY TIME BY DESTROYING IT, BY DIRECTING ANOTHER PERSON TO DESTROY IT IN YOUR PRESENCE OR BY SIGNING A WRITTEN AND DATED STATEMENT EXPRESSING YOUR INTENT TO REVOKE THIS DOCUMENT. IF YOU REVOKE THIS DOCUMENT, YOU SHOULD NOTIFY YOUR AGENT AND ANY OTHER PERSON TO WHOM YOU HAVE GIVEN A COPY OF THE FORM. YOU ALSO SHOULD NOTIFY ALL PARTIES HAVING CUSTODY OF YOUR ASSETS. THESE PARTIES HAVE NO RESPONSIBILITY TO YOU UNLESS YOU ACTUALLY NOTIFY THEM OF THE REVOCATION. IF YOUR AGENT IS YOUR SPOUSE AND YOUR MARRIAGE IS ANNULLED, OR YOU ARE DIVORCED AFTER SIGNING THIS DOCUMENT, THIS DOCUMENT IS INVALID.

SINCE SOME 3RD PARTIES OR SOME TRANSACTIONS MAY NOT PERMIT USE OF THIS DOCUMENT, IT IS ADVISABLE TO CHECK IN ADVANCE, IF POSSIBLE, FOR ANY SPECIAL REQUIREMENTS THAT MAY BE IMPOSED.

YOU SHOULD SIGN THIS FORM ONLY IF THE AGENT YOU NAME IS RELIABLE, TRUSTWORTHY AND COMPETENT TO MANAGE YOUR AFFAIRS.

I _____

(insert your name and address) appoint _____

_____ (insert the name and address of the person appointed) as my agent to act for me in any lawful way with respect to the powers initialed below. If the person appointed is unable or unwilling to act as my agent, I appoint _____ _____ (insert name and address of alternate person appointed) to act for me in any lawful way with respect to the powers initialed below.

TO GRANT ONE OR MORE OF THE FOLLOWING POWERS, INITIAL THE LINE IN FRONT OF EACH POWER YOU ARE GRANTING.

TO WITHHOLD A POWER, DO NOT INITIAL THE LINE IN FRONT OF IT. YOU MAY, BUT NEED NOT, CROSS OUT EACH POWER WITHHELD.

Handling My Money And Property
Initials

_____ 1. PAYMENTS OF BILLS: My agent may make payments that are necessary or appropriate in connection with the administration of my affairs.

_____ 2. BANKING: My agent may conduct business with financial institutions, including endorsing all checks and drafts made payable to my order and collecting the proceeds; signing in my name checks or orders on all accounts in my name or for my benefit; withdrawing funds from accounts in my name; opening accounts in my name; and entering into and removing articles from my safe deposit box.

_____ 3. INSURANCE: My agent may obtain insurance of all types, as considered necessary or appropriate, settle and adjust insurance claims and borrow from insurers and 3rd parties using insurance policies as collateral.

_____ 4. ACCOUNTS: My agent may ask for, collect and receive money, dividends, interest, legacies and property due or that may become due and owing to me and give receipt for those payments.

_____ 5. REAL ESTATE: My agent may manage real property; sell, convey and mortgage realty for prices and on terms as considered advisable; foreclose mortgages and take title to property in my name; and execute deeds, mortgages, releases, satisfactions and other instruments relating to realty.

_____ 6. BORROWING: My agent may borrow money and encumber my assets for loans as considered necessary.

_____ 7. SECURITIES: My agent may buy, sell, pledge and exchange securities of all kinds in my name; sign and deliver in my name transfers and assignments of securities; and consent in my name to reorganizations, mergers or exchange of securities for new securities.

_____ 8. INCOME TAXES: My agent may make and sign tax returns; represent me in all income tax matters before any federal, state, or local tax collecting agency; and receive confidential information and perform any acts that I may perform, including receiving refund checks and the signing of returns.

_____ 9. TRUSTS: My agent may transfer at any time any of my property to a living trust that has been established by me before the execution of this document.

Professional and Technical Assistance
Initials

_____ 10. LEGAL ACTIONS: My agent may retain attorneys on my behalf; appear for me in all actions and proceedings to which I may be a party; commence actions and proceedings in my name; and sign in my name all documents or pleadings of every description.

_____ 11. PROFESSIONAL ASSISTANCE: My agent may hire accountants, attorneys, clerks, workers and others for the management, preservation and protection of my property and estate.

General Authority
Initials

_____ 12. GENERAL: My agent may do any act or thing that I could do in my own proper person if personally present, including managing or selling tangible assets, disclaiming a probate or nonprobate inheritance and providing support for a minor child or dependent adult. The specifically enumerated powers of the basic power of attorney for finances and property are not a limitation of this intended broad general power except that my agent may not take any action prohibited by law and my agent under this document may not:

a. Make medical or health care decisions for me.
b. Make, modify or revoke a will for me.
c. Other than a burial trust agreement under section 445.125, Wisconsin Statutes, enter into a trust agreement on my behalf or amend or revoke a trust agreement, entered into by me.

d. Change any beneficiary designation of any life insurance policy, qualified retirement plan, individual retirement account or payable on death account or the like whether directly or by canceling and replacing the policy or rollover to another plan or account.

e. Forgive debts owed to me or disclaim or waive benefits payable to me, except a probate or nonprobate inheritance.

f. Appoint a substitute or successor agent for me.

g. Make gifts.

Compensation To Agent From Principal's Funds
Initials

_____ 13. COMPENSATION: My agent may receive compensation only in an amount not greater than that usual for the services to be performed if expressly authorized in the special instructions portion of this document.

Accounting
Initials

_____ 14. ACCOUNTING: My agent shall render an accounting (monthly) (quarterly) (annually) (CIRCLE ONE) to me or to _____ (insert name and address) during my lifetime and a final accounting to the personal representative of my estate, if any is appointed, after my death.

Nomination of Guardian
Initials

_____ 15. GUARDIAN: If necessary, I nominate _____ (name) of _____ (address) as guardian of my person and I nominate _____ (name) of _____ (address) as guardian of my estate.

Special Instructions
Initials

_____ 16. SPECIAL INSTRUCTIONS: On the following lines you may give special instructions regarding the powers granted to your agent.

TO ESTABLISH WHEN, AND FOR HOW LONG, THE BASIC POWER OF ATTORNEY FOR FINANCES AND PROPERTY IS IN EFFECT, YOU MUST

INITIAL ONLY ONE OF THE FOLLOWING 3 OPTIONS. IF YOU DO NOT INITIAL ONE, OR IF YOU INITIAL MORE THAN ONE, THIS BASIC POWER OF ATTORNEY FOR FINANCES AND PROPERTY WILL NOT TAKE EFFECT. Initials

_____ This basic power of attorney for finances and property becomes effective when I sign it and will continue in effect as a durable power of attorney under section 243.07, Wisconsin Statutes, if I become disabled or incapacitated.

_____ This basic power of attorney for finances and property becomes effective only when both of the following apply:

a. I have signed it; and

b. I become disabled or incapacitated.

_____ This basic power of attorney for finances and property becomes effective when I sign it but will cease to be effective if I become disabled or incapacitated.

I agree that any 3rd party who receives a copy of this document may act under it. Revocation of this basic power of attorney is not effective as to a 3rd party until the 3rd party learns of the revocation. I agree to reimburse the 3rd party for any loss resulting from claims that arise against the 3rd party because of reliance on this basic power of attorney.

Signed this _____ day of _____ (month), _____ (year)

_____
(Your Signature)

_____
(Your Social Security Number)

Statement of Witnesses
By signing as a witness, I am acknowledging the signature of the principal who signed in my presence and the presence of the other witness, and the fact that he or she has stated that this power of attorney reflects his or her wishes and is being executed voluntarily. I believe him or her to be of sound mind and capable of creating this power of attorney. I am not related to him or her by blood, marriage or adoption, and, to the best of my knowledge, I am not entitled to any portion of his or her estate under his or her will.

Witness 1
Dated: _____
Signature: _____
Print Name: _____
Address: _____

Witness 2
Dated: _____
Signature: _____
Print Name: _____
Address: _____

Notary
State of _____
County of _____

This document was acknowledged before me on _____ (date) by _____ (name of principal).

_____
(Signature of Notarial Officer)

(Seal, if any)

_____
(Title)
[My commission is permanent or expires: _____]

Agents
BY ACCEPTING OR ACTING UNDER THE APPOINTMENT, THE AGENT AS-
SUMES THE FIDUCIARY AND OTHER LEGAL RESPONSIBILITIES AND LI-
ABILITIES OF AN AGENT.

_____
(Name of Agent)

_____
(Signature of Agent)

Preparer

This document was drafted by _____
(signature of person preparing the document).

Chapter 7

Durable Health Care Power of Attorney

Traditionally, financial and property matters were the type of actions handled with powers of attorney. Increasingly people are using a specific type of power of attorney to authorize other persons to make health care decisions on their behalf in the event of a disability which makes the person unable to communicate their wishes to doctors or other health care providers. This broad type of power of attorney is called a *health care power of attorney*. It is different from *durable power of attorney for financial affairs*, which gives another person the authority handle a person's financial affairs, but is intended to remain in effect even if a person becomes disabled or incompetent. A *durable power of attorney for financial affairs* does not confer authority on another person to make health care decisions on someone else's behalf. Only a *durable health care power of attorney* can do that.

> ⚡**Toolkit Tip!**
>
> A health care power of attorney is the only type of power of attorney that can be used to authorize someone to make health care decisions for you if you are unable to communicate.

When Should You Use a Health Care Power of Attorney?

Health care powers of attorney are useful documents that go beyond the provisions of a living will. They provide for health care options that living wills do not cover, and are important additions to the use of a living will. Basically, a health care power of attorney allows you to appoint someone to act for you in making health care decisions when you are unable to make them for yourself. A living will does not provide for this. Also, a health care power of attorney generally applies to all medical decisions (unless you specifically limit the power). Most living wills only apply to certain decisions regarding life support at the end of your life and are most useful in "terminal illness" or "permanent unconsciousness" situations. Note that a health care power of attorney is also a 'durable' type power of attorney, the term durable meaning that the power of attorney is not effected by your incapacitation and will remain in effect during any such incapacitation. Health care powers of attorney will be referred to as durable for the rest of this discussion.

> **⊘ Definition:**
>
> **Durable:**
> When used to describe a power of attorney, this means that the document is still effective if the maker is incapacitated. A standard (non-durable) power of attorney becomes invalid if the maker is incapacitated.

Additionally, a durable health care power of attorney can provide your chosen agent with a valuable flexibility in making decisions regarding medical choices that may arise. Often, during the course of medical treatment, unforeseen situations may occur that require immediate decision-making. If you are unable to communicate your desires regarding such choices, the appointment of a *health care representative* for you (appointed with a durable health care power of attorney) will allow such decisions to be made on your behalf by a trusted person.

Finally, a durable health care power of attorney can provide specific detailed instructions regarding what you would like done by your attending physician in specific circumstances. Generally, living wills are limited to options for the withholding of life support. In order to be certain that you have made provisions for most potential health care situations, it is recommended you prepare both a living will and a durable health care power of attorney. Not everyone, however, has a trusted person available to serve as their health care representative. In these situations, the use of a living will alone will be necessary. It is, of course, possible to add additional instructions to any living will to clearly and specifically indicate your desires. Please see Chapter 10 for information regarding living wills. Also note that advance health care directives also contain both living wills and durable health care powers of attorney. For further information regarding advance health care directives, please see Chapter 9.

Your health care representative can be a relative or close friend. It should be someone who knows you very well and whom you trust completely. Your representative should be someone who is not afraid to ask questions of health care providers and is able to make difficult decisions. Your representative may need to be assertive on your behalf. You should discuss your choice with your representative and make certain that he or she understands the responsibilities involved.

All states have enacted legislation regarding this type of form and recognize the validity of this type of legal document. In some states, they are called Appointment of Health Care Agent; in others, they are referred to as a Health Care Proxy. The form included in this book is officially titled Durable Health Care Power of Attorney and Appointment of Health Care Agent and Proxy, and is designed to be legally valid in all states. Information regarding each state's provisions are included in the Appendix.

The durable health care power of attorney included in this chapter is intended to be used to confer a very powerful authority to another person. In some cases, this may actually mean that you are giving that other person the power of life or death over you. This is not a power that should be conferred lightly. Very serious thought should be given to both who you appoint as your health care attorney-in-fact (the person you authorize to act on your behalf) and to any specific directions that you may want to give to that person regarding health care decisions.

You may revoke your durable health care power of attorney at any time prior to your incapacitation (and even during any incapacitation if you are able to make your desire to revoke the power known). Remember, however, that should you become disabled or incapacitated and unable to communicate your wishes to anyone, you may be unable to communicate your desire to revoke your durable health care power of attorney.

Please note that this form also provides a release for your health care representative to receive your medical records under the federal HIPAA regulations relating to the privacy of health care records. Also, at the beginning of the form is a notice that clearly explains the importance of caution in the use of this form and is applicable to all states. Please read it carefully before you sign your durable health care power of attorney.

> **Toolkit Tip!**
>
> Typically, in financial powers of attorney, the person appointed is called the "attorney-in-fact". In health care powers of attorney, the person appointed is generally called either the "health care representative", "health care agent", or "health care proxy".

There are two methods for preparing a durable health care power of attorney with this book. This chapter contains a general, standardized durable health care power of attorney. The enclosed CD contains state-specific health care powers of attorney as part of the state-specific advance health care directives that have been taken directly from the most recent legislation regarding health care powers of attorney in each state. (Note: these are explained in Chapter 9). A few states do not currently have specific legislation providing express statutory recognition of health care powers of attorney. For those states, the durable health care power of attorney in this chapter has been prepared by legal professionals to comply with the basic requirements that courts in that state or other states have found important. In such states, be assured that courts, health care professionals, and physicians will be guided by this expression of your desires concerning life support as expressed in the durable health care power of attorney prepared using this book. You may use either (1) the general durable health care power of attorney form or (2) the state-specific advance health care directive form for your state. Please compare your state's form (in your state's advance health care directive on the CD) with the standardized form in this chapter and select the appropriate form that you feel best expresses your wishes regarding the appointment of a health care agent to make your health care decisions for you if you are unable to make those decisions for yourself.

The Federal Patient Self-Determination Act encourages all people to make their own decisions about the type of medical care they wish to receive. This act also requires all health care agencies (hospitals, long-term care facilities, and home health agencies) receiving Medicare and Medicaid reimbursement to recognize a living will and/or health care power of attorney as advance directives. Under this Act, all health care agencies must ask you if you have advance directives and must give you materials with information about your rights under state law. The durable health care power of attorney included in this chapter and/or the state-specific health care power of attorney included in the state-specific advance health care directives on the CD *must* be recognized by all health care agencies and health care providers.

> ## ⚡ Warning!
>
> Be very careful as to who you appoint as your health care representative. They will have the authority to make life and death decisions if you are unable to make them yourself.

Finally, in all states, either laws or judicial case law have established that both the health care agent that you appoint and any health care providers who are following reasonable decisions made by your health care agent will not be held liable for any civil or criminal liability as long as they act in good faith. In addition, most state laws provide that attending physicians who act under the direction of a duly-appointed health care agent and follow generally-recognized health care procedures can not be found to have committed professional misconduct, even for the withholding or withdrawal of life-sustaining procedures. These laws are designed to allow your health care agent to make major health care decisions, including decisions that might end your life, without fear of civil or criminal liability for any such decisions. In addition, these laws have also developed to insure health care providers that they themselves will not be subject to any liability because they are following the directions of your appointed health care representative.

Revoking Your Durable Health Care Power of Attorney

All states have provided methods for the easy revocation of durable health care powers of attorney. Since such forms provide authority to medical personnel to withhold life-support technology that will likely result in death to the patient, great care must be taken to insure that a change of mind by the patient is heeded. For the revocation of a durable power of attorney for health care, any one of the following methods of revocation is generally acceptable:

- Physical destruction of the durable power of attorney for health care, such as tearing, burning, or mutilating the document.

- A written revocation of the durable power of attorney for health care by you or by a person acting at your direction. A form for this is provided in the next chapter and on the enclosed CD.

- An oral revocation in the presence of a witness who signs and dates an affidavit confirming a revocation. This oral

> **♀ Toolkit Tip!**
>
> If you use the revocation forms in this chapter or if you physically destroy your health care power of attorney, make sure that you provide a copy (or notice) of this revocation to anyone or any health care facility that has a copy or original of the durable power of attorney for health care that you are revoking.

declaration may take in any manner (verbal or non-verbal). Most states allow for a person to revoke such a document by any indication (even non-verbal) of the intent to revoke a durable power of attorney for health care, regardless of his or her physical or mental condition. A form for this (Witness Affidavit of Oral Revocation of Durable Health Care Power of Attorney) is included in the next chapter and on the enclosed CD.

Instructions for Durable Health Care Power of Attorney and Appointment of Health Care Agent and Proxy

This Power of Attorney goes into effect immediately and remains in effect even upon your incapacitation

This form should be used for preparing a durable health care power of attorney that appoints another person whom you chose to have the authority to make health care decisions for you in the event that you become incapacitated and unable communicate your own decisions. The grant of power under this document is very broad and may include the power to withdraw medical care that could potentially end your life.

This form also provides a HIPPA medical records privacy release that will allow the person that you appoint to access any hospital or medical records on you behalf to provide them sufficient information to make any required medical decisions on your behalf. The authority granted by this power of attorney may be revoked by you at any time and is automatically revoked if you die. If there is anything about this form that you do not understand, you should ask a lawyer to explain it to you.

To complete this form, fill in the following:

1. Name and address of person granting power of attorney
2. Name and address of person appointed as the "health care representative" (same as the "attorney-in-fact for health care decisions")

(3)   State whose laws will govern the powers granted

(4)   Signature of person granting power of attorney. IMPORTANT NOTE: You should only sign this section if you have carefully read and agree with the statement that grants your health care representative the authority to order the withholding of nutrition, hydration, and any other medical care when you are diagnosed as being in a persistent vegetative state.

(5)   Any additional terms or conditions that you wish to add

(6)   Date of signing of durable health care power of attorney

(7)   Your signature and printed name (do not sign unless in front of a notary public and witnesses)

(8)   Signature and printed name of witnesses (signed in front of a notary)

(9)   The notary acknowledgment section (to be completed by notary public)

(10)   Signature and printed name of person appointed as health care representative (This signature need not be witnessed or notarized)

In California, Delaware, Georgia, and Vermont, an additional statement is required to be signed by a patient advocate, ombudsman (in California, Delaware and Vermont) or facility director (in Georgia or Vermont, if the principal is a patient in a skilled nursing facility.

Durable Health Care Power of Attorney and Appointment of Health Care Agent and Proxy

NOTICE TO ADULT SIGNING THIS DOCUMENT: This is an important legal document. Before executing this document, you should know these facts: This document gives the person you designate (the attorney-in-fact) the power to make MOST health care decisions for you if you lose the capacity to make informed health care decisions for yourself. This power is effective only when your attending physician determines that you have lost the capacity to make informed health care decisions for yourself. Regardless of this document, as long as you have the capacity to make informed health care decisions for yourself, you retain the right to make all medical and other health care decisions for yourself. You may include specific limitations in this document on the authority of the attorney-in-fact to make health care decisions for you. Subject to any specific limitations you include in this document, if your attending physician determines that you have lost the capacity to make an informed decision on a health care matter, the attorney-in-fact GENERALLY will be authorized by this document to make health care decisions for you to the same extent as you could make those decisions yourself, if you had the capacity to do so. The authority of the attorney-in-fact to make health care decisions for you GENERALLY will include the authority to give informed consent, to refuse to give informed consent, or to withdraw informed consent to any care, treatment, service, or procedure to maintain, diagnose, or treat a physical or mental condition. Additionally, when exercising authority to make health care decisions for you, the attorney-in-fact will have to act consistently with your desires or, if your desires are unknown, to act in your best interest. You may express your desires to the attorney-in-fact by including them in this document or by making them known to the attorney-in-fact in another manner. When acting pursuant to this document, the attorney-in-fact GENERALLY will have the same rights that you have to receive information about proposed health care, to review health care records, and to consent to the disclosure of health care records. You can limit that right in this document if you so choose. GENERALLY, you may designate any competent adult as the attorney-in-fact under this document. You have the right to revoke the designation of the attorney-in-fact and the right to revoke this entire document at any time and in any manner. Any such revocation generally will be effective when you express your intention to make the revocation. However, if you made your attending physician aware of this document, any such revocation will be effective only when you communicate it to your attending physician, or when a witness to the revocation or other health care personnel to whom the revocation is communicated by such a witness communicates it to your attending physician. If you execute this document and create a valid Health Care Power of Attorney with it, this will revoke any prior, valid power of attorney for health care that you created, unless you indicate otherwise in this document. **This document is not valid as a Health Care Power of Attorney unless it is acknowledged before a notary public or is signed by at least two adult witnesses who are present when you sign or acknowledge your signature. No person who is related to you by blood, marriage, or adoption may be a witness. The attorney-in-fact, your attending physician, and the administrator of any nursing home in which you are receiving care also are ineligible to be witnesses. If there is anything in this document that you do not understand, you should ask a lawyer to explain it to you.**

① I, _____ (printed name) ,
residing at _____,
appoint the following person as my attorney-in-fact for health care decisions, my health care agent, and confer upon this person my health care proxy. This person shall hereafter referred to as my "health care representative":
② _____ (printed name) ,
residing at _____.

③ I grant my health care representative the maximum power under law to perform any acts on my behalf regarding health care matters that I could do personally under the laws of the State of _____, including specifically the power to make any health decisions on my behalf, upon the terms and conditions set forth below. My health care representative accepts this appointment and agrees to act in my best interest as he or she considers advisable. This health care power of attorney and appointment of health care agent and proxy may be revoked by me at any time and is automatically revoked on my death. However, this power of attorney shall not be affected by my present or future disability or incapacity.

This health care power of attorney and appointment of health care agent and proxy has the following terms and conditions:

If I have signed a Living Will or Directive to Physicians, and it is still in effect, I direct that my health care representative abide by the directions that I have set out in that document. If at any time I should have an incurable injury, disease, or illness which has been certified as a terminal condition by my attending physician and one additional physician, both of whom have personally examined me, and such physicians have determined that there can be no recovery from such condition and my death is imminent, and where the application of life prolonging procedures would serve only to artificially prolong the dying process, then:

I direct my health care representative to assure that such procedures be withheld or withdrawn, and that I be permitted to die naturally with only the administration of medication, the administration of nutrition and/or hydration, or the performance of any medical procedure deemed necessary to provide me with comfort, care, or to alleviate pain. If at any time I should have been diagnosed as being in a persistent vegetative state which has been certified as incurable by my attending physician and one additional physician, both of whom have personally examined me, and such physicians have determined that there can be no recovery from such condition, and where the application of life prolonging procedures would serve only to artificially prolong the dying process, then: I direct that my health care representative assure that such procedures be withheld or withdrawn, and that I be permitted to die naturally with only the administration of medication, the administration of nutrition and/or hydration, or the performance of any medical procedure deemed necessary to provide me with comfort, care, or to alleviate pain.

④ **THE FOLLOWING INSTRUCTIONS (IN BOLDFACE TYPE) ONLY APPLY IF I HAVE SIGNED MY NAME IN THIS SPACE:** _____

However, if at any time I should have been diagnosed as being in a persistent vegetative state which has been certified as incurable by my attending physician and one additional physician, both of whom have personally examined me, and such physicians have determined that there can be no recovery from such condition, I also direct that my health care representative have sole authority to order the withholding of any aid, including the administration of nutrition, hydration, and any other medical procedure deemed necessary to provide me with comfort, care, or to alleviate pain.

If I am able to communicate in any manner, including even blinking my eyes, I direct that my health care representative try and discuss with me the specifics of any proposed health care decision.

⑤ If I have any further terms or conditions, I state them here:

I have discussed my health care wishes with the person whom I have herein appointed as my health care representative, I am fully satisfied that the person who I have herein appointed as my health care representative will know my wishes with respect to my health care and I have full faith and confidence in their good judgement.

I further direct that my health care representative shall have full authority to do the following, should I lack the capacity to make such a decision myself, provided however, that this listing shall in no way limit the full authority that I give my health care representative to make health care decisions on my behalf:

a. to give informed consent to any health care procedure;

b. to sign any documents necessary to carry out or withhold any health care procedures on my behalf, including any waivers or releases of liabilities required by any health care provider;

c. to give or withhold consent for any health care or treatment;

d. to revoke or change any consent previously given or implied by law for any health care treatment;

e. to arrange for or authorize my placement or removal from any health care facility or institution;

f. to require that any procedures be discontinued, including the withholding of any medical treatment and/or aid, including the administration of nutrition, hydration, and any other medical procedure deemed necessary to provide me with comfort, care, or to alleviate pain, subject to the conditions earlier provided in this document;

g. to authorize the administration of pain-relieving drugs, even if they may shorten my life.

I desire that my wishes with respect to all health care matters be carried out through the authority that I have herein provided to my health care representative, despite any contrary wishes, beliefs, or opinions of any members of my family, relatives, or friends. I have read the Notice that precedes this document. I understand the full importance of this appointment, and I am emotionally and mentally competent to make this appointment of health care representative. I intend for my health care representative to be treated as I would be with respect to my rights regarding the use and disclosure of my individually identifiable health information or other medical records. This release authority applies to any information governed by the Health Insurance Portability and Accountability Act of 1996 (aka HIPAA), 42 USC 1320d and 45 CFR 160-164.

I declare to the undersigned authority that I sign and execute this instrument as my health care power of attorney and that I sign it willingly, or willingly direct another to sign for me, that I execute it as my free and voluntary act for the purposes expressed in this document and that I am nineteen years of age or older, of sound mind and under no constraint or undue influence ,and that I have read and understand the contents of the notice at the beginning of this document, and .that I understand the purpose and effect of this document.

⑥ Dated _____ , 20_____

⑦ **Signature of person granting health care power of attorney**

_____

Signature of person granting health care power of attorney and appointing health care representative

_____

Printed name of person granting health care power of attorney and appointing health care representative

⑧ **Witness Attestation**

I, _____(printed name),
the first witness, and I, _____(printed name), the second witness, sign my name to the foregoing power of attorney being first duly sworn and do declare to the undersigned authority that the principal signs and executes this instrument as his/her power of attorney and that he/she signs it willingly, or willingly directs another to sign for him/her, and that I, in the presence and hearing of the principal, sign this power of attorney as witness to the principal's signing and that to the best of my knowledge the principal is nineteen years of age or older, of sound mind and under no constraint or undue influence. I am nineteen years of age or older. I am not appointed as the health care representative or attorney-in-fact by this document. I am not related to the principal by blood, adoption or marriage, nor am I entitled to any portion of the principal's estate under the laws of intestate succession or under any will or codicil of the principal. I also do not provide health care services to the principal, nor an employee of any health care facility in which the principal is a patient and am not financially responsible for the principal's health care.

_____   _____
Signature of First Witness   Address of First Witness

_____   _____
Signature of Second Witness   Address of Second Witness

⑨ **Notary Acknowledgment**
State of _____
County of _____

Subscribed, sworn to and acknowledged before me on this date _____ ,
20_____ by _____, the principal, who came before me personally, and under oath, stated that he or she is the person described in the above document and he or she signed the above document in my presence, or willingly directed another to sign for him or her. I declare under penalty of perjury that the person whose name is subscribed to this instrument appears to be of sound mind and under no duress, fraud, or undue influence. This document was also subscribed and sworn to before me on this date by _____, the first witness, and _____ ,the second witness .

_____
Notary Signature
Notary Public, In and for the County of _____   State of _____
My commission expires: _____   Notary Seal

Acceptance of Appointment as Health Care Attorney-in-Fact and Health Care Representative

I have read the attached durable health care power of attorney and am the person identified as the attorney-in-fact and health care representative for the principal. I hereby acknowledge that I accept my appointment as health care attorney-in-fact and health care representative and that when I act as agent I shall exercise the powers in the best interests of the principal.

⑩_____

Signature of person granted health care power of attorney and appointed health care representative

_____

Printed name of person granted health care power of attorney and appointed as health care representative

In California, Delaware, Georgia, and Vermont, the following statement is required to be signed by a patient advocate, ombudsman (in California, Delaware and Vermont) or facility director (in Georgia or Vermont, if the principal is a patient in a skilled nursing facility):

Statement of Patient Advocate or Ombudsman: I declare under penalty of perjury under the laws of the State of _____ that I am a patient advocate or ombudsman (or medical facility director) and am serving as a witness required by the laws of this state and that the principal appeared to be of sound mind and under no duress, fraud, or undue influence.
Dated _____

_____   _____
Signature of Patient Advocate or Ombudsman   Printed name and title of witness

Chapter 8

Revocation of Powers of Attorney

This chapter contains three forms for use in situation when it may be necessary to revoke a power of attorney. The first form is a general revocation form that can be used for revoking most powers of attorney. The next two forms are designed specifically to be used for a revocation of a health care power of attorney. Also note that, in the case of health care powers of attorney, any one of the following methods of revocation is generally acceptable:

- Physical destruction of the durable power of attorney for health care, such as tearing, burning, or mutilating the document.

- A written revocation of the durable power of attorney for health care by you or by a person acting at your direction. A form for this is provided in this chapter and on the CD.

- An oral revocation in the presence of a witness who signs and dates an affidavit confirming a revocation. This oral declaration may take in any manner (verbal or non-verbal). Most states allow for a person to revoke such a document by any indication (even non-verbal) of the intent to revoke a durable power of attorney for health care, regardless of his or her physical or mental condition. A form for this (Witness Affidavit of Oral Revocation of Durable Health Care Power of Attorney) is included in this chapter and on the CD.

Finally, please note that a Revocation of Advance Health Care Directive and a Witness Affidavit of Oral Revocation of Advance Health Care Directive is also provide in Chapter 9 for use with that specific type of document.

Instructions for Revocation of Power of Attorney

This document may be used with any of the previous power of attorney forms. The revocation is used to terminate the original authority that was granted to the other person in the first place. Some limited powers of attorney specify that the powers that are granted will end on a specific date. If that is the case, you will not need a revocation unless you wish the powers to end sooner than the date specified. If the grant of power was for a limited purpose and that purpose is complete but no date for the power to end was specified, this revocation should be used as soon after the transaction as possible. In any event, if you choose to revoke a power of attorney, a copy of this revocation should be provided to the person to whom the power was given. Copies should also be given to any party that may have had dealings with the attorney-in-fact before the revocation and to any party with whom the attorney-in-fact may be expected to attempt to deal with after the revocation. If you feel that it is important to verify the revocation of your power of attorney, you should have any third party that you supply with a copy of the revocation sign another copy for you to keep. If that is not possible, you should mail a copy of the revocation to that person or institution by first class mail, with a return receipt requested that requires a signature to verify delivery.

Although this revocation may be used to revoke a health care power of attorney, please also note that there are other acceptable methods to revoke a health care power of attorney (as noted on the previous page).

To complete this document, fill in the following information:

(1) Printed name and address of person who originally granted power (principal)
(2) Date of original power of attorney
(3) Printed name and address of person granted power (attorney-in-fact)
(4) Date of revocation of power of attorney
(5) Signature of person revoking power of attorney (principal) (signed in front of notary)
(6) Notary to complete the notary acknowledgement

Revocation of Power of Attorney

① I, _____ (printed
name), address: _____
do revoke the power of attorney dated ② _____ , 20 _____ ,
which was granted to ③ _____ (printed name),
address: _____ ,

to act as my attorney-in-fact.

④ This Revocation is dated _____ , 20 _____

⑤ _____
Signature of Person Revoking Power of Attorney

⑥ Notary Acknowledgement

State of _____
County of _____

On _____ , 20 _____ , _____ personally
came before me and, being duly sworn, did state that he or she is the person described in the
above document and that he or she signed the above document in my presence.

_____
Signature of Notary Public

Notary Public, In and for the County of _____
State of _____

My commission expires: _____   Notary Seal

Instructions for Revocation of a Durable Health Care Power of Attorney

On the following page, there is included a revocation of health care power of attorney. You have the right at any time to revoke your health care power of attorney. Remember, however, that should you become disabled or incapacitated and unable to communicate your wishes to anyone, you may be unable to communicate your desire to revoke your health care power of attorney. In any event, if you choose to revoke your health care power of attorney, a copy of this revocation should be provided to the person to whom the power was originally given. Copies should also be given to any party that may have had dealings with the attorney-in-fact before the revocation and to any party with whom the attorney-in-fact may be expected to attempt to deal with after the revocation, for example, your family physician.

Also note that you may also revoke a health care power of attorney by an oral revocation that takes place in the presence of a witness who then signs and date a written statement that confirms the revocation. Your oral declaration may take any manner, even a non-verbal indication (such as nodding your head or blinking your eyes) that signifies your intent to revoke the health care power of attorney. Such revocation can take place regardless of your physical or mental condition, as long as you are able to communicate, in some recognizable manner, your clear intent to revoke the power that was granted. For an oral revocation, use the Witness Affidavit of Oral Revocation of Durable Health Care Power of Attorney.

If you are able to, this form should be filled out and signed by the person revoking the health care power of attorney. It should also be notarized.

①   Name and address of person granting original health care power of attorney
②   Date of original durable health care power of attorney (that is now being revoked)
③   Name and address of person originally appointed as the "health care representative"
④   Date of signing of Revocation of Durable Health Care Power of Attorney
⑤   Your signature and printed name

Revocation of Durable Health Care Power of Attorney

① I, _____ (printed name),

of (address) _____

② do revoke the Durable Health Care Power of Attorney dated _____ , 20_____ ,

③ which was granted to _____ (printed name),

of (address) _____ , to act

as my attorney-in-fact for health care decisions and I revoke any appointment of the above person as my health care agent, health care representative, or health care proxy.

④ Dated _____ , 20_____

⑤ _____

Signature of person revoking power of attorney

_____

Printed name of person revoking power of attorney

Instructions for Witness Affidavit of Oral Revocation of Durable Health Care Power of Attorney

If it is necessary to use the Witness Affidavit of Oral Revocation of Durable Health Care Power Of Attorney form, the witness should actually observe your indication of an intention to revoke your durable health care power of attorney. This may take the form of any verbal or non-verbal direction, as long as your intent to revoke is clearly and unmistakably evident to the witness. This form does not need to be notarized to be effective. Make sure that you provide a copy of this revocation to anyone or any health care facility that has a copy or original of the durable health care power of attorney that you are revoking.

To complete this document, fill in the following information:

① Name and address of person who originally signed health care power of attorney (principal)
② Date of original health care power of attorney
③ State in which health care power of attorney was originally signed
④ Printed name of witness to act of revocation
⑤ Date of act of revocation
⑥ Witness signature
⑦ Date of witness signature
⑧ Printed name of witness

Witness Affidavit of Oral Revocation of Durable Health Care Power of Attorney

The following person ① _____,
referred to as the Principal, was the maker and signatory of a Durable Health Care Power of Attorney which was dated ② _____ , and which was executed by him or her for use in the State of ③ _____ .

By this written affidavit, I, ④ _____ , the witness, hereby affirm that on the date of ⑤ _____ , I personally witnessed the above-named declarant make known to me, through verbal and/or non-verbal methods, his or her clear and unmistakable intent to entirely revoke such Durable Health Care Power of Attorney, or any other appointment or designation of a person to make any health care decisions on his or her behalf. It is my belief that the above-named principal fully intended that all of the above-mentioned documents no longer have any force or effect whatsoever.

Witness Acknowledgment

The declarant is personally known to me and I believe him or her to be of sound mind and under no duress, fraud, or undue influence.

Witness Signature ⑥ _____   Date ⑦ _____

Printed Name of Witness ⑧ _____

Chapter 9

Advance Health Care Directives

What is an Advance Health Care Directive?

An advance health care directive is a legal document that may be used in any state and that allows you to provide written directions relating to your future health care should you become incapacitated and unable to speak for yourself. Advance health care directives give you a direct voice in medical decisions in situations when you cannot make those decisions yourself. Your advance health care directive will not be used as long as you are able to express your own decisions. You can always accept or refuse medical treatment and you always have the legal right to revoke your advance health care directive at any time. Instructions regarding revocations are discussed later in these instructions. The Federal Patient Self-Determination Act encourages all people to make their own decisions about the type of medical care they wish to receive. This act also requires all health care agencies (hospitals, long-term care facilities, and home health agencies) receiving Medicare and Medicaid reimbursement to recognize a living will and health care power of attorney as advance directives. Under this Act, all health care agencies must ask you if you have advance directives and must give you materials with information about your rights under state law.

Advance health care directives are not only for senior citizens. Serious life-threatening accidents or disease can strike anyone and leave them unable to communicate their desires. In fact, the rise of the use of advance health care directives can be attributed, in part, to legal cases involving medical care to young people, particularly Karen Ann Quinlan and Nancy Cruzan, and most recently, Terry Schiavo. Anyone over the age of 18 (19 in Alabama) who is mentally competent should complete an advance health care directive. Be aware, however, that advance health care directives are intended for non-emergency medical treatment. Most often, there is no time for health care providers to consult and analyze the provisions of an advance health care directive in an emergency situation.

The advance health care directives that are contained on the CD that is enclosed with this book all contain four separate sections, each dealing with different aspects of potential situations that may arise during a possible period of incapacitation:

- Living will
- Selection of health care agent (generally, by health care power of attorney)
- Designation of primary physician
- Organ donation

In addition, this book also provides (in Chapters 5 and 6) a fifth legal form that may be useful in many health care situations if you are unable to handle your own financial affairs: a durable power of attorney for financial affairs. A brief explanation of each of these forms follows:

Living Will: A *living will* is a document that can be used to state your desire that extraordinary life support means not be used to artificially prolong your life in the event that you are stricken with a terminal disease or injury. Its use has been recognized in all states in recent years. The purpose of a living will is to provide doctors and other health care workers with clear directions regarding how you would like your medical care handled toward the end of your life. A living will makes it possible for you to specify, in advance, exactly what your preferences are regarding the use of life-sustaining medical procedures if you are ever in a terminal medical condition or in a vegetative state, and are unable to give such directions yourself.

☼ Toolkit Tip!

Advance health care directives are not only for senior citizens. Serious life-threatening accidents or disease can strike anyone and leave them unable to communicate their desires.

Health Care Power of Attorney: This relatively new legal document has been developed to allow a person to appoint another person to make health care decisions on one's behalf, in the event that he or she becomes incapacitated or incompetent. Generally, a *health care power of attorney* will only take effect upon a person becoming unable to manage his or her own affairs, and only after this incapacitation has been certified by an attending physician. The person appointed will then have the authority to view your medical records, consult with your doctors and make any required decisions regarding your health care. This document may be carefully tailored to fit your needs and concerns and can be used in conjunction with a living will. It can be a valuable tool for dealing with difficult healthcare situations. For instructions and forms for preparing an individual durable health care power of attorney that is not part of an advance health care directive, please refer to Chapter 7.

Designation of Primary Physician: Through the use of this document, you will be able to designate your choice for your primary physician in the event you are unable to communicate your wishes after an accident or during an illness. Although your family may know your personal doctor, it may still be a good idea to put this choice in writing so that there is no question regarding who your choice for a doctor may be.

Organ Donation: You may also wish that your vital organs or, indeed, your entire body be used after your death for various medical purposes. Every year, many lives are saved and much medical research is enhanced by organ donations. All states allow for you to personally declare your desires regarding the use of your body and/or organs after death.

Durable Power of Attorney for Financial Affairs: (*You will need to prepare this form separately if desired as it is not part of the Advance Health Care Directives.)* Situations may arise when you are unable to handle your own financial affairs due to an incapacitating illness or accident. For those situations, a durable power of attorney for financial affairs has been developed to allow you to give authority to another person to take care of your financial affairs. *Durable* refers to the fact that the authority that you give to another will be in effect even if you are incapacitated. Such a document provides another person that you appoint with the same powers and authority that you, yourself, have over your property. Your appointed person can sign checks, pay bills, sign contracts, and handle all of your affairs on your behalf. In general, there are two types of durable powers of attorney for financial affairs: one that is immediately in effect and that will *remain* in effect in the event of your incapacitation, and another that *only* goes into effect if you become incapacitated. Note that this form is not contained in any of the advance health care directives that are provided on the enclosed CD. For information on preparing a durable power of attorney for financial affairs, please see Chapters 5 or 6.

The combination of these five forms provides a comprehensive method by which you may provide, in advance, for a situation in which you may be unable to communicate your desires to your family, your friends, and your health care providers. It is an opportunity to carefully plan how you would like various medical situations to be handled should they arise.

You may choose to complete an entire comprehensive advance health care directive or you may simply wish to prepare a separate durable health care power of attorney, and/or a separate durable power of attorney for financial affairs. Either method is acceptable. Note that a separate living will form is also provided in Chapter 10. If you would like to prepare a living will, you are encouraged to use the state-specific advance health care directive for your state, which contains a state-specific living will form as part of that document. This will allow the provisions in your living will and the provisions in your health care power of attorney (both as part of your complete advance health care directive) to complement each other. It is important that these two documents be coordinated so that the actions that your health care agent may be asked to take on your behalf when you are unable to communicate are in line with your stated desires as shown in your living will. Keeping these two documents together as part of a comprehensive advance health care directive makes such coordination much more likely.

These forms are provided on the enclosed CD in two separate formats: either as PDF forms that may be filled in on your computer, but not altered, or as text forms that may be carefully altered to more closely fit your individual wishes and desires. The individual forms have been prepared to meet the minimum legal requirements in all states and are legally-valid in all states. Please see the detailed instructions in the Introduction concerning how to complete either the PDF or text versions of these individual forms, If you choose to complete the separate individual forms, please see Chapters 5 and 6 for durable power of attorney for financial affairs forms, and Chapters 7 for durable health care power of attorney forms.

When Should You Use an Advance Health Care Directive?

A *'state-specific advance health care directive'* is a form that has been taken directly from the laws of your particular state. The legal effects of the language in such a document have been approved by the legislature of the state. This provides an advantage in that the legal language in such a 'statutory' form is generally familiar to health care providers in the particular state and they know that such language has been approved. This does not mean, however, that other 'non-statutory' forms are not legally valid in the state as well. Anyone may use a 'non-statutory' legal form with language that they find appropriate to their own situation, as long as the document meets certain minimum legal standards for a particular state.

You need not necessarily adopt all four sections of the document for your own use. You may select and complete any or all of the four separate sections of the form. For example, if you choose not to select a health care agent, you may use the other three parts of the form and not complete that section. Instructions for filling in the forms are contained later in this chapter. Many people find using a single comprehensive document easier than completing each separate form as an individual document. This method also provides a simple compact package that contains your entire advance health care directive with forms using legal language that most health care providers in your state are familiar with. In a few states, the legislatures have not developed specific language for one or more of the forms. These few instances are noted under the state's heading in the appendix of this book. In addition, in such situations, an appropriate and legally-valid form has been added to the directives for those states. Any such forms have been prepared following any guidelines set out by the state's legislature.

Important Note: The state-specific advance health care directive forms *do not* contain a durable power of attorney for financial affairs. As this form is not directly related to health care decision issues, it is left as a separate form located in Chapters 5 and/or 6. Should you desire to use this type of document to authorize someone to handle your financial affairs in the event of your disability or incapacitation, you should use one of the forms provided in Chapters 5 or 6.

Witness and Notary Requirements

All states have provided protections to ensure the validity of the advance health care directive. They have also provided legal protections against persons using undue influence to force or coerce someone into signing an advance health care directive. There are various requirements regarding who may be a witness to your signing of your advance health care directive. In general, these protections are for the purpose of ensuring that the witnesses have no actual or indirect stake in your death. These witnesses should have no connection with you from a health care or beneficiary standpoint. In most states, the witnesses must:

- Not be under 18 years of age (19 in Alabama)
- Not be related to you in any manner either by blood, marriage, or adoption
- Not be your attending physician
- Not be a patient or employee of your attending physician
- Not be a patient, physician, or employee of the healthcare facility in which you may be a patient

- Not be entitled to any portion of your estate upon your death under any laws of intestate succession, nor under your will or any codicil
- Not have a claim against any portion of your estate upon your death
- Not be directly financially responsible for your medical care
- Not have signed the advance health care directive for you, even at your direction
- Not be paid a fee for acting as a witness

In addition, please note that several states and the District of Columbia (Washington D.C.) have laws in effect regarding witnesses when the *declarant* (the person signing the advance health care directive) is a patient in a nursing home, boarding facility, hospital, or skilled or intermediate health care facility. In those situations, it is advisable to have a patient ombudsman, patient advocate, or the director of the health care facility act as the third witness to the signing of an advance health care directive.

These restrictions on who may be a witness to your signing of an advance health care directive require, in most cases, that the witnesses either be 1) friends who will receive nothing from you under your will, or 2) strangers. Please review the requirements for your own state in the witness statements on your particular state's form.

In addition, all of the forms included in this book, including all of the advance health care directives, are designed to be notarized. This is a requirement in most states for most forms and has been made mandatory on all of the forms in this book. The purpose of notarization in this instance is to add another level of protection against coercion or undue pressure being exerted to force anyone to sign any of these legal forms against their wishes. Sadly, such undue pressure has been applied in some cases to force senior citizens to sign legal documents against their own wishes. The requirement that one sign a document in front of a notary and in front of two additional witnesses can significantly lessen the opportunity for such abuse.

Instructions for Your Advance Health Care Directive

① Select the appropriate form from the CD. Carefully read through each section of your Advance Health Care Directive. You may wish to make two copies of the form(s) that you choose. This will allow you to use one form as a draft copy and the other form for a final copy that you, your witnesses , and a notary will sign.

② You will need to initial your choices in the first section of the form as to which sections of the entire Advance health care directive you wish to be effective. The choices are:

- Living will
- Selection of health care agent
- Designation of primary physician
- Organ donation

Please note that you may choose to exclude any of the above portions of your form and the remaining portions will be valid. If you wish to exclude one or more portions, DO NOT place your initials in the space before the section that you wish to exclude. Be careful so that you are certain you are expressing your desires exactly as you wish on these very important matters. If you do not wish to use a particular main section of the entire form, cross out that section of the form clearly and do not initial that section in either the first paragraph of the Directive or in the paragraph directly before your signature near the end of the Directive. If you do not wish to use a particular paragraph within one of the four main sections of the form, cross out that paragraph also.

Make the appropriate choices in each section where indicated by initialing the designated place or filling in the appropriate information. Depending on which form that you use, you may have many choices to initial or you may have no choices to initial. Please carefully read through the paragraphs and clauses that require choices to be certain that you understand the choices that you will be making. If you wish to add additional instructions or limitations in the places indicated on the form, please type or clearly print your instructions. If you need to add additional pages, please use the form titled "Additional Information for Advance Health Care Directive" which is also provided on the CD. If you need and use additional pages, be certain that you initial and date each added page and that you clearly label each additional page regarding which paragraph or section of the form to which it pertains.

③ In the form or section on organ donations, you may choose to either donate all of your organs or limit your donation to certain specific organs. Likewise, you may provide that the organs be used for any purpose or you may limit their use to certain purposes.

④ Finally, you will need to complete the signature and witness/notary sections of your forms. When you have a completed original with no erasures or corrections, staple all of the pages together in the upper left-hand corner. Do not sign this document or fill in the date yet. You should now assemble your witnesses and a notary public to witness your signature. Be certain that your witnesses meet your specific state requirements. In addition, please note that several states and the District of Columbia have laws in effect regarding witnesses when the declarant is a patient in a nursing home, boarding facility, hospital, or skilled or intermediate health care facility. In those situations, it is advisable to have a patient ombudsman, patient advocate, or the director of the health care facility to act as the third witness to the signing of an advance health care directive. In order that your advance health care directive be accepted by all legal and medical authorities with as little difficulty as possible, it is highly recommended that you have your signing of this important document witnessed by both your appropriate witnesses and a notary public.

⑤ In front of all of the witnesses and the notary public, the following should take place in the order shown:

(a) There is no requirement that the witnesses know any of the terms of your advance health care directive or other legal forms, or that they read any of your advance health care directive or legal forms. All that is necessary is that they observe you sign your advance health care directive and that they also sign the advance health care directive as witnesses in each other's presence.

(b) You will sign your legal form at the end where indicated, exactly as your name is written on the form, in ink using a pen. At this time, if you are using a state-specific form, you should also again initial your choices as to which sections you have chosen (directly before your signature space). You will also need to fill in the date on the first page of the directive or form, date and initial each additional information page (if you have used any), and fill in your address after your signature. Once you have signed and completed all of the necessary information, pass your advance health care directive or other legal form to the first witness, who should sign and date the acknowledgment where indicated and also print his or her name.

(c) After the first witness has signed, have the advance health care directive or other legal form passed to the second witness, who should also sign and date the acknowledgment where indicated and print his or her name.

(d) Throughout this ceremony, you and all of the witnesses must remain together. The final step is for the notary public to sign in the space where indicated and complete the notarization block on the form.

(e) If you have chosen individuals to act as your health care agent (durable power of attorney for health care), you should have them sign the form at the end where shown acknowledging that they accept their appointment.

⑥ When this step is completed, your advance health care directive or individual legal form that you have signed is a valid legal document. Have several photo-copies made and, if appropriate, deliver a copy to your attending physician to have placed in your medical records file. You should also provide a copy to any person who was selected as either your health care agent or your agent for financial affairs. You may also desire to give a copy to the person you have chosen as the executor of your will, your clergy, and your spouse or other trusted relative.

If you need to add additional pages to your advance health care directive, please use the form titled "Additional Information for Advance Health Care Directive" at the end of this chapter. If you need and use additional pages, be certain that you initial and date each added page and that you clearly label each additional page regarding which paragraph or section of the form to which it pertains. You should also note in the form itself that you are using additional pages by printing or writing "See attached additional page which is incorporated by reference" in the section of the form where you wish to insert additional instructions or information.

Revoking Your Advance Health Care Directive

All states have provided methods for the easy revocation of advance health care directives and the forms that they contain. Since such forms provide authority to medical personnel to withhold life-support technology that will likely result in death to the patient, great care must be taken to insure that a change of mind by the patient is heeded. Any one of the following methods of revocation is generally acceptable:

• Physical destruction of the advance health care directive, such as tearing, burning, or mutilating the document.

• A written revocation of the advance health care directive by you or by a person acting at your direction. A form for this is provided later in this chapter and on the CD.

• An oral revocation in the presence of a witness who signs and dates an affidavit confirming a revocation. This oral declaration may take place in any manner (verbal or non-verbal). Most states allow for a person to revoke such a document by any indication (even non-verbal) of the intent to revoke an advance health care directive, regardless of his or her physical or mental condition. A form for this effect is included later in this chapter and on the CD, titled "Witness Affidavit of Oral Revocation of Advance Health Care Directive."

If your revoke your advance health care directive, make sure that you provide a copy (or notice) of this revocation to anyone or any health care facility that has a copy or original of the advance health care directive that you are revoking.

Instructions for Revocation of Advance Health Care Directive

To complete this document, fill in the following information:

① Name of person who originally signed the advance health care directive (principal or declarant)
② Date of original advance health care directive
③ State in which original advance health care directive was signed
④ Signature of person revoking advance health care directive
⑤ Date of revocation of advance health care directive

Revocation of Advance Health Care Directive

① I, _____ , am the maker and signatory of an Advance Health Care Directive which was dated ② _____ , and which was executed by me for use in the State of ③_____ .

By this written revocation, I hereby entirely revoke such Advance Health Care Directive, any Living Will, any Durable Power of Attorney for Health Care, any Organ Donation, or any other appointment or designation of a person to make any health care decisions on my behalf. I intend that all of the above mentioned documents have no force or effect whatsoever.

BY SIGNING HERE I INDICATE THAT I UNDERSTAND THE PURPOSE AND EFFECT OF THIS DOCUMENT.

④ Signature _____   ⑤ Date _____

Instructions for Witness Affidavit of Oral Revocation of Advance Health Care Directive

If it is necessary to use the Witness Affidavit of Oral Revocation of Advance Health Care Directive form, the witness should actually observe your indication of an intention to revoke your Advance Health Care Directive. This may take the form of any verbal or non-verbal direction, as long as your intent to revoke is clearly and unmistakably evident to the witness. This form does not need to be notarized to be effective. Make sure that you provide a copy of this revocation to anyone or any health care facility that has a copy or original of the Advance Health Care Directive that you are revoking.

To complete this document, fill in the following information:

① Name of person who originally signed the advance health care directive (principal or declarant)
② Date of original advance health care directive
③ State in which original advance health care directive was signed
④ Printed name of witness
⑤ Date of act of revocation
⑥ Signature of witness to the oral or non-verbal revoking of advance health care directive
⑦ Date of witness signature
⑧ Printed name of witness

Witness Affidavit of Oral Revocation of Advance Health Care Directive

The following person, ① _____ , herein referred to as the declarant, was the maker and signatory of an Advance Health Care Directive which was dated ② _____ , and which was executed by him or her for use in the State of ③ _____ .

By this written affidavit, I, ④ _____ , the witness, hereby affirm that on the date of ⑤ _____ , I personally witnessed the above-named declarant make known to me, through verbal and/or non-verbal methods, their clear and unmistakable intent to entirely revoke such Advance Health Care Directive, any Living Will, any Durable Power of Attorney for Health Care, any Organ Donation, or any other appointment or designation of a person to make any health care decisions on his or her behalf. It is my belief that the above-named declarant fully intended that all of the above-mentioned documents no longer have any force or effect whatsoever.

Witness Acknowledgment

The declarant is personally known to me and I believe him or her to be of sound mind and under no duress, fraud, or undue influence.

Witness Signature ⑥ _____ Date ⑦ _____

Printed Name of Witness ⑧ _____

Instructions for Additional Information for Advance Health Care Directives

If you need to add additional pages to your advance health care directive document, please use the form titled "Additional Information for Advance Health Care Directive" which is provided on the following page and on the CD. If you need to use additional pages, be certain that you initial and date each added page and that you clearly label each additional page regarding which paragraph or section of the form to which it pertains. You should also note in the form itself that you are using additional pages by printing or writing "See attached additional information page, which is incorporated by reference" in the section of the form where you wish to insert additional instructions or information. Note that this form should be attached to the original advance health care directive document prior to the signing and notarization of the original document.

To complete this document, fill in the following information:

1. Date of original advance health care directive
2. Name and address of person who originally signed advance health care directive (declarant)
3. Detailed statement of any additional information or instructions in advance health care directive (Be certain that you note the paragraph or section of the original advance health care directive where the additional information or instructions will apply).
4. Initials of declarant and date of advance health care directive

Additional Information for Advance Health Care Directive

The following information is incorporated by reference and is to be considered as a part of the Advance Health Care Directive, dated ① _____ _____, which was signed by the following declarant ② _____,

Declarant must initial and date at bottom of form and insert additional information here: ③

④ Initials of Declarant _____   Date _____

Chapter 10

Preparing a Living Will

In this chapter, you will be given instructions on how to prepare a *living will,* a document that states your desires regarding end-of-life medical care. A living will is a relatively new legal document that has been made necessary due to recent technological advances in the field of medicine. These advances can allow for the continued existence of a person on advanced life support systems long after any normal semblance of "life," as many people consider it, has ceased.

The inherent problem that is raised by this type of extraordinary medical life support is that the person whose life is being artificially continued by such means may not wish to be kept alive beyond what they may consider to be the proper time for their life to end. However, since a person in such condition has no method of communicating their wishes to the medical or legal authorities in charge, a living will was developed that allows one to make these important decisions in advance of the situation.

The purpose of a living will is to provide doctors and other health care workers with clear directions regarding how you would like your medical care handled toward the end of your life. A living will makes it possible for you to specify, in advance, exactly what your preferences are regarding the use of life-sustaining medical procedures if you are ever in a terminal medical condition or in a vegetative state, and are unable to

> **∅ Definition:**
>
> **Terminal Condition:**
> An incurable medical condition that will cause imminent death and where the use of life support systems will only prolong the moment of death.

⌀ Definition:

Vegetative State:
A medical condition of complete and irreversible loss of brain function; a permanent coma.

⚡ Warning!
VERY IMPORTANT: You should read the provisions of your proposed living will very carefully, as they authorize actions that will *end your life.* If you do not fully understand the terms of your living will, you should consult an attorney.

give such directions yourself. *Terminal* is generally defined as an incurable condition that will cause imminent death such that the use of life-sustaining procedures only serve to prolong the moment of death. Likewise, a *vegetative state* is generally defined as a complete and irreversible loss of cognitive brain function and consciousness. Thus, a living will comes into effect only when there is no medical hope for a recovery from a particular injury or illness which will prove fatal or leave one in a permanent and irreversible coma.

As more and more advances are made in the medical field in terms of the ability to prevent "clinical" death, the difficult situations envisioned by a living will are destined to occur more often. The legal acceptance of a living will is currently at the forefront of law. Living wills are accepted in all states, but they must adhere to certain legal conditions. A few states do not currently have specific legislation providing express statutory recognition of living wills, but courts in those states have ruled that living wills are legally valid. Although a living will does not address all possible contingencies regarding terminally-ill patients, it does provide a written declaration for the individual to make known her or his decisions on life-prolonging procedures. A living will declares your wishes not to be kept alive by artificial or mechanical means if you are suffering from a terminal condition and your death would be imminent without the use of such artificial means. It provides a legally-binding written set of instructions regarding your wishes about this important matter.

In most states, in order to qualify for the use of a living will, you must meet the following criteria:

• You must be at least 19 years of age
• You must be of "sound mind"
• You must be able to comprehend the nature of your action in signing such a document

A living will becomes valid when it has been properly signed and witnessed. However, it is very important to remember that as long as you are capable of making decisions and giving directions regarding your medical care, your stated wishes must be followed—*not* those directions that are contained in your living will. Your living will only comes into force when you are in a terminal or vegetative condition, with no likelihood of recovery, and are unable to provide directions yourself. Until that time, *you*–and not your living will–will provide the directions for your health care. Generally, a licensed physician is required to determine when your condition has become terminal or vegetative with no likelihood of recovering.

There are 3 separate methods for preparing a living will in this book. First, this chapter contains a general, standardized living will (this standard living will is also contained on the CD). Next, the Forms-on-CD that accompanied this book also contains state-specific living will forms that have been taken directly from the most recent legislation regarding living wills in each state. A few states do not currently have specific legislation providing express statutory recognition of living wills. For those states, a living will has been prepared by legal professionals to comply with the basic requirements that courts in that state or other states have found important. In such states, be assured that courts, health care professionals, and physicians will be guided by this expression of your desires concerning life support as expressed in the living will prepared using this book and CD.

> **♀ Toolkit Tip!**
>
> This book provides 3 methods for completing a living will: 1) a standardized living will, 2) a state-specific living will (on the CD), and 3) a living will that is part of a state-specific advance health care directive (also on the CD).

Finally, a living will is also part of the state-specific advance health care directives that were explained in Chapter 9 and these forms are also contained on the enclosed CD. You may use either the general living will form or the state-specific statutory form for your state explained in this chapter, or you may choose to use the living will in the advance health care directive for your state. Please compare your state's specific living will form in the advance health care directives with the standardized form in this chapter and on the CD and select the appropriate form that you feel best expresses your wishes regarding health care if you are in a terminal or vegetative condition.

Typical Living Will Provisions

Nearly all states have passed legislation setting up a statutorily-accepted living will form. Those states that have not expressed a preference for a specific type of living will have, nevertheless,

☀ Toolkit Tip!

You should usually prepare a living will and a health care power of attorney. Note that the advance health care directives explained in Chapter 9 contain both of these important forms.

accepted living wills that adhere to general legal requirements. There are many different types of living wills, from very brief statements such as the following from the State of Illinois:

> "If at any time I should have an incurable and irreversible injury, disease, or illness judged to be a terminal condition by my attending physician who has personally examined me and has determined that my death is imminent except for death-delaying procedures, I direct that such procedures which would only prolong the dying process be withheld or withdrawn, and that I be permitted to die naturally with only the administration of medication, sustenance, or the performance of any medical procedure deemed necessary by my attending physician to provide me with comfort care."

to lengthy and elaborate multi-page forms with detailed and very specific instructions. All of the various state forms try to assure that a person's own wishes are followed regarding health care decisions. Many states have drafted their legislation with the intention that people prepare both a living will and a health care power of attorney (or similar form) which appoints a person of your choosing to act on your behalf in making health care decisions when you are unable to make such decisions for yourself. It is advisable that you prepare both of these advance health care forms in order to cover most, if not all, eventualities that may arise regarding your health care in difficult situations. Health care powers of attorney are explained in Chapter 7.

In general, the purpose of your living will is to convey your wishes regarding life-prolonging treatment and artificially provided nutrition and hydration if you no longer have the capacity to make your own decisions, and have either a terminal condition, or become permanently unconscious. You should very carefully think about your own personal desires should either of these conditions arise. Please also note that the basic living will included in this book also contains a release of medical information under the federal HIPAA guidelines for privacy of medical information.

You should also read through this statement concerning the importance of the decisions that you make in a living will (This notice is also part of the living will itself):

Notice to the Adult Signing this Document:

This is an important legal document. This document directs the medical treatment you are to receive in the event you are unable to participate in your own medical decisions and you are in a terminal condition. This document may state what kind of treatment you want or do not want to receive. This document can control whether you live or die. Prepare this document carefully. If you use this form, read it completely.

You may want to seek professional help to make sure the form does what you intend and is completed without mistakes. This document will remain valid and in effect until and unless you revoke it. Review this document periodically to make sure it continues to reflect your wishes. You may amend or revoke this document at any time by notifying your physician and other health-care providers. You should give copies of this document to your physician and your family. This form is entirely optional. If you choose to use this form, please note that the form provides signature lines for you, the three witnesses whom you have selected and a notary public.

Finally, the Federal Patient Self-Determination Act encourages all people to make their own decisions about the type of medical care they wish to receive. This act also requires all health care agencies (hospitals, long-term care facilities, and home health agencies) receiving Medicare and Medicaid reimbursement to recognize a living will and/or health care power of attorney as advance directives that indicate the patient's wishes. Under this Act, all health care agencies must ask you if you have advance directives and must give you materials with information about your rights under state law. The living will in this chapter and/or the state-specific living wills on the CD must be recognized by all health care agencies.

> **⌯̇Toolkit Tip!**
>
> If you decide to use a state-specific living will (found on the CD), please use the instructions outlined on the following pages and also in the Introduction for completing these forms.

Instructions for Preparing and Signing a Living Will

If you desire that your life not be prolonged artificially when there is no reasonable chance for recovery and death is imminent, please follow the instructions below for completion of your living will. The entire following form is should be used if you choose to use this form. It has been adapted to be valid in all states. Courts, health care professionals, members of your family, and physicians will be guided by this expression of your desires concerning life support. Please consult the Appendix for further information regarding recognition of living wills in your state.

1. Make a photo-copy or printout a copy of the entire living will form from this chapter or the state-specific living will form from the Forms-on-CD. Using the photo-copy as a worksheet, please fill in the correct information in the appropriate blanks as noted below:

    ① Name of person making living will
    ② Name of person making living will
    ③ State whose laws will govern the living will
    ④ Any additional directions, terms or conditions that you wish to add
    ⑤ Number of pages of entire living will (fill in after printing out final copy)
    ⑥ Date of signing of living will (fill in upon signing)
    ⑦ Your signature and printed name (do not sign unless in front of a notary public)
    ⑧ Date, signatures and printed names of witnesses to signing of living will
    ⑨ The notary acknowledgment section (to be completed by notary public)

2. On clean, white, 8 1/2 x 11" paper, type or printout the entire living will exactly as shown with your information added. Carefully re-read this original living will to be certain that it exactly expresses your desires on this very important matter. When you have a clean, clear original version, staple all of the pages together in the upper left-hand corner. Do not yet sign this document or fill in the date.

3. You should now assemble two or three witnesses and a Notary Public to witness your signature. Note that the standardized living will provides for three witnesses so that it will be legally valid in all states. Most of the state-specific living wills provide for only two witnesses, although some will require three. As noted on the document itself, these witnesses should have no connection with you from a health care or beneficiary standpoint (exception: see note following). Specifically, the witnesses must:

- Be at least 19 years of age
- Not be related to you in any manner: by blood, marriage, or adoption
- Not be your attending physician, or a patient or employee of your attending physician; or a patient, physician, or employee of the health care facility in which you may be a patient. However, please see below.
- Not be entitled to any portion of your estate on your death under any laws of intestate succession, nor under your will or any codicil
- Have no claim against any portion of your estate on your death
- Not be directly financially responsible for your medical care
- Not have signed the living will for you, even at your direction
- Not be paid a fee for acting as a witness

Note: a few states have laws in effect regarding witnesses when the declarant is a patient in a nursing home, boarding facility, hospital, or skilled or intermediate health care facility. In those situation, it is advisable to have a patient ombudsman, patient advocate, or the director of the health care facility to act as the third witness to the signing of a living will. Please check the Appendix for your state's requirements.

4. In front of all of the witnesses and in front of the Notary Public, the following should take place in the order shown:

- You will then sign your living will at the end, exactly as your name is typewritten on your living will, where indicated, in ink using a pen.
- After you have signed, pass your living will to the first witness, who should sign where indicated and fill in his or her address.
- After the first witness has signed, have the living will passed to the second witness, who should also sign where indicated.
- If you are using a living will that requires a third witness, then after the second witness has signed, have the living will passed to the third and final witness, who also signs where indicated and fills in his or her address. Throughout this ceremony, you and all of the witnesses must remain together.

The final step is for the notary public to sign in the space indicated. When this step is completed, your living will is a valid legal document. Have several copies made and, if appropriate, deliver a copy to your attending physician to have placed in your medical records file. You may also desire to give a copy to the person you have chosen as the executor of your will (or successor trustee of your living trust), a copy to your clergy, and a copy to your spouse or other trusted relative.

Living Will Declaration and Directive to Physicians of

① _____

Notice to Adult Signing This Document: This is an important legal document. This document directs the medical treatment you are to receive in the event you are unable to participate in your own medical decisions and you are in a terminal condition. This document may state what kind of treatment you want or do not want to receive. This document can control whether you live or die. Prepare this document carefully. If you use this form, read it completely. You may want to seek professional help to make sure the form does what you intend and is completed without mistakes. This document will remain valid and in effect until and unless you revoke it. Review this document periodically to make sure it continues to reflect your wishes. You may amend or revoke this document at any time by notifying your physician and other health-care providers. You should give copies of this document to your physician and your family. This form is entirely optional. If you choose to use this form, please note that the form provides signature lines for you, the three witnesses whom you have selected and a notary public.

② I, _____ , being of sound mind, willfully and voluntarily make known my desire that my life not be artificially prolonged under the circumstances set forth below, and, ③ pursuant to any and all applicable laws in the State of _____ , I declare that:

If at any time I should have an incurable injury, disease, or illness which has been certified as a terminal condition by my attending physician and one additional physician, both of whom have personally examined me, and such physicians have determined that there can be no recovery from such condition and my death is imminent, and where the application of life prolonging procedures would serve only to artificially prolong the dying process, then:

I direct that such procedures be withheld or withdrawn, and that I be permitted to die naturally with only the administration of medication, the administration of nutrition and/or hydration, or the performance of any medical procedure deemed necessary to provide me with comfort, care, or to alleviate pain.

If at any time I should have been diagnosed as being in a persistent vegetative state which has been certified as incurable by my attending physician and one additional physician, both of whom have personally examined me, and such physicians have determined that there can be no recovery from such condition, and where the application of life prolonging procedures would serve only to artificially prolong the dying process, then:

I direct that such procedures be withheld or withdrawn, and that I be permitted to die naturally with only the administration of medication, the administration of nutrition and/or hydration, or the performance of any medical procedure deemed necessary to provide me with comfort, care, or to alleviate pain.

In the absence of my ability to give directions regarding my treatment in the above situations, including directions regarding the use of such life prolonging procedures, then:

It is my intention that this declaration shall be honored by my family, my physician, and any court of law, as the final expression of my legal right to refuse medical and surgical treatment. I declare that I fully accept the consequences for such refusal.

④ If I have any additional directions, I will state them here:

If I have also signed a Health Care Power of Attorney, Appointment of Health Care Agent, or Health Care Proxy, I direct the person who I have appointed with such instrument to follow the directions that I have made in this document. I intend for my agent to be treated as I would be with respect to my rights regarding the use and disclosure of my individually identifiable health information or other medical records. This release authority applies to any information governed by the Health Insurance Portability and Accountability Act of 1996 (aka HIPAA), 42 USC 1320d and 45 CFR 160-164.

If I am diagnosed as pregnant, this document shall have no force and effect during my pregnancy.

I understand the full importance of this declaration, and I am emotionally and mentally competent to make this declaration and Living Will. I also understand that I may revoke this document at any time.

⑤ I publish and sign this Living Will and Directive to Physicians, consisting of _____ ⑥ typewritten pages, on _____, 20_____ , and declare that I do so freely, for the purposes expressed, under no constraint or undue influence, and that I am of sound mind and of legal age.

⑦ _____
Declarant's Signature

_____
Printed Name of Declarant

⑧ On _____, 20_____ , in the presence of all of us, the above-named Declarant published and signed this Living Will and Directive to Physicians, and then at the Declarant's request, and in the Declarant's presence, and in each other's presence, we all signed below as witnesses, and we each declare, under penalty of perjury, that, to the best of our knowledge:

1. The Declarant is personally known to me and, to the best of my knowledge, the Declarant signed this instrument freely, under no constraint or undue influence, and is of sound mind and memory and legal age, and fully aware of the possible consequences of this action.

2. I am at least 19 years of age and I am not related to the Declarant in any manner: by blood, marriage, or adoption.

3. I am not the Declarant's attending physician, or a patient or employee of the Declarant's attending physician; or a patient, physician, or employee of the health care facility in which the Declarant is a patient, unless such person is required or allowed to witness the execution of this document by the laws of the state in which this document is executed.

4. I am not entitled to any portion of the Declarant's estate on the Declarant's death under the laws of intestate succession of any state or country, nor under the Last Will and Testament of the Declarant or any Codicil to such Last Will and Testament.

5. I have no claim against any portion of the Declarant's estate on the Declarant's death.

6. I am not directly financially responsible for the Declarant's medical care.

7. I did not sign the Declarant's signature for the Declarant or on the direction of the Declarant, nor have I been paid any fee for acting as a witness to the execution of this document.

⑨

_____
Signature of Witness #1

_____
Printed name of Witness #1

_____
Address of Witness #1

_____

Signature of Witness #2

_____

Signature of Witness #3

_____

Printed name of Witness #2

_____

Printed name of Witness #3

_____

Address of Witness #2

_____

Address of Witness #3

Notary Acknowledgement

⑪ County of _____
State of _____

On _____ , 20_____, before me personally appeared _____ , the Declarant, and _____ , the first witness, _____ , the second witness, _____ , the third witness, and, being first sworn on oath and under penalty of perjury, state that, in the presence of all the witnesses, the Declarant published and signed the above Living Will Declaration and Directive to Physicians, and then, at Declarant's request, and in the presence of the Declarant and of each other, each of the witnesses signed as witnesses, and stated that, to the best of their knowledge, the Declarant signed said Living Will Declaration and Directive to Physicians freely, under no constraint or undue influence, and is of sound mind and memory and legal age and fully aware of the potential consequences of this action. The witnesses further state that this affidavit is made at the direction of and in the presence of the Declarant.

_____

Signature of Notary Public

_____

Printed name of Notary Public

Notary Public,
In and for the County of _____
State of _____
My commission expires: _____   Notary Seal

Instructions for Revoking a Living Will

All states which have recognized living wills have provided methods for the easy revocation of them. Since they provide authority for medical personnel to withhold life-support technology which will likely result in death to the patient, great care must be taken to insure that a change of mind by the patient is heeded.

If revocation of your living will is an important issue, please consult your state's law directly. The name of your particular state's law relating to living wills is provided in the Appendix of this book.

For the revocation of a living will, any one of the following methods of revocation is generally acceptable:

• Physical destruction of the living will, such as tearing, burning, or mutilating the document.

• A written revocation of the living will by you or by a person acting at your direction. A form for this is provided at the end of this chapter. You may use two witnesses on this form, although most states do not require the use of witnesses for the written revocation of a living will to be valid.

• An oral revocation in the presence of a witness who signs and dates a writing confirming a revocation. This oral declaration may take any manner. Most states allow for a person to revoke such a document by any indication (even non-verbal) of the intent to revoke a living will, regardless of their physical or mental condition.

To use the Revocation of Living Will form provided on the next page, simply fill in the following information:

① Name of person revoking living will
② Date of original living will
③ Date of signing revocation of living will
④ Signature and printed name of person revoking living will
⑤ Signatures and printed names of two witnesses to signing of revocation

Revocation of Living Will

① I, _____ , am the Declarant and maker of a Living Will and Directive to
② Physicians, dated _____ , 20_____ .

By this written revocation, I hereby entirely revoke such Living Will and Directive to Physicians and intend that it no longer have any force or effect whatsoever.

③ Dated _____ , 20_____ .

④ _____
Declarant's Signature

_____
Printed Name of Declarant

⑤ _____
Signature of Witness

_____
Printed name of Witness

_____
Address of Witness

_____
Signature of Witness

_____
Printed name of Witness

_____
Address of Witness

Chapter 11

Preparing a Designation of Primary Physician

This form allows you to make known your personal choice of the doctor whom you would like to care for you should you be unable to make known your choice. Generally, people desire that their personal family physician be designated as their primary physician since this person is most aware of their personal wishes and desires concerning health care issues. This form may also be useful in conjunction with other estate planning forms that may call for a certification by a primary physician of a person's disability or incapacitation, such as with a durable power of attorney or health care power of attorney. The use of this form is optional. You should keep a copy of this document attached to any such form that may require action by your primary physician. In addition, you should request that a copy of this document be placed into your main medical files. This form need not be acknowledged by a notary public.

☀️Toolkit Tip!

This form is also part of the state-specific advance health care directives explained in Chapter 9. Use the form in this chapter if you choose to prepare this form as a separate document.

Instructions for Designation of Primary Physician

To complete this form, fill in the following information:

1. Your name and address
2. Name and address of doctor selected as your primary physician
3. Date of signing of Designation of Primary Physician
4. Your signature and printed name

Designation of Primary Physician

①   I, _____, address:

do hereby designate the following doctor as my primary physician for all medical issues:

②   _____, address:

③   Date _____

④ _____
     Signature of person designating primary physician

_____
     Printed name of person designating primary physician

Chapter 12

Preparing an Organ Donation Form

The use of this form allows you to make a donation of your organs for medical use after your death. Using this form, you may make choices about whether and how you may wish any of your organs to be donated for medical, scientific, or educational uses after your death. All states have versions of a state law usually referred to as an "Anatomical Gift Act," which provides that individuals may make personal choices about whether and how to provide for the gift of their organs after death. Because of the many lives that can be saved though the use of transplanted donated organs, many states actually actively encourage such donations. This form allows for a selection of which of your organs or body parts you wish to donate and a selection of how those items that you have chosen to donate may be used (such as for any purpose, for research, therapy, transplantation, medical education, or other limitations on their use).

Please read through this carefully and make your appropriate decisions. You may choose to select the donation of your whole body or only of specific parts. You may also choose to allow your donation to be used for any medical or scientific purpose or you may limit the uses of your donation in any way. Naturally, the use of this form is entirely optional. If you do complete this form, it is a good idea to leave a copy of this form with your will and/or living trust and, additionally, to have a copy placed in your main medical file of your primary family physician. As the viability of organs for donation is very time-sensitive, it may also be a good

◌ Toolkit Tip!

Make certain that any organ donation that you make using this form is identical to any organ donation decision that you may have made previously (for example, on your driver's license.

idea to inform your closest relatives of your decision regarding the use of your organs after your death. This form is designed to be notarized.

Please note that this form specifically states that such donation be made regardless of the objections of any family member. This clause is included because there have been many successful efforts by surviving family members to prevent organ donations after the death of a person who has signed a valid organ donation form. This clause makes known your desire that such donations are your strong personal desire, regardless of the objections of any family members.

Also note that you should be certain that the choices that you make using this document should be identical to any choices that you may have made in any other document, including in your will or on a driver's license organ donation designation.

> ### ☼ Toolkit Tip!
>
> An organ donation form is also part of the advance health care directives explained in Chapter 9 of this book. You should complete either one, *but not both*, of these forms to make your organ donation decision.

Instructions for Organ Donation Form

To complete this form, fill in the following information:

① Your name and address

② Initial your selection of either any organs/parts or which specific organs or parts

③ Initial your selection of either any purposes or which specific purposes limitations on the use of your organs or parts

④ Date of signing of organ donation form

⑤ Your signature and printed name (Sign in front of notary public)

⑥ The notary acknowledgement section is completed by a notary public

Organ Donation Form

①   I, _____, address:

being of sound mind, do hereby donate the following organs for the noted medical purposes, and I specifically intend that such donations take place regardless of any objections of any of my family member:

② In the event of my death, I have placed my *initials* next to the following part(s) of my body that I wish donated for the purposes that I have *initialed* below:

[   ] any organs or parts **OR**

[   ] eyes   [   ] bone and connective tissue   [   ] skin

[   ] heart   [   ] kidney(s)   [   ] liver

[   ] lung(s)   [   ] pancreas   [   ] other _____

③ for the purposes of:

[   ] any purpose authorized by law **OR**

[   ] transplantation   [   ] research   [   ] therapy

[   ] medical education   [   ] other limitations

④ Dated _____

⑤ _____

      Signature of person donating organs

      _____

      Printed name of person donating organs

⑥ **Notary Acknowledgement**

State of _____

County of _____

On _____ , 20_____ , _____ came before me personally and, under oath, stated that he/she is the person described in the above document and he/she signed the above document in my presence.

_____

Notary Public

In and for the County of _____   State of _____

My commission expires: _____   Notary Seal

Appendix: State Power of Attorney Laws

This Appendix contains a summary of the laws relating to power of attorney, living will, and advance health care directive issues for all states and the District of Columbia (Washington D.C.). It has been compiled directly from the most recently-available statutes and has been abridged for clarity and succinctness. It is recommended that you review the listing that pertains to your home state. As you review your state's particular laws, keep in mind that your power of attorney or other documents are going to be interpreted under the laws of the state where you reside at the time you prepare your documents and, perhaps, in a different state where you may be hospitalized. Every effort has been made to ensure that the information contained in this Appendix is as complete and up-to-date as possible. However, state laws are subject to constant change. While most laws relating to powers of attorney are relatively stable, it is advisable to check your particular state statutes to be certain there have been no major modifications since this book was prepared, especially for those legal points that are particularly important in your situation. To simplify this process as much as possible, the exact name of the statute and the chapter or section number of where the information can be found is noted after each section of information. Any of these official statute books should be available at any public library or on the internet. A librarian will be glad to assist you in locating the correct book and in finding the appropriate pages. The correct terminology for each state is used in these listings. However, some states use certain language interchangeably. In those states, the most commonly-used language is stated. The state-by-state listings following in this Appendix contain the following information for each state:

State Website: This listing provides the internet website address of the location of the state's statutes. The addresses were current at the time of this book's publication; however, like most websites, the page addresses are subject to change. If an expired state webpage is not automatically redirected to a new site, laws can be searched at http://www.findlaw.com

State Law Description: This is the title where most of the relevant state laws on powers of attorney are contained.

Living Will Form: Under this listing, the exact state title and statutory location of a state's Living Will Form is provided. State-specific forms for all states are provided on the CD.

Other Directives: The existence and location of additional official state directives relating to advance health care and powers of attorney are indicated in this listing. Examples of such forms are Anatomical Gift Act forms (organ donation forms), Designation of Primary Physician, and other related forms.

Living Will Effective: This listing indicates the requirements of state law regarding when a living will becomes effective. Most states require that two physicians must diagnose and document that a patient either has a terminal illness with no hope of recovery or is in a permanent state of unconsciousness, or some similar diagnosis.

Living Will/Advance Health Care Directive Witness Requirements: Under this listing are noted the specific state requirements for witnesses to the signing of a living will and any related advance health care directives. In general, most states require that there are two witnesses, and that the witnesses be over eighteen, not related by blood or marriage to the declarant, not entitled to any part of the declarant's estate, and not financially responsible for the declarant's health care costs. Note that a few states require that, if the declarant is a patient in a nursing home or hospital, one of the witnesses be a patient advocate or patient ombudsman. In some states, the patient advocate or ombudsman is required to be a third witness, in addition to the other two required witnesses.

Advance Health Care Directive Form: Under this listing, the exact location of a state's official Advance Health Care Directive Form is shown, if the state provides one. Also noted is the availability of any such form on the enclosed CD.

Durable Health Care Power of Attorney: The existence and location of official state health care powers of attorney are indicated in this listing. Also noted are details of state law regarding agent's powers, revocation, and physician's immunity. Also noted is the availability of such form in the book and on the enclosed CD.

Durable Financial Power of Attorney: This listing indicates the requirements of state law regarding durable powers of attorney for financial affairs. If the state legislature provides the form, this is also noted. Also noted is the availability of state-supplied or other statutory and legally-valid form in the book and on the enclosed CD.

Alabama

State Website: www.legislature.state.al.us/CodeofAlabama/1975/coatoc.htm
State Law Reference: Code of Alabama.
Living Will Form: Living Will (Section 22-8A-4). This form is provided on the CD.
Other Directives: An organ donation form is provided on the CD under the Anatomical Gift Act (Section 22-19-40).
Living Will Effective: Two (2) physicians, one being the attending physician, must diagnose and document in the medical records that you either have a terminal illness or injury or are in a permanent state of unconsciousness. Not valid if pregnant. (Section 22-8A-4).
Living Will/Advance Health Care Directive Witness Requirements: Living will must be signed in the presence of two (2) or more witnesses at least nineteen (19) years of age. Witnesses cannot be related by blood, adoption, or marriage, entitled to any part of your estate, or be directly financially responsible for your health care. (Section 22-8A-4).
Advance Health Care Directive: State-specific form is provided by legislature and is included on CD. State-specific form is provided by legislature and is included on CD. Referred to as a Living Will. (Section 22-8A-4).
Durable Health Care Power of Attorney: Agent may authorize withholding or withdrawal of life-sustaining treatment, and make all other health care decisions. Directives prepared in other states are valid if in compliance with Alabama law. Health care providers who rely in good faith on agent's directions are immune from civil and criminal liability. Revocable by written revocation, destruction of document, or verbal expression of intent to cancel. Directives prepared in other states are valid if in compliance with Alabama law. Health care providers who rely in good faith on agent's directions are immune from civil and criminal liability. State-specific form is part of Advance Health Care Directive. See Chapters 7 and 9 for instructions for form on CD. (Section 22-8A-4). Follow signature, witness, and notary requirements as noted on form. Follow signature, witness, and notary requirements as noted on form.
Durable Financial Power of Attorney: No state-specific form provided by legislature. See Chapter 5 for legally-valid power of attorney forms to use. (Section 26-1-2). Follow signature, witness, and notary requirements as noted on form.

Alaska

State Website: www.legis.state.ak.us/folhome.htm
State Law Reference: Alaska Statutes.
Living Will Form: Declaration Relating to Use of Life-Sustaining Procedures serves as Living Will (Section 13.52.300). This form is provided on the CD.
Other Directives: An organ donation form is provided on the CD under the Anatomical Gift Act (Section 13.52.170 through 13.52.280).
Living Will Effective: Two (2) physicians determine that you are in a terminal condition and your death will result without using life-sustaining procedures. Your physician must then record your diagnosis and the contents of your Declaration in your medical records.

(Section 13.52.300).

Living Will/Advance Health Care Directive Witness Requirements: Sign your Declaration, or direct another to sign it, in the presence of two (2) adult witnesses or a notary public. Witnesses cannot be related by blood or marriage. (Section 13.52.300).

Advance Health Care Directive: State-specific form is provided by legislature and is included on CD. (Section 13.52.300).

Durable Power of Attorney for Health Care: Agent may consent or refuse to consent to medical care or relief for the principal from pain but agent may not authorize the termination of life-sustaining procedures; may include provision indicating whether a living will has been executed. Revocable at any time. A third party who relies on reasonable representations of an attorney-in-fact does not incur a liability to the principal or principal's heirs, assigns, or estate. State-specific form is part of Advance Health Care Directive. See Chapters 7 and 9 for instructions for form on CD. (Section 13.52.300). Follow signature, witness, and notary requirements as noted on form.

Durable Financial Power of Attorney: State-specific form is provided by legislature and is included on CD. See Chapter 6 for sample form. You may also use a generic durable financial power of attorney form in Chapter 5. You may also use a generic durable financial power of attorney form in Chapter 5. (Sections 13.26.332 and 13.26.353). Follow signature, witness, and notary requirements as noted on form.

Arizona

State Website: www.azleg.state.az.us/

State Law Reference: Arizona Revised Statutes Annotated.

Living Will Form: Living Will (Sections 36-3261 and 36-3262). This form is provided on the CD. Arizona maintains a Living Will/Advance Directive Registry at www.azsos.gov/adv_dir/.

Other Directives: An organ donation form is provided on the CD under the Anatomical Gift Act (Sections 36-841 through 36-850).

Living Will Effective: For the living will to become operative, a physician must certify that your condition is terminal, irreversible, or incurable. (Section 36-3251)

Living Will/Advance Health Care Directive Witness Requirements: Sign in the presence of one (1) or more witnesses or a notary public. Witnesses cannot be related by blood, adoption, or marriage, entitled to any part of your estate, or be directly financially responsible for your health care. (Section 36-3261 and 36-3221).

Advance Health Care Directive: State-specific form is provided by legislature and is included on CD. Referred to as a Living Will. (Sections 36-3261 and 36-3261).

Durable Health Care Power of Attorney: Agent has power to give or refuse consent to all medical, surgical, hospital, and make health care decisions on that person's behalf. Person may revoke health care directive or disqualify a surrogate by (1) written revocation; (2) orally notifying surrogate or health care provider; (3) making new health care directive; (4) any other act demonstrating specific intent to revoke. Health care directive prepared in another state is valid in this state if it was valid where and at the time it was adopted to the extent it does not conflict with the criminal laws of Arizona. Health care provider making good faith decisions in reliance on apparently genuine health care directive or decision of a surrogate is immune from civil, criminal, and professional discipline for that reliance. State-specific form is part of Advance Health Care Directive. See Chapters 7 and 9 for instructions for form on CD. (Sections 36-3221 through 36-3224). Follow signature, witness, and notary requirements as noted on form.

Durable Financial Power of Attorney: No state-specific form provided by legislature. See Chapter 5 for legally-valid power of attorney forms to use (Section 14-5501). Follow signature, witness, and notary requirements as noted on form.

Arkansas

State Website: http://www.arkleg.state.ar.us/
State Law Reference: Arkansas Code.
Living Will Form: Declaration serves as Living Will (Section 20-17-202). This form is provided on the CD.
Other Directives: An organ donation form is provided on the CD under the Anatomical Gift Act (Section 20-17-1201+).
Living Will Effective: Declaration applies when two (2) physicians diagnose you to have an incurable or irreversible condition that will cause death in a relatively short time. Not valid if pregnant. (20-17-203).
Living Will/Advance Health Care Directive Witness Requirements: Sign in the presence of two (2) witnesses. No other restrictions apply. (Section 20-17-202).
Advance Health Care Directive: State-specific form is provided by legislature and is included on CD. Referred to as a Declaration. (Section 20-17-202).
Durable Power of Attorney for Health Care: Agent may authorize withholding of any medical procedure or intervention that will serve only to prolong the dying process or to maintain the patient in a condition of permanent unconsciousness, Revocable at any time in any manner by the declarant without regard to declarant's mental/physical condition. Revocation is effective upon communication to attending physician. A declaration executed in another state in compliance with the laws of that state or Arkansas law is valid. Physician whose actions are in accord with reasonable medical standards is not subject to criminal, civil, or professional liability with respect to them. No state-specific form provided by legislature. See Chapter 6 for legally-valid form to use; form also provided on CD. Also may use Advance Health Care Directive. See Chapter 9 for instructions for this form on CD. (Section 20-13-104). Follow signature, witness, and notary requirements as noted on form.
Durable Financial Power of Attorney: State-specific form is provided by legislature and is included on CD. See Chapter 6 for sample form. You may also use a generic durable financial power of attorney form in Chapter 5. (Section 28-68-402). Follow signature, witness, and notary requirements as noted on form.

California

State Website: www.leginfo.ca.gov/

State Law Reference: California Law.

Living Will Form: California Advanced Health Care Directive serves as Living Will (Probate Code, Section 4701). This form is provided on the CD.

Other Directives: An organ donation form is provided on the CD under the Anatomical Gift Act (Health and Safety Code, Sections 7150 +).

Living Will Effective: This Directive becomes effective in the event that you have an incurable and irreversible condition that will result in death within a relatively short time, become unconscious and, to a reasonable degree of medical certainty, will not regain consciousness, or the likely risks and burdens of treatment would outweigh the expected benefits. Not valid if pregnant. (Probate Code, Section 4701).

Living Will/Advance Health Care Directive Witness Requirements: Sign in the presence of two (2) adult witnesses. A witness cannot be the person you appointed as your agent, your health care provider or an employee of your health care provider, or the operator or employee of a residential care facility for the elderly. Witnesses cannot be related to you by blood, marriage, or adoption, or be entitled to any part of your estate. A third witness, who must be a patient advocate or ombudsman, is required if the patient is in a skilled nursing facility (Probate Code, Section 4701).

Advance Health Care Directive: State-specific form is provided by legislature and is included on CD. (Probate Code, Section 4701).

Power of Attorney for Health Care: Agent may make decisions on any care, treatment, service, or procedure to maintain, diagnose, or treat an individual's physical or mental condition; including decision to begin, continue, increase, limit, discontinue or not begin any health care. Agent has same right as principal to receive information and consent regarding health care decisions and records except to consent to commitment, convulsive treatment, or psychosurgery, sterilization or abortion. No authority while principal can give informed consent to a health care decision. Anytime while principal has capacity to give a durable power of attorney, he may (1) revoke the appointment of the attorney-in-fact orally or in writing; (2) revoke the agent's authority by notifying the physician orally or in writing; (3) a subsequent durable power of attorney revokes prior one; (4) divorce revokes any designation of former spouse. Enforceable if executed in another state or jurisdiction in compliance with the laws of that state or jurisdiction or in substantial compliance with the laws of California. State-specific form is part of Advance Health Care Directive. See Chapters 7 and 9 for instructions for form on CD. (Probate Code, Sections 4701, 4673, 4674, and 4675). Follow signature, witness, and notary requirements as noted on form.

Durable Financial Power of Attorney: State-specific form is provided by legislature and is included on CD. See Chapter 6 for sample form. You may also use a generic durable financial power of attorney form in Chapter 5. (Probate Code, Sections 4120 +). Follow signature, witness, and notary requirements as noted on form.

Colorado

State Website: www.leg.state.co.us/
State Law Reference: Colorado Revised Statutes.
Living Will Form: Colorado Declaration as to Medical or Surgical Treatment serves as Living Will (Section 15-18-103). This form is provided on the CD.
Other Directives: An organ donation form is provided on the CD under the Anatomical Gift Act (Section 12-34-101).
Living Will Effective: Two (2) physicians must determine that you are in a terminal condition and your death will result without using life-sustaining procedures. Your physician must then record your diagnosis and the contents of your Declaration in your medical records. Not valid if pregnant. (Sections 15-18-103 and 15-18-104).
Living Will/Advance Health Care Directive Witness Requirements: Sign in the presence of two (2) adult witnesses. A witness cannot be a person who has claim against your estate upon your death, stands to inherit from your estate, or a physician, an employee of your attending physician or treating health care facility, or a patient of your treating health care facility. (Sections 15-18-105 and 15-18-106).
Advance Health Care Directive: State-specific form is provided by legislature and is included on CD. Referred to as a Declaration as to Medical or Surgical Treatment. (Section 15-18-104).
Durable Power of Attorney for Health Care: Agent has authority to act on behalf of principal who lacks decisional capacity in consenting to or refusing medical treatment including artificial nourishment and hydration; may include conditions or limitations of agent's authority. Divorce, dissolution, annulment, or legal separation revokes any designation of former spouse as agent; otherwise can be revoked at any time. A durable power of attorney executed in another state shall be presumed to comply with this law and may, in good faith, be relied on by a health care provider. No criminal or civil liability or regulatory sanction for complying in good faith with medical treatment decision of agent acting in accordance with advanced medical directive. State-specific form is part of Advance Health Care Directive. See Chapters 7 and 9 for instructions for form on CD. (Section 15-14-506). Follow signature, witness, and notary requirements as noted on form.
Durable Financial Power of Attorney: State-specific form is provided by legislature and is included on CD. See Chapter 6 for sample form. You may also use a generic durable financial power of attorney form in Chapter 5. (Sections 15-1-1301+, 15-14-501+, and 15-14-601+). Follow signature, witness, and notary requirements as noted on form.

Connecticut

State Website: www.cga.ct.gov/
State Law Reference: Connecticut General Statutes Annotated.
Living Will Form: Connecticut Health Care Instructions serves as Living Will (Section 19a-575). This form is provided on the CD.
Other Directives: An organ donation form is provided on the CD under the Anatomical Gift

Act (Section 19a-279+).

Living Will Effective: When you have an incurable or irreversible medical condition which, without the use of life support, will result in death in a relatively short period of time, or you are in a permanent coma or a persistent vegetative state. Not valid if pregnant. (Section 19a-575).

Living Will/Advance Health Care Directive Witness Requirements: Sign in the presence of two (2) adult witnesses. Your appointed agent cannot be a witness. If you reside in a resident facility operated or licensed by the department of mental health or department of mental retardation, additional Living Will/Advance Health Care Directive Witness Requirements: must be met and you should consult an attorney. (Sections 19a-575 and 19a-576).

Advance Health Care Directive: State-specific form is provided by legislature and is included on CD. Referred to as Connecticut Health Care Instructions. (Section 19a-575).

Durable Health Care Power of Attorney: Agent may consent, refuse consent, or withdraw consent to any medical treatment other than that designed solely to maintain physical comfort, the withdrawal of life support systems, or of nutrition or hydration; does not apply to pregnant patient. May be revoked at any time, in any manner; automatically revoked by divorce, legal separation, annulment, or dissolution of marriage if spouse is appointed as health care agent, unless principal specifies otherwise. Physician withholding, removing life-support system of an incapacitated patient shall not be civilly or criminally liable if decision was based on physician's (1) best medical judgment; (2) physician deems patient in a terminal condition; (3) patient's wishes were considered according to an executed document. Connecticut Health Care Instructions also contain Appointment of Health Care Agent and Appointment of Attorney-In-Fact for Health Care Decisions. State-specific form is part of Advance Health Care Directive. See Chapters 7 and 9 for instructions for form on CD. (Sections 1-54a and 19a-575). Follow signature, witness, and notary requirements as noted on form.

Durable Financial Power of Attorney: State-specific form is provided by legislature and is included on CD. See Chapter 6 for sample form. You may also use a generic durable financial power of attorney form in Chapter 5. (Section 45a-562). Follow signature, witness, and notary requirements as noted on form.

Delaware

State Website: www.delcode.delaware.gov/index.shtml

Living Will Form: Instructions for Health Care serves as Living Will (Section 16-2503). This form is provided on the CD.

Other Directives: An organ donation form is provided on the CD under the Anatomical Gift Act (Sections 16-2710 - 16-2719).

Living Will Effective: Two (2) physicians determine in writing that you have a terminal condition and/or are in a permanent state of unconsciousness. (Section 16-2505).

Living Will/Advance Health Care Directive Witness Requirements: Sign in the presence of two (2) adult witnesses. A witness cannot be a person who has claim against your estate upon your death, stands to inherit from your estate, be directly financially responsible for your health care, or be an owner, operator, or employee of a residential long-term health care institution in which you reside. If declarant is a patient in a nursing home, one of the witnesses must be a patient advocate or ombudsman. (Sections 16-2503 and 16-2505).

Advance Health Care Directive: State-specific form is provided by legislature and is included on CD. Referred to as Instructions for Health Care. Delaware Advance Directive contains Power of Attorney for Health Care and Instructions for Health Care. (Section 16-2503).

Durable Health Care Power of Attorney: Agent may grant, refuse, withdraw consent to provision of medical treatment, including right to refuse medical treatment which would extend appointer's life. Revocable at any time without regard to declarant's mental state or competency by (1) destruction of declaration with intent to revoke; (2) oral statement in presence of 2 persons 18 years or older expressing intent to revoke; (3) written revocation signed and dated by declarant or (4) new declaration with contrary intent. Directives of other states in compliance with the laws of that state or of Delaware are valid. Physicians or nurses acting in reliance on properly executed document are presumed to be acting in good faith and there is no civil or criminal liability unless negligent. State-specific form is part of Advance Health Care Directive. See Chapters 7 and 9 for instructions for form on CD. (Section 16-2503). Follow signature, witness, and notary requirements as noted on form.

Durable Financial Power of Attorney: No state-specific form is provided. See Chapter 5 for legally-valid power of attorney forms to use. (Section 12-4901+). Follow signature, witness, and notary requirements as noted on form.

District of Columbia (Washington D.C.)

State Website: http://government.westlaw.com/linkedslice/default.asp?SP=DCC-1000
State Law Reference: District of Columbia Code Annotated.
Living Will Form: District of Columbia Declaration serves as Living Will (Section 7-622). This form is provided on the CD.
Other Directives: An organ donation form is provided on the CD under the Anatomical Gift Act (Section 7-1521.04).
Living Will Effective: Two (2) physicians determine that you are in a terminal condition and your death will result without using life-sustaining procedures. Your physician must then record your diagnosis and the contents of your Declaration in your medical records. (Sections 7-621 and 7-622).
Living Will/Advance Health Care Directive Witness Requirements: Sign in the presence of two (2) adult witnesses. A witness cannot be your appointed attorney-in-fact, health care provider, or an employee of your health care provider. Witnesses also cannot be related by blood, marriage, or adoption, stand to inherit from your estate, or be financially responsible for your health care. (Section 7-622).
Advance Health Care Directive: State-specific form is provided by legislature and is included on CD. Referred to as a Declaration. (Section 7-622).
Durable Health Care Power of Attorney: Agent may grant, refuse, withdraw consent to

the provision of any health-care service, treatment, or procedure if principal is incapable of making or communicating decisions himself. Revocable at any time by notifying health care provider or attorney-in-fact orally or in writing. Divorce automatically revokes designation of former spouse. State-specific form is part of Advance Health Care Directive. See Chapters 7 and 9 for instructions for form on CD. (Section 21-2207). Follow signature, witness, and notary requirements as noted on form.

Durable Financial Power of Attorney: State-specific form is provided by legislature and is included on CD. See Chapter 6 for sample form. You may also use a generic durable financial power of attorney form in Chapter 5. (Section 21-2081). Follow signature, witness, and notary requirements as noted on form.

Florida

State Website: http://www.flsenate.gov/statutes/index.cfm
State Law Reference: Florida Statutes Annotated.
Living Will Form: Living Will (Section 765-303). This form is provided on the CD.
Other Directives: An organ donation form is provided on the CD under the Anatomical Gift Act (Sections 765.510 - 765.546).
Living Will Effective: Two (2) physicians determine in writing that you have a terminal condition, and/or are in a permanent state of unconsciousness and can no longer make your own health care decisions. (Section 765.306).
Living Will/Advance Health Care Directive Witness Requirements: Sign in the presence of two (2) adult witnesses. At least one (1) of your witnesses must not be related to you by marriage or blood. (Section 765.302).
Advance Health Care Directive: State-specific form is provided by legislature and is included on CD. Referred to as a Living Will. (Section 765.303).
Durable Health Care Power of Attorney: Agent may make all health care decisions regarding principal's health care during principal's incapacity, including life-prolonging procedures: any medical procedure, treatment, or intervention which utilizes mechanical or other artificial means to sustain, restore, supplant a spontaneous vital function and serves only to prolong the dying process of a patient in terminal condition. Does not include medication or medical procedure to provide comfort care or to alleviate pain; cannot withhold or withdraw life prolonging procedures from pregnant patient prior to viability. Revocable at any time by principal by (1) signed, dated writing; (2) destruction of declaration; (3) oral expression of intent to revoke; (4) subsequent advance health care directive materially different from the previously executed advance directive; (5) divorce revokes any designation of the former spouse as surrogate. An advance directive executed in another state in compliance with the laws of that state or Florida is validly executed. Health care facility, provider, or other person acting under their direction is not subject to criminal, civil, or professional liability for carrying out health care decision. State-specific form is part of Advance Health Care Directive. See Chapters 7 and 9 for instructions for form on CD. (Section 765.203). Follow signature, witness, and notary requirements as noted on form.

Durable Financial Power of Attorney: No state-specific form provided by legislature. See Chapter 5 for legally-valid power of attorney forms to use. (Section 709.08). Follow signature, witness, and notary requirements as noted on form.

Georgia

State Website: www.legis.state.ga.us
State Law Reference: Code of Georgia Annotated.
Living Will Form: Georgia Living Will (Section 31-32-3). This form is provided on the CD.
Other Directives: An organ donation form is provided on the CD under the Anatomical Gift Act (Section 44-5-140).
Living Will Effective: Two (2) physicians determine in writing that you have a terminal condition, and/or are in a permanent state of unconsciousness. Not valid if pregnant. (Sections 31-32-2 and 31-32-8).
Living Will/Advance Health Care Directive Witness Requirements: Sign in the presence of two (2) adult witnesses. A witness cannot be a person who has claim against your estate upon your death, stands to inherit from your estate, be directly financially responsible for your health care, or be an owner, operator, or employee of a health care institution in which you are a patient. Witnesses also cannot be related by blood or marriage. (Section 31-32-5).
Advance Health Care Directive: State-specific form is provided by legislature and is included on CD. Referred to as Georgia Advance Directive for Health Care. (Section 31-32-4).
Durable Health Care Power of Attorney: Agent has all powers the principal may have to be informed about and to consent or refuse to consent to, including any type of health care for the principal including withholding or withdrawal of life-sustaining or death-delaying procedures or after death, anatomical gifts, autopsies or disposition of remains. Revocable at any time by principal without regard to physical or mental condition by (1) destruction of the document; (2) written revocation signed and dated by the principal; (3) by oral or any other expression of intent to revoke in presence of an adult witness who within 30 days must sign and date in writing confirming the expression of such intent; (4) divorce revokes agency in former spouse. No health care provider subject to any civil, criminal, or professional liability solely for complying with decision of agent. State-specific form is part of Advance Health Care Directive. See Chapters 7 and 9 for instructions for form on CD. (Section 31-32-4). Follow signature, witness, and notary requirements as noted on form.
Durable Financial Power of Attorney: State-specific form is provided by legislature and is included on CD. See Chapter 6 for sample form. You may also use a generic durable financial power of attorney form in Chapter 5. (Sections 10-6-140 through 10-6-142). Follow signature, witness, and notary requirements as noted on form.

Hawaii

State Website: http://www.capitol.hawaii.gov/
State Law Reference: Hawaii Revised Statutes.

Living Will Form: Instruction for Health Care serves as Living Will (Section 327E-3). This form is provided on the CD.

Other Directives: An organ donation form is provided on the CD under the Anatomical Gift Act (Section 327-1).

Living Will Effective: In the event that you have an incurable and irreversible condition that will result in death within a relatively short time, become unconscious and, to a reasonable degree of medical certainty, will not regain consciousness, or the likely risks and burdens of treatment would outweigh the expected benefits. Not valid if pregnant. (Section 327E-3).

Living Will/Advance Health Care Directive Witness Requirements: Sign in the presence of two (2) adult witnesses. At least one (1) of your witnesses cannot be related to you by marriage or blood or entitled to any part of your estate. A witness cannot be the person you appoint as your agent, health care provider, or an employee of your health care provider. (Section 327E-3).

Advance Health Care Directive: State-specific form is provided by legislature and is included on CD. Referred to as Instructions for Health Care. (Section 327E-3).

Durable Health Care Power of Attorney: Agent authorized to make any lawful health care decisions that could have been made by principal at time of election. Agent may decide that principal's life should not be prolonged through surgery, resuscitation, life-sustaining medicine, or procedures for provision of nutrition or hydration if explicitly appointed. Effective only during period of incapacity of principal as determined by licensed physician. Not revoked until notice of actual death or disability of principal is given to attorney-in-fact (durable or otherwise). State-specific form is part of Advance Health Care Directive. See Chapters 7 and 9 for instructions for form on CD. (Section 327E-3). Follow signature, witness, and notary requirements as noted on form.

Durable Financial Power of Attorney: No state-specific form provided by legislature. See Chapter 5 for legally-valid power of attorney forms to use. (Sections 551D-1 through 551D-7). Follow signature, witness, and notary requirements as noted on form.

Idaho

State Website: http://www3.state.id.us/

State Law Reference: Idaho Code.

Living Will Form: Idaho Living Will (Section 39-4510). This form is provided on the CD.

Other Directives: An organ donation form is provided on the CD under the Anatomical Gift Act (Section 39-3401).

Living Will Effective: Two (2) physicians determine that you are in a terminal condition, your death will result without using life-sustaining procedures, or you are in a persistent vegetative state. Not valid if pregnant. May submit to optional state registry of Living Wills. (Section 39-4510).

Living Will/Advance Health Care Directive Witness Requirements: Although Idaho does not have any witness requirements, we suggest that you sign in the presence of two adult witnesses or a notary public, and we suggest that witnesses should not be your appointed attorney-in-fact, your health care provider, or a person related to you by blood, marriage or adoption.

Advance Health Care Directive: State-specific form is provided by legislature and is included on CD. Referred to as Idaho Living Will. (Section 39-4510).

Durable Health Care Power of Attorney: Agent may make health care decisions for principal, meaning consent, refusal of consent, or withdrawal of consent to any care, treatment, services, or procedure to maintain, diagnose, or treat an individual's physical condition. Also includes life-prolonging care decisions. Effective only when competent person is unable to communicate rationally. Revocable at any time by the maker without regard to competence by (1) destruction of the document; (2) by written, signed revocation; (3) by verbal expression of intent to revoke. No civil or criminal liability for physician acting in accordance with wishes of patient as expressed by statutory procedure. State-specific form is part of Advance Health Care Directive. See Chapters 7 and 9 for instructions for form on CD. (Section 39-4510). Follow signature, witness, and notary requirements as noted on form.

Durable Financial Power of Attorney: No state-specific form provided by legislature. See Chapter 5 for legally-valid power of attorney forms to use. (Section 15-5-501+). Follow signature, witness, and notary requirements as noted on form.

Illinois

State Website: http://www.ilga.gov/
State Law Reference: Illinois Compiled Statutes.
Living Will Form: Illinois Declaration serves as Living Will (755 ILCS 35/3). This form is provided on the CD.
Other Directives: An organ donation form is provided on the CD under the Anatomical Gift Act (755 ILCS 50).
Living Will Effective: If death would occur without the use of death-delaying procedures. Your physician must personally examine you and certify in writing that you are terminally ill. Not valid if pregnant. (755 ILCS 35/2).
Living Will/Advance Health Care Directive Witness Requirements: Sign in the presence of two (2) adult witnesses. Witnesses cannot be entitled to any part of your estate or financially responsible for your medical care. (755 ILCS 35/3).
Advance Health Care Directive: State-specific form is provided by legislature and is included on CD. Referred to as Illinois Declaration (755 ILCS 35/3)
Durable Health Care Power of Attorney: Health care powers may be delegated to an agent and include consent or refusal or withdrawal of any type of health care for individual. May extend beyond principal's death if necessary to permit anatomical gift, autopsy, or disposition of remains. Revocable at any time by principal without regard to mental or physical condition by (1) written revocation signed and dated; (2) oral expression in presence of witness who signs and dates a written confirmation; (3) destruction of power of attorney in manner indicating intent to revoke. Living will not operative as long as properly authorized

agent is available. Revocable at any time by principal without regard to mental or physical condition by (1) written revocation signed and dated; (2) oral expression in presence of witness who signs and dates a written confirmation; (3) destruction of power of attorney in manner indicating intent to revoke. No civil, criminal, or professional liability if good faith reliance on any decision or direction by agent not clearly contrary to terms of a health care agency. State-specific form is part of Advance Health Care Directive. See Chapters 7 and 9 for instructions for form on CD. **(**755 ILCS 45/4-1+). Follow signature, witness, and notary requirements as noted on form.

Durable Financial Power of Attorney: State-specific form is provided by legislature and is included on CD. See Chapter 6 for sample form. You may also use a generic durable financial power of attorney form in Chapter 5. (755 ILCS 45/2-1+). Follow signature, witness, and notary requirements as noted on form.

Indiana

State Website: http://www.in.gov/legislative/ic/code/

State Law Reference: Indiana Code Annotated.

Living Will Form: Indiana Living Will Declaration (Section 16-36-4-10). This form is provided on the CD.

Other Directives: An organ donation form is provided on the CD under the Anatomical Gift Act (Section 29-2-16-1).

Living Will Effective: Your physician must certify in writing that you are in a terminal condition and your death would occur within a short period of time without the use of life-sustaining medical care. (Section 16-36-4-10).

Living Will/Advance Health Care Directive Witness Requirements: Sign in the presence of two (2) adult witnesses. Witnesses cannot be entitled to any part of your estate, related to you by blood or marriage, financially responsible for your medical care, or be the person who signed the Declaration on your behalf. (Section 16-36-4-8).

Advance Health Care Directive: State-specific form is provided by legislature and is included on CD. Referred to as Indiana Living Will Declaration. (Section 16-36-4-10).

Durable Health Care Power of Attorney: Agent may act in matters affecting the principal's health care: any care, treatment, service, or procedure to maintain, diagnose, or treat an individual's physical or mental condition including admission to a health care facility and disclosure of medical records to health care provide; this appointment does not affect individual's authorization re: life-prolonging measures (i.e. a living will). Individual capable of consenting to health care may revoke appointment at any time by notifying representative or health care provider orally or in writing. Individual who may consent to his own health care may disqualify others from consenting or revoking appointment for the individual (disqualification must be in writing). No criminal, civil, or professional liability for a physician acting in good faith in reliance on the agent's direction. State-specific form is part of the Advance Health Care Directive. See Chapters 7 and 9 for instructions for form on CD. (Section 16-36-4-10).

Follow signature, witness, and notary requirements as noted on form.

Durable Financial Power of Attorney: No state-specific form provided by legislature. See Chapter 5 for legally-valid power of attorney forms to use. (Section 29-3-5). Follow signature, witness, and notary requirements as noted on form.

Iowa

State Website: http://www.legis.state.ia.us/

State Law Reference: Iowa Code Annotated.

Living Will Form: Iowa Declaration serves as Living Will (Section 144A.3). This form is provided on the CD.

Other Directives: An organ donation form is provided on the CD under the Anatomical Gift Act (Section 142C).

Living Will Effective: Two (2) physicians must certify in writing that you are in a terminal condition and your death would occur within a short period of time without the use of life-sustaining medical care. Not valid if pregnant. (Section 144A.5).

Living Will/Advance Health Care Directive Witness Requirements: Sign in the presence of two (2) witnesses eighteen (18) years or older or a notary public. A witness cannot be your health care provider or an employee of your health care provider. (Section 144A.3).

Advance Health Care Directive: State-specific form is provided by legislature and is included on CD. Referred to as Iowa Declaration. (Section 144A.3)

Durable Health Care Power of Attorney: Agent has power of consent, refusal of consent, or withdrawal of consent to health care. Attorney-in-fact has priority over court-appointed guardian to make health care decisions; does not include provision of nutrition or hydration except when required through intubation. May be revoked at any time in any manner by which principal is able to communicate intent to revoke. Power revoked in case of divorce where spouse designated durable power of attorney for health care. Similar document executed in another state in compliance with the laws of that state is valid and enforceable in Iowa; to the extent the document is consistent with Iowa law. Health care provider not subject to civil or criminal liability or professional disciplinary action if acting in good faith on decision of attorney-in-fact. State-specific form is part of Advance Health Care Directive. See Chapters 7 and 9 for instructions for form on CD. (Section 144B.2). Follow signature, witness, and notary requirements as noted on form.

Durable Financial Power of Attorney: No state-specific form is provided. See Chapter 5 for legally-valid power of attorney forms to use. (Section 633B.1+). Follow signature, witness, and notary requirements as noted on form.

Kansas

State Website: http://www.kslegislature.org/

State Law Reference: Kansas Statutes Annotated.

Living Will Form: Kansas Declaration serves as Living Will (Section 65-28,103). This form is provided on the CD.

Other Directives: An organ donation form is provided on the CD under the Anatomical Gift Act (Section 65-3209+).

Living Will Effective: Two (2) physicians must certify in writing that you are in a terminal condition and your death would occur within a short period of time without the use of life-sustaining medical care. (Section 65-28,103).

Living Will/Advance Health Care Directive Witness Requirements: Sign in the presence of two (2) witnesses eighteen (18) years or older or a notary public. Witnesses cannot be entitled to any part of your estate, be financially responsible for your medical care, be related to you by blood or marriage, or be the person who signed the Declaration on your behalf. (Section 65-28,103).

Advance Health Care Directive: State-specific form is provided by legislature and is included on CD. Referred to as Kansas Declaration. (Section (65-28,103).

Durable Health Care Power of Attorney: Agent may consent, refuse consent, or withdraw consent to any care, treatment, service, or procedure to maintain, diagnose, or treat a physical or mental condition and make decisions about organ donation, autopsy, and disposition of body; make all necessary arrangements for principal at any hospital/facility and employ health care personnel; request and review and execute any information regarding principal's affairs, including medical and hospital records. By an instrument in writing witnessed as required for power of attorney or "set out another manner of revocation, if desired." Any durable power of attorney for health care decisions which is valid under the laws of the state of the principal's residence at the time it was signed is valid under the act. State-specific form is part of Advance Health Care Directive. See Chapters 7 and 9 for instructions for form on CD. (Section 58-629). Follow signature, witness, and notary requirements as noted on form.

Durable Financial Power of Attorney: No state-specific form provided by legislature. See Chapter 5 for legally-valid power of attorney forms to use. (Section 58-650+). Follow signature, witness, and notary requirements as noted on form.

Kentucky

State Website: http://lrc.ky.gov/

State Law Reference: Kentucky Revised Statutes.

Living Will Form: Living Will Directive (Section 311.625). This form is provided on the CD

Other Directives: An organ donation form is provided on the CD under the Anatomical Gift Act (Sections 311.165 through 311.235).

Living Will Effective: When you become unable to make your own medical decisions. Not valid if pregnant. (Section 311.625).

Living Will/Advance Health Care Directive Witness Requirements: Sign in the presence of two (2) witnesses eighteen (18) years or older or a notary public. Witnesses cannot be entitled to any part of your estate, financially responsible for your medical care, or related to you by blood or marriage. (Section 311.625).

Advance Health Care Directive: State-specific form is provided by legislature and is included on CD. Referred to as Living Will Directive. (Section 311.625).

Durable Health Care Power of Attorney: Surrogate may make health care decisions grantor could make if he or she had decisional capacity, provided all decisions are in accordance with granter's wishes and surrogate has considered recommendations of attending physician; these decisions include withholding or withdrawal of artificial nutrition or hydration if (1) death is imminent (i.e. death is expected within a few days); (2) provision of nutrition cannot be physically assimilated; (3) burden or provision of such nutrition and hydration outweighs benefit. (Artificial nutrition or hydration not to be withdrawn if needed for comfort or relief of pain.); (4) When patient is in permanently unconscious state and advanced directive has authorized withdrawal or withholding of such nutrition and hydration. May be revoked in whole or in part or surrogate's powers reduced or limited at any time if grantor has decisional capacity; by (1) oral statement of intent to revoke in presence of 2 adults, one of whom is a health care provider; (2) destruction of declaration with intent to revoke; (3) effective immediately for attending physician once revocation received; (4) oral statement by grantor with decisional capacity to revoke overrides previous written directive. Directives made outside the provisions of this act does not restrict health care providers from following such directives if they are consistent with accepted medical practice. Any health professional is not subject to criminal prosecution or civil liability or deemed to have engaged in unprofessional conduct as a result of withholding or withdrawing life prolonging treatment in accordance with directive unless there was bad faith. State-specific form is part of Advance Health Care Directive. See Chapters 7 and 9 for instructions for form on CD. (Section 311.625). Follow signature, witness, and notary requirements as noted on form.

Durable Financial Power of Attorney: No state-specific form provided by legislature. See Chapter 5 for legally-valid power of attorney forms to use. (Section 386.093). Follow signature, witness, and notary requirements as noted on form.

Louisiana

State Website: http://www.legis.state.la.us/

State Law Reference: Louisiana Revised Statutes and Louisiana Civil Code Annotated.

Living Will Form: Louisiana Declaration serves as Living Will (Revised Statutes, Section 40:1299.58.3). This form is provided on the CD.

Other Directives: An organ donation form is provided on the CD under the Anatomical Gift Act (Revised Statutes, Section 17:2354).

Living Will Effective: Two (2) physicians must certify in writing that you are in a terminal condition and your death would occur within a short period of time without the use of life-sustaining medical care. (Revised Statutes, Section 40:1299.58.2).

Living Will/Advance Health Care Directive Witness Requirements: Sign in the presence of two (2) adult witnesses. Witnesses cannot be entitled to any part of your estate or related by blood or marriage. (Revised Statutes, Sections 40:1299.58.2 and 40:1299.58.3).

Advance Health Care Directive: State-specific form is provided by legislature and is included on CD. Referred to as Louisiana Declaration. (Revised Statutes, Section 40:1299.58.3).

Durable Health Care Power of Attorney: Agent may authorize any medical procedure or intervention, including but not limited to invasive administration of nutrition and hydration, which would serve only to prolong the dying process for a person diagnosed as having a terminal and irreversible condition. Does not include any measure necessary for comfort care. Revocable at any time by declarant without regard to mental state or competency by (1) destruction of document; (2) written revocation signed and dated by declarant; (3) oral or nonverbal expression by declarant of intent to revoke. Effective upon communication to physician. Declaration properly executed in and under the laws of another states is deemed to be validly executed. Any health care facility, physician or other person acting under their direction shall not be criminally, civilly, or professionally liable for withholding life-sustaining procedures in accordance with the provisions of this chapter, No state-specific form provided by legislature. See Chapter 7 for form. Also may use Advance health Care Directive. See Chapters 7 and 9 for instructions for form on CD. (Revised Statutes, Section 40:1299.53). Follow signature, witness, and notary requirements as noted on form..

Durable Financial Power of Attorney: No state-specific form provided by legislature. See Chapter 5 for legally-valid forms to use. (Civil Code, Section 3026). Follow signature, witness, and notary requirements as noted on form.

Maine

State Website: http://janus.state.me.us/legis/statutes/

State Law Reference: Maine Revised Statutes Annotated.

Living Will Form: Instructions for Health Care serves as Living Will (Section 18A-5-804). This form is provided on the CD

Other Directives: An organ donation form is provided on the CD under the Anatomical Gift Act (Section 22-2-2901+).

Living Will Effective: The Living Will becomes effective in the event that you have an incurable and irreversible condition that will result in death within a relatively short time, become unconscious and, to a reasonable degree of medical certainty, will not regain consciousness, or the likely risks and burdens of treatment would outweigh the expected benefits. (Section 18A-5-804).

Living Will/Advance Health Care Directive Witness Requirements: Sign in the presence of two (2) adult witnesses. No other restrictions apply. (Section 18A-5-804).

Advance Health Care Directive: State-specific form is provided by legislature and is included on CD. Referred to as Instructions for Health care. (Section 18A-5-801).

Durable Health Care Power of Attorney: Agent may consent or withhold consent or approval relating to any medical or other health care treatment of the principal including life-sustaining treatment when principal is in terminal condition or persistent vegetative state. May be revoked or terminated by a fiduciary of principal only with prior approval of court upon petition by any interested person. Declaration executed in another state in compliance with laws of that state and Maine is valid. Physician or other health care provider whose action is in accord with reasonable medical standards and in good faith is not subject to criminal or civil liability or discipline for unprofessional conduct. State-specific form is part of Advance Health Care Directive. See Chapters 7 and 9 for instructions for form on CD. (Section 18A-5-506). Follow signature, witness, and notary requirements as noted on form.

Durable Financial Power of Attorney: No state-specific form provided by legislature. See Chapter 5 for legally-valid power of attorney forms to use. (Section 18A-5-508). Follow signature, witness, and notary requirements as noted on form.

Maryland

State Website: http://mlis.state.md.us/

State Law Reference: Maryland Code.

Living Will Form: Advance Medical Directive Health Care Instructions serve as Living Will (Health General, Section 5-603). This form is provided on the CD.

Other Directives: An organ donation form is provided on the CD under the Anatomical Gift Act (Estates & Trusts, Section 4-501).

Living Will Effective: Two (2) physicians must agree in writing that you are incapable of making an informed health care decision, but you are not unconscious or unable to communicate by any other means. (Health General, Section 5-606).

Living Will/Advance Health Care Directive Witness Requirements: Sign in the presence of two (2) adult witnesses. The person you assign as your agent cannot be a witness. At least one (1) of your witnesses must be a person who is not entitled to any portion of your estate or financial benefit by reason of your death. (Health General, Section 5-603).

Advance Health Care Directive: State-specific form is provided by legislature and is included on CD. Referred to as Maryland Advance Directive: Planning for future Health Care Decisions. (Health General, Section 5-603).

Durable Health Care Power of Attorney: Agent may make health care decisions for declarant under circumstances stated in directive based on wishes of declarant; decision regarding the provision, withholding of life-sustaining procedures should be based, in whole or in part, on the patients preexisting, long-term mental or physical disability or a patient's economic disadvantage; can't authorize sterilization or treatment for mental disorder. Revocable at any time by (1) signed and dated writing; oral statement to health care practitioner; (3) execution of subsequent directive. Declaration executed out-of-state by nonresident is effective if declaration is in compliance with the laws of Maryland or the laws of the state where executed (to the extent permitted by the laws of Maryland). Any health-care provider who withholds or withdraws health care or life-sustaining procedures in accordance with this subtitle and in good faith, is not subject to civil or criminal liability and may not be found to have committed professional misconduct. State-specific form is part of Advance Health Care Directive. See Chapters 7 and 9 for instructions for form on CD. (Health General, Section 5-603). Follow signature, witness, and notary requirements as noted on form.

Durable Financial Power of Attorney: No state-specific form provided by legislature. See Chapter 5 for legally-valid power of attorney forms to use. (Estates and Trusts, Section 13-601). Follow signature, witness, and notary requirements as noted on form.

Massachusetts

State Website: http://www.mass.gov/legis/laws/mgl/

State Law Reference: Massachusetts General Laws.

Living Will Form: No state statute governing the use of Living Wills. However, you have a constitutional right to state your wishes about medical care. A basic living will form is provided in this book. This form is also provided on the CD as a state-specific Massachusetts Living Will form.

Other Directives: An organ donation form is provided on the CD under the Anatomical Gift Act.

Living Will Effective: In the event that you develop an irreversible condition that prevents you from making your own medical decisions.

Living Will/Advance Health Care Directive Witness Requirements: Because Massachusetts does not have a statute governing the use of Living Wills, there are no specific requirements to make your Living Will legally binding. We suggest that you sign in the presence of two (2) witnesses eighteen (18) years or older or a notary public. A witness should not be your health care provider or an employee of your health care provider. Witnesses should not be entitled to any part of your estate, financially responsible for your medical care, or related to you by blood or marriage.

Advance Health Care Directive: No state statute. Form provided on CD.

Durable Health Care Power of Attorney: Agent may make any and all health care decisions on principal's behalf that principal could make including decisions about life-sustaining treatment (which do not include those procedures to provide comfort care or pain alleviation), subject to any express limitations of health care proxy's authority (proxy has priority over other persons, including one with durable power of attorney unless limited by principal or court order). Revocable by (1) notification of agent or health care provider orally or in writing or by any other act evidencing specific intent to revoke the proxy; (2) execution of subsequent health care proxy; (3) divorce or legal separation where spouse was principal's agent under health care proxy. Effective if executed in another state or jurisdiction if in compliance with laws of that state or jurisdiction. No civil, criminal, or professional liability for carrying out in good faith a health care decision by an agent pursuant to a health care proxy. No state-specific form provided by legislature. See Chapter 7 for legally-valid for to use; form also provided on CD. Also may use Advance Health Care Directive. See Chapter 9 for instructions for this form on CD. (Chapter 201D, Sections 1-17). Follow signature, witness, and notary requirements as noted on form.

Durable Financial Power of Attorney: No state-specific form provided by legislature. See Chapter 5 for legally-valid power of attorney forms to use. Follow signature, witness, and notary requirements as noted on form.

Michigan

State Website: http://www.michiganlegislature.org/

State Law Reference: Michigan Compiled Laws Annotated.

Living Will Form: No state statute governing the use of Living Wills. However, you have a constitutional right to state your wishes about medical care. A basic living will form is provided in this book. This form is also provided on the CD as a state-specific Michigan Living Will form.

Other Directives: An organ donation form is provided on the CD under the Anatomical Gift Act

Living Will Effective: In the event that you develop an irreversible condition that prevents you from making your own medical decisions.

Living Will/Advance Health Care Directive Witness Requirements: Because Michigan does not have a statute governing the use of Living Wills, there are no specific requirements to make your Living Will legally binding. We suggest that you sign in the presence of two (2) witnesses eighteen (18) years or older or a notary public. A witness should not be your health care provider or an employee of your health care provider. Witnesses should not be entitled to any part of your estate, be financially responsible for your medical care, or be related to you by blood or marriage.

Advance Health Care Directive: No state statute. Form provided on CD.

Durable Health Care Power of Attorney: May authorize patient advocate to exercise 1 or more powers concerning patient's care, custody, and medical treatment that patient could have exercised on own behalf. Patient advocate may make decision to withhold or withdraw treatment which would allow patient to die only if patient has expressed in a clear and convincing manner that patient advocate is allowed to do so and that patient acknowledges that such a decision would allow death. (1) Revocable at any time and in any manner sufficient to communicate intent by patient to revoke; (2) resignation or removal of patient advocate; (3) subsequent designation that revokes prior designation, either expressly or by inconsistency; (4) divorce revokes designation of patient advocate in former spouse; (5) death of patient; (6) order of probate court; (7) occurrence of provision for revocation contained in designation; (8) any current desires of patient are binding on patient advocate. Person providing, performing, withholding, withdrawing medical treatment reasonably relying on decisions of patient advocate is liable in same manner and to same extent as if patient had made decision on his or her own behalf. No state-specific form provided by legislature. See Chapter 7 for legally-valid for to use; form also provided on CD. Also may use Advance Health Care Directive. See Chapter 9 for instructions for this form on CD. (Sections 700.5506+). Follow signature, witness, and notary requirements as noted on form.

Durable Financial Power of Attorney: No state-specific form provided by legislature. See Chapter 5 for legally-valid power of attorney forms to use. (Sections 700.5501+). Follow signature, witness, and notary requirements as noted on form.

Minnesota

State Website: http://www.revisor.leg.state.mn.us/stats/

State Law Reference: Minnesota Statutes Annotated.

Living Will Form: Health Care Living Will (Section 145B-04). This form is provided on the CD.

Other Directives: An organ donation form is provided on the CD under the Anatomical Gift Act (Sections 525.9211+).

Living Will Effective: Living Will becomes effective in the event that you can no longer make your own medical decisions. Not valid if pregnant. (Sections 145B.02 and 145B.04).

Living Will/Advance Health Care Directive Witness Requirements: Sign in the presence of two (2) witnesses eighteen (18) years or older or a notary public. A witness cannot be the person whom you appointed as your agent. At least one (1) witness cannot be your health care provider or an employee of your health care provider. (Section 145B.03).

Advance Health Care Directive: Agent may consent, refuse to consent, withdraw consent to any care, treatment, procedure or health care decision to maintain, diagnose, or treat mental or physical condition of principal including food and water by artificial means. Divorce revokes any designation of former spouse as agent to make health care decisions. Revocable at any time by (1) destroying; (2) written statement expressing intent to revoke; (3) verbally expressing intent to revoke in presence of 2 witnesses; (4) executing subsequent instrument. Power of attorney document, when executed in another state in compliance with that state's law is valid and enforceable in Minnesota to the extent it is consistent with Minnesota law. Health care provider is not subject to criminal prosecution, civil liability or professional disciplinary action if they rely in good faith on health care decision made by agent; no criminal, civil, or professional liability for health care provider who administers health care to keep patient alive (despite agent's decision) if all reasonable steps were promptly taken to transfer patient to complying provider. State-specific form is provided by legislature and is included on CD. Referred to as Health Care Living Will. (Section 145B.04).

Durable Health Care Power of Attorney: State-specific form is part of Advance Health Care Directive. See Chapters 7 and 9 for instructions for form on CD. (Section 145B.04). Follow signature, witness, and notary requirements as noted on form.

Durable Financial Power of Attorney: State-specific form provided by legislature allows choice as to whether Power of Attorney will be durable or non-durable. See Chapter 6 for sample. May also use generic durable power of attorney forms in Chapter 5. (Section 523.07). Follow signature, witness, and notary requirements as noted on form. Also included on CD is Minnesota Affidavit by Attorney-in-Fact of Nontermination or Nonrevocation, to be used to verify to a third party that Power of Attorney is still in full force and effect.

Mississippi

State Website: http://www.mscode.com/

State Law Reference: Mississippi Code Annotated.

Living Will Form: Instructions for Health Care serves as Living Will (Section 41-41-209). This form is provided on the CD.

Other Directives: An organ donation form is provided on the CD under the Anatomical Gift Act (Sections 41-39-31+).

Living Will Effective: In the event that you have an incurable and irreversible condition that will result in death within a relatively short time, become unconscious and, to a reasonable degree of medical certainty, will not regain consciousness, or the likely risks and burdens of treatment would outweigh the expected benefits. (Section 41-41-209).

Living Will/Advance Health Care Directive Witness Requirements: Sign in the presence of two (2) witnesses eighteen (18) years or older or a notary public. A witness cannot be the person whom you appointed as your agent, health care provider, or an employee of your health care provider. At least one (1) witness cannot be related to you by blood or marriage or entitled to your estate upon your death. (Section 41-41-209).

Advance Health Care Directive: State-specific form is provided by legislature and is included on CD. (Section 41-41-209).

Durable Health Care Power of Attorney: Agent may consent, refuse consent, or withdraw consent to any care, treatment, service, or procedure to maintain, diagnose, or treat an individual's physical or mental condition; may include decisions after death such as anatomical gift, autopsy, etc. Does not affect health care treatment in an emergency. Unless the document provides a shorter time, it shall be effective until revoked by principal. Durable power of attorney revocable at any time the principal has capacity to give a durable power of attorney for health care by notifying the attorney-in-fact in writing or notifying the health care provider in writing or by executing subsequent valid durable power of attorney for health care (revokes prior durable power of attorney for health care). No civil, criminal, or professional responsibility if health care provider relies in good faith on health care decision. State-specific form is part of Advance Health Care Directive. See Chapters 7 and 9 for instructions for form on CD. (Section 41-41-209). Follow signature, witness, and notary requirements as noted on form.

Durable Financial Power of Attorney: No state-specific form provided by legislature. See Chapter 5 for legally-valid power of attorney forms to use. (Sections 87-3-105). Follow signature, witness, and notary requirements as noted on form.

Missouri

State Website: http://www.moga.state.mo.us/STATUTES/STATUTES.HTM#T

State Law Reference: Missouri Annotated Statutes.

Living Will Form: Missouri Declaration serves as Living Will (Section 459.015). This form is provided on the CD.

Other Directives: An organ donation form is provided on the CD under the Anatomical Gift Act (Sections 194.210+).

Living Will Effective: The Declaration becomes effective in the event that you have an incurable or irreversible medical condition which, without the use of life support, will result in death in a relative short period of time, or you are in a permanent coma or persistent vegetative state. (Section 459.025)

Living Will/Advance Health Care Directive Witness Requirements: Sign in the presence of two (2) adult witnesses. If you have someone sign the Declaration on your behalf, that person cannot serve as a witness. (Section 459.015).

Advance Health Care Directive: State-specific form is provided by legislature and is included on CD. Referred to as Missouri Declaration. (Section 459.015).

Durable Health Care Power of Attorney: Agent may make health care decisions, but no agent may authorize withdrawal of artificially supplied nutrition and hydration which the patient may ingest through natural means. Revocable at any time in any manner by which patient is able to communicate the intent to revoke. Revocation is effective upon communication to agent or to physician. Any third party acting in good faith may rely on the instructions of the attorney-in-fact without liability to the patient or the patient's successors-in-interest. No state-specific form provided by legislature. See Chapter 7 for legally-valid form, which is also provided on the enclosed CD. Also may use Advance Health Care Directive. See Chapter 9 for instructions for this form on CD. (Section 404.822). Follow signature, witness, and notary requirements as noted on form.

Durable Financial Power of Attorney: No state-specific form provided by legislature. See Chapter 5 for legally-valid power of attorney forms to use. (Section 404.705). Follow signature, witness, and notary requirements as noted on form.

Montana

State Website: http://data.opi.state.mt.us/bills/mca_toc/index.htm

State Law Reference: Montana Code Annotated.

Living Will Form: Montana Declaration serves as Living Will (Section 50-9-103). This form is provided on the CD.

Other Directives: An organ donation form is provided on the CD under the Anatomical Gift Act (Section 72-17-101+).

Living Will Effective: Becomes effective when you have an incurable or irreversible medical condition which, without the use of life support, will result in death in a relatively short period of time, or you are in a permanent coma or persistent vegetative state. (Section 50-9-105).

Living Will/Advance Health Care Directive Witness Requirements: Sign in the presence of two (2) adult witnesses. No other restrictions apply. Do not use your appointed health care agent as one of your witnesses. (Section 50-9-103).

Advance Health Care Directive: State-specific form is provided by legislature and is included on CD. Referred to as Montana Declaration. (Section 50-9-103).

Durable Health Care Power of Attorney: Agent may authorize withholding or withdrawal of life-sustaining treatment, defined as any medical procedure or intervention that will serve only to prolong the dying process. Qualified patient may designate another individual to make decisions governing withholding or withdrawal of life-sustaining treatment. Life-sustaining procedures may not be withdrawn when qualified patient is known to be pregnant and when it is likely fetus will result in live birth. Revocable at any time in any manner without regard to physical or mental condition. Revocation is effective upon notice. Declarations made in another state in compliance with that state's laws executed in a substantially similar manner to laws of Montana are effective. Individuals appointed under this section are not criminally or civilly liable for decisions made pursuant to executed declaration; attending physicians or health care providers are not subject to civil or criminal liability or guilty of unprofessional conduct if acting in accordance with reasonable medical standards and in good faith. State-specific form is part of Advance Health Care Directive. See Chapters 7 and 9 for instructions for form on CD. (Section 50-9-103). Follow signature, witness, and notary requirements as noted on form.

Durable Financial Power of Attorney: State-specific form is provided by legislature and is included on enclosed CD. See Chapter 6 for sample form. You may also use a generic durable financial power of attorney form in Chapter 5. (Section 72-5-501). Follow signature, witness, and notary requirements as noted on form.

Nebraska

State Website: http://www.unicam.state.ne.us/web/public/home

State Law Reference: Revised Statutes of Nebraska.

Living Will Form: Nebraska Declaration serves as Living Will (Section 20-404). This form is provided on the CD.

Other Directives: An organ donation form is provided on the CD under the Anatomical Gift Act (Section 71-4804).

Living Will Effective: Declaration becomes effective when your attending physician determines you to have an incurable or irreversible medical condition which, without the use of life support, will result in death in a relatively short period of time, or you are in a permanent coma or persistent vegetative state. (Section 20-405).

Living Will/Advance Health Care Directive Witness Requirements: Sign in the presence of two (2) adult witnesses. Witnesses cannot be employees of your life or health insurance provider and at least one (1) witness must not be an administrator or employee of your treating health care provider. (Section 20-404).

Advance Health Care Directive: State-specific form is provided by legislature and is included on CD. Referred to as Nebraska Declaration. (Section 20-404).

Durable Health Care Power of Attorney: Agent may consent, refuse consent, or withdraw of consent to health care. However, powers do not include (1) withdrawal of routine comfort care; (2) withdrawal of usual and typical provision of nutrition and hydration; (3) withdrawal or withholding of life-sustaining procedures or artificially administered nutrition or hydration except if declarant gives that authority. Revocable at any time by competent principal in any manner he/she is able to communicate an intent to revoke; withdrawal at any time by attorney-in-fact. Otherwise, effective until death of principal; divorce or legal separation, unless otherwise noted in divorce decree, shall be deemed to revoke power of attorney for health care in spouse. Declaration executed in another state is valid according to its terms if valid under the laws of that state. No criminal, civil, or professional liability for attending physician following agent's direction if acting in good faith. Does not limit liability for negligence. State-specific form is part of Advance Health Care Directive. See Chapters 7 and 9 for instructions for form on CD. (Section 30-3408). Follow signature, witness, and notary requirements as noted on form.

Durable Financial Power of Attorney: State-specific form is provided by legislature and is included on enclosed CD. See Chapter 6 for sample form. You may also use a generic durable financial power of attorney form in Chapter 5. (Section 49-1522). Follow signature, witness, and notary requirements as noted on form.

Nevada

State Website: http://www.leg.state.nv.us/NRS/

State Law Reference: Nevada Revised Statutes Annotated.

Living Will Form: Nevada Declaration serves as Living Will (Section 449-610). This form is provided on the CD. Nevada maintains a Living Will/Advance Directive Registry at www.nvsos.gov/index.aspx?page=214

Other Directives: An organ donation form is provided on the CD under the Anatomical Gift Act (Sections 451.500+).

Living Will Effective: Declaration becomes effective when your doctor determines that your death would occur without the use of life-sustaining medical care. (Section 449.617).

Living Will/Advance Health Care Directive Witness Requirements: Sign in the presence of two (2) adult witnesses. No other restrictions apply. (Section 449.610).

Advance Health Care Directive: State-specific form is provided by legislature and is included on CD. Referred to as Nevada Declaration. (Section 449.610).

Durable Health Care Power of Attorney: Attorney-in-fact has power to make health care decisions before or after death for disabled principal including consent, refusal of consent, or withdrawal of consent to any care, treatment, service, or procedure to maintain, diagnose, or treat physical or mental condition except treatment specifically stated: commitment to mental facility, convulsive treatment, psychosurgery, sterilization, or abortion or any other specifically designated treatments. Divorce revokes designation of former spouse. Power of attorney remains valid indefinitely unless principal designates shorter period or it is revoked or another power of attorney is executed subsequently. State-specific form is part of Advance Health Care Directive. See Chapters 7 and 9 for instructions for form on CD. (Section 449.830). Follow signature, witness, and notary requirements as noted on form.

Durable Financial Power of Attorney: No state-specific form provided by legislature. See Chapter 5 for legally-valid power of attorney forms to use. (Section 111.460). Follow signature, witness, and notary requirements as noted on form.

New Hampshire

State Website: http://gencourt.state.nh.us/rsa/html/indexes/default.asp

State Law Reference: New Hampshire Revised Statutes.

Living Will Form: New Hampshire Declaration serves as Living Will (Section 137-J:20). This form is provided on the CD.

Other Directives: An organ donation form is provided on the CD under the Anatomical Gift Act (Section 291-A).

Living Will Effective: Two (2) physicians must certify in writing that you are in a terminal condition and your death would occur within a short period of time without the use of life-sustaining medical care. (Section 137-J:20).

Living Will/Advance Health Care Directive Witness Requirements: Sign in the presence of two (2) witnesses eighteen (18) years or older or a notary public. A witness cannot be a person who has a claim against your estate, stands to inherit from your estate, be your spouse, or be your doctor or a person acting under direction or control of your doctor. If you are a resident of a health care facility or a patient in a hospital, one of your witnesses may be your doctor or an employee of your doctor. (Section 137-J:14).

Advance Health Care Directive: State-specific form is provided by legislature and is included on CD. Referred to as New Hampshire Declaration. (Section 137-J:19).

Durable Health Care Power of Attorney: Agent may consent, refuse to consent or withdraw consent to any care, treatment, admission to a health care facility, any service or procedure to maintain, diagnose or treat an individual's physical or mental condition. Artificial nutrition and hydration may not be withdrawn or withheld unless clear expression of such power in document. Does not include power to consent to voluntary admission to state institution, voluntary sterilization or consent to withholding of life-sustaining treatment for pregnant patient unless treatment will not permit continuing development and live birth of unborn child. Revocable by (1) notifying attorney-in-fact or health care provider orally or in writing or in any other way communicating specific intent to revoke; (2) execution of subsequent durable power of attorney; (3) filing of action of divorce if spouse is agent. Revocation effective upon notice to health care provider or to attorney-in-fact. Person who is directly interested or related to patient may file an action to revoke durable power of attorney on grounds that principal was not of sound mind or under duress, fraud, or undue influence. Documents executed in another state are enforceable if they are in compliance with the law of that state or jurisdiction. No state-specific form provided by legislature. See Chapter 7 for legally-valid for to use; form also provided on CD. Also may use Advance Health Care Directive. See Chapter 9 for instructions for this form on CD. (Section 137-J:19). Follow signature, witness, and notary requirements as noted on form.

Durable Financial Power of Attorney: State-specific form is provided by legislature and is included on enclosed CD. See Chapter 6 for sample form. You may also use a generic durable financial power of attorney form in Chapter 5. (Section 506:6). Follow signature, witness, and notary requirements as noted on form.

New Jersey

State Website: http://www.njleg.state.nj.us
State Law Reference: New Jersey Revised Statutes.
Living Will Form: New Jersey Instruction Directive serves as Living Will (Section 26-2H-55). This form is provided on the CD.
Other Directives: An organ donation form is provided on the CD under the Anatomical Gift Act (Section 26:6-57+).
Living Will Effective: Your doctor or treating health care institution must receive this document. Your attending physician and one (1) other physician must confirm that you are unable to make health care decisions. (Sections 26:2H-59 and 26:2H-60).
Living Will/Advance Health Care Directive Witness Requirements: Sign in the presence of two (2) witnesses eighteen (18) years or older or a notary public. A witness cannot be the person whom you appointed as your agent. (Section 26:2H-56).
Advance Health Care Directive: State-specific form is provided by legislature and is included on CD. Referred to as Advance Directive for Health Care. (Section 26:2H-58).
Durable Health Care Power of Attorney: Agent may make decisions to accept or refuse treatment, service, or procedure used to diagnose, treat, or care for a patient's physical or mental condition including life-sustaining treatment. Includes decisions on acceptance or rejection of services of particular physician or health care provider or transfer of care; on the use of any medical device or procedure, artificially provided fluids and nutrition, drugs, surgery or therapy that uses mechanical or other artificial means to sustain, restore, or supplant a vital bodily function and thereby increase the expected life span of a patient; does not include provision of comfort care or alleviation of pain. Revocable by (1) oral or written notification; (2) execution of subsequent directive; (3) divorce revokes former spouse's designation as representative. Patient's clearly expressed wishes take precedent over any patient's decision or proxy directive. Effective if executed in compliance with New Jersey law or the laws of that state. No civil, criminal, or professional liability for any physician acting in good faith and pursuant to agent's decisions. No state-specific form provided by legislature. See Chapter 7 for legally-valid for to use; form also provided on CD. Also may use Advance Health Care Directive. See Chapter 9 for instructions for this form on CD. (Section 26:2H-56). Follow signature, witness, and notary requirements as noted on form.
Durable Financial Power of Attorney: No state-specific form provided by legislature. See Chapter 5 for legally-valid power of attorney forms to use. (Section 46:2B-8.1). Follow signature, witness, and notary requirements as noted on form.

New Mexico

State Website: http://www.legis.state.nm.us/
State Law Reference: New Mexico Statutes Annotated.
Living Will Form: Optional Advance Health Care Directive (Section 24-7A-4). This form is provided on the CD.

Other Directives: An organ donation form is provided on the CD under the Anatomical Gift Act (Sections 24-6B-1+).

Living Will Effective: This document becomes effective in the event that you have an incurable and irreversible condition that will result in death within a relatively short time, become unconscious and, to a reasonable degree of medical certainty, will not regain consciousness, or the likely risks and burdens of treatment would outweigh the expected benefits. (Section 24-7A-4).

Living Will/Advance Health Care Directive Witness Requirements: The law does not require that your advance directive be witnessed. To avoid future concerns, we recommend that you sign in the presence of two (2) witnesses eighteen (18) years or older or a notary public. A witness should not be the person whom you appointed as your agent. (Section 24-7A-4)

Advance Health Care Directive: State-specific form is provided by legislature and is included on CD. (Section 24-7A-4).

Durable Health Care Power of Attorney: Agent may make health care decisions including selection and discharge of health care providers, approval and disapproval of diagnostic tests, surgical procedures, programs of medication, orders not to resuscitate, and directions to provide, withhold or withdraw artificial nutrition and hydration and all others forms of treatment or health care which maintains, diagnoses, or otherwise affects an individual's mental or physical condition. Individual with capacity may revoke by (1) signed writing; (2) personally informing supervising health care provider; (3) in any manner that communicates intent to revoke; (4) filing for divorce or legal separation revokes designation of spouse as agent (revived by remarriage); (5) conflicting earlier health care directive (to the extent of the conflict). Out-of-state document is valid if it complies with provisions of Uniform Health Care Decisions Act of New Mexico regardless of where it was executed or communicated. No civil or criminal liability or discipline for unprofessional conduct if health care provider acting in good faith and in accordance with generally accepted health care standards. State-specific form is part of Advance Health Care Directive. See Chapters 7 and 9 for instructions for form on CD. Follow signature, witness, and notary requirements as noted on form.

Durable Financial Power of Attorney: State-specific form is provided by legislature and is included on enclosed CD. See Chapter 6 for sample form. You may also use a generic durable financial power of attorney form in Chapter 5. (Section 46B-1-104). Follow signature, witness, and notary requirements as noted on form.

New York

State Website: http://assembly.state.ny.us/leg/

State Law Reference: New York Consolidated Laws.

Living Will Form: Order Not to Resuscitate acts as Living Will. (Public Health, Section 2960+). This form is provided on the CD.

Other Directives: An organ donation form is provided on the CD under the Anatomical Gift Act (Public Health, Section 4300+).

Living Will Effective: The Living Will becomes effective when you become terminally ill, permanently unconscious, or minimally conscious due to brain damage and will never regain the ability to make decisions. (Public Health, Section 2965).

Living Will/Advance Health Care Directive Witness Requirements: Order not to resuscitate acts as Living Will in New York. You must sign in the presence of two (2) adult witnesses who do not benefit from your estate. (Public Health, Section 2964).

Advance Health Care Directive: State-specific form is provided by legislature and is included on CD. Referred to as Order Not To Resuscitate. (Public Health, Sections 2960+).

Durable Health Care Power of Attorney: Agent may make any decision to consent or refuse consent of any treatment, service, or procedure to diagnose or treat an individual's physical or mental condition. Proxy document may provide that it expires on a specified date or occurrence of condition; otherwise in effect until revoked. Revocable by (1) notifying agent or health care provider orally, in writing, or any other act evidencing intent to revoke; (2) divorce if former spouse was agent; (3) upon execution of a subsequent health care proxy. Out-of-state document is effective if executed in another state in compliance with laws of that state. No criminal, civil, or professional liability for acting in good faith pursuant to statute. State-specific form is part of Advance Health Care Directive. See Chapters 7 and 9 for instructions for form on CD. (Public Health, Sections 2980+). Follow signature, witness, and notary requirements as noted on form.

Durable Financial Power of Attorney: State-specific form is provided by legislature and is included on enclosed CD. See Chapter 6 for sample form. You may also use a generic durable financial power of attorney form in Chapter 5. (General Obligations, Sections 5-1501+). Follow signature, witness, and notary requirements as noted on form. Note that a New York Statutory Major Gifts Rider is required to be signed by the principal at the same time as the underlying Power of Attorney if the principal wishes to authorize the attorney-in-fact to make major gifts or changes to the principal's ownership interest in property.

North Carolina

State Website: http://www.ncga.state.nc.us/

State Law Reference: North Carolina General Statutes.

Living Will Form: Declaration of a Desire for a Natural Death serves as Living Will (Section 90-321). This form is provided on the CD.

Other Directives: An organ donation form is provided on the CD under the Anatomical Gift Act (Section 130A-402+).

Living Will Effective: Two (2) physicians must certify in writing that you are in a terminal condition and your death would occur within a short period of time without the use of life-sustaining medical care. Not valid if pregnant. (Section 90-321).

Living Will/Advance Health Care Directive Witness Requirements: Sign in the presence of two (2) adult witnesses and a notary public. A witness cannot be a person who has claim against your estate upon your death, stands to inherit from your estate, be directly financially responsible for your health care, or be an owner, operator, or employee of a health care institution in which you are a patient. Witnesses also cannot be related by blood or marriage. (Section 90-321).

Advance Health Care Directive: State-specific form is provided by legislature and is included on CD. Referred to as Declaration of a Desire for a Natural Death. (Section 90-321).

Durable Health Care Power of Attorney: Agent may make decisions regarding life-sustaining procedures, including those which serve to artificially prolong the dying process and may include mechanical ventilation, dialysis, antibiotics, artificial nutrition and hydration and other forms of treatment which sustain, restore, or supplant vital bodily functions but do not include care necessary to provide comfort or alleviate pain. May be revoked at anytime by principal capable of making and communicating health care decisions or by death of principal or by execution of a subsequent instrument or written instrument of revocation or any other method where intent to revoke is communicated (effective upon communication). Revoked on decree of divorce if spouse is agent, except if alternate has been appointed. If all health care attorneys-in-fact are unwilling or unable to act, the health care power of attorney will cease to be effective. No person acting on the authority of the health care agent shall be liable for actions taken pursuant to decision of health care agent. Withholding or discontinuing life-sustaining procedures shall not be considered suicide or cause of death for criminal or civil purpose. State-specific form is part of Advance Health Care Directive. See Chapters 7 and 9 for instructions for form on CD. (Sections 32A-15+). Follow signature, witness, and notary requirements as noted on form.

Durable Financial Power of Attorney: State-specific form is provided by legislature and is included on enclosed CD. See Chapter 6 for sample form. You may also use a generic durable financial power of attorney form in Chapter 5. (Section 32A-1+). Follow signature, witness, and notary requirements as noted on form.

North Dakota

State Website: http://www.legis.nd.gov/information/statutes/cent-code.html
State Law Reference: North Dakota Century Code.
Living Will Form: Declaration serves as Living Will (Section 23-06.5-17). This form is provided on the CD.
Other Directives: An organ donation form is provided on the CD under the Anatomical Gift Act (Sections 23-06.6-01+).
Living Will Effective: Two (2) physicians must certify in writing that you are in a terminal condition and your death would occur within a short period of time without the use of life-sustaining medical care. Not valid if pregnant. (Section 23-06.5-17).
Living Will/Advance Health Care Directive Witness Requirements: Sign in the presence of two (2) adult witnesses and a notary public. A witness cannot be a person who has claim against your estate upon your death, stands to inherit from your estate, be directly financially responsible for your health care, or be your doctor. Witnesses also cannot be related by blood or marriage. If you are presently living in a nursing home or other long-term care

facility, one (1) of your witnesses must be one (1) of the following: a member of the clergy, a lawyer licensed to practice in North Dakota, or a person designated by the Department of Human Services or the county court for the county in which the facility is located. (Section 23-06.5-17).

Advance Health Care Directive: State-specific form is provided by legislature and is included on CD. (Section 23-06.5-17).

Durable Health Care Power of Attorney: Agent has power to make any health care decisions principal could if he did not lack capacity (lack of capacity must be certified in writing by principal's attending physician), decisions including consent, refusal to consent or withdrawal of consent or request any care, treatment, service, or procedure to maintain, diagnose, or treat individual's physical or mental condition; does not include admission to mental health facility, psychosurgery, abortion, or sterilization. Revocable by (1) notification of agent orally, in writing, or any other act evidencing specific intent to revoke; (2) execution of subsequent durable power of attorney; (3) divorce where spouse was principal's agent. Out-of-state document is effective if executed in another state in compliance with the law of that state. No civil, criminal, or professional liability if acting in good faith and with ordinary care pursuant to directives of durable power of attorney. State-specific form is part of Advance Health Care Directive. See Chapters 7 and 9 for instructions for form on CD. (Section 23-06.5-17). Follow signature, witness, and notary requirements as noted on form.

Durable Financial Power of Attorney: No state-specific form provided by legislature. See Chapter 5 for legally-valid power of attorney forms to use. (Section 30.1-30). Follow signature, witness, and notary requirements as noted on form.

Ohio

State Website: http://codes.ohio.gov/

State Law Reference: Ohio Revised Code Annotated.

Living Will Form: Living Will Declaration (Section 2133-04). This form is provided on the CD.

Other Directives: An organ donation form is provided on the CD under the Anatomical Gift Act (Section 2108.01+).

Living Will Effective: Two (2) physicians determine that you are in a terminal condition and your death will result without using life-sustaining procedures, including the determination that there is no reasonable possibility that you will regain the ability to make your own health care decisions. Not valid if pregnant, unless pregnancy will not develop live birth. (Section 2133.03).

Living Will/Advance Health Care Directive Witness Requirements: Sign in front of two (2) witnesses eighteen (18) years or older or a notary public. Witnesses cannot be related to you by blood, marriage, or adoption, or be your doctor or the administrator of a nursing home in which you are receiving treatment. (Section 2133.02).

Advance Health Care Directive: State-specific form is provided by legislature and is included on CD. (Section 2133.02 does not provide a statutory form, but it provides suggestions for phrasing the directive.)

Durable Health Care Power of Attorney: Agent may make decisions regarding medical procedure, treatment, intervention, or other measure that will serve to prolong the process of dying, including right to give informed consent and make other decisions principal could if s/he had capacity. Does not expire unless principal specifies an expiration date in the instrument. Revocable at any time in any manner; effective when expressed, but if physician had knowledge of the durable power of attorney, revocation is effective on communication to physician. Valid Durable Power of Attorney for health care revokes any prior instrument. Effective if document complies with the laws of the state where executed and that substantially complies with Ohio law. No civil, criminal, or professional liability for good faith reliance which is in accordance with reasonable medical standards on agent's health care decisions. No state-specific form provided by legislature. See Chapter 7 for legally-valid for to use; form also provided on CD. Also may use Advance Health Care Directive. See Chapter 9 for instructions for this form on CD. (Sections 1337.11+). Follow signature, witness, and notary requirements as noted on form.

Durable Financial Power of Attorney: No state-specific form provided by legislature. See Chapter 5 for legally-valid power of attorney forms to use. (Section 1337.09). Follow signature, witness, and notary requirements as noted on form.

Oklahoma

State Website: http://www.lsb.state.ok.us/

State Law Reference: Oklahoma Statutes Annotated.

Living Will Form: Living Will is Part 1 of Advance Directive for Health Care (Section 63-3101.4). This form is provided on the CD.

Other Directives: An organ donation form is provided on the CD under the Anatomical Gift Act (Sections 63-2201+).

Living Will Effective: This Directive goes into effect once it is given to your doctor and you are unable to make your own medical decisions. In order to follow your instructions regarding life-sustaining treatment, your doctor must first consult another doctor to determine that you are persistently unconscious or suffering from a terminal condition. Not valid if pregnant. (Section 63-3101.3)

Living Will/Advance Health Care Directive Witness Requirements: Sign in the presence of two (2) adult witnesses. A witness cannot be any person who would inherit from you under any existing will or by operation of law. (Section 63-3101.4).

Advance Health Care Directive: State-specific form is provided by legislature and is included on CD. (Section 63-3101.4).

Durable Health Care Power of Attorney: Agent may grant complete or limited authority to make health and medical care decisions but not life-sustaining treatment decisions unless the power complies with requirements for a "health care proxy" under Oklahoma law. Revocable in whole or in part in any manner at any time without regard to declarant's mental or physical condition. Effective upon communication to physician. Out -of-state document is effective if executed in another state if it substantially complies with the Uniform Durable Power of Attorney Act. No civil, criminal, or professional liability for carrying out the directives of durable power of attorney in good faith and in accordance with reasonable medical standards. May use generic form in Chapter 7. State-specific form is provided by legislature and is included on enclosed CD as part of Advance Health Care Directive. See Chapter 9 for instructions for Advance Health Care Directive form on CD. (Section 63-3101.4). Follow signature, witness, and notary requirements as noted on form.

Durable Financial Power of Attorney: State-specific form is provided by legislature and is included on enclosed CD. See Chapter 6 for sample form. You may also use a generic durable financial power of attorney form in Chapter 5. (Sections 15-1001+). Follow signature, witness, and notary requirements as noted on form.

Oregon

State Website: http://www.leg.state.or.us/ors/
State Law Reference: Oregon Revised Statutes.
Living Will Form: Health Care Instructions serves as Living Will (Section 127.531). This form is provided on the CD.
Other Directives: An organ donation form is provided on the CD under the Anatomical Gift Act (Sections 97.950 through 97.964).
Living Will Effective: Two (2) physicians agree that you have an incurable and irreversible condition that will result in death within a relatively short time, will become unconscious and, to a reasonable degree of medical certainty, will not regain consciousness, or the likely risks and burdens of treatment would outweigh the expected benefits.
Living Will/Advance Health Care Directive Witness Requirements: Sign in the presence of two (2) adult witnesses. If you have someone sign the Declaration on your behalf, that person cannot serve as a witness. Your attending physician cannot be a witness. At least one (1) of your witnesses cannot be related to you by blood, marriage, or adoption, entitled to any portion of your estate, or be an owner, operator, or employee of your treating health care facility. (Section 127.515).
Advance Health Care Directive: State-specific form is provided by legislature and is included on CD. (Section 127.531).
Durable Health Care Power of Attorney: Agent may make health care decisions for principal regarding life-sustaining procedures including any medical procedure or intervention that uses mechanical or other artificial means to sustain, restore, or supplant a vital function only when authorized or when principal is terminally ill and such treatment only serves to artificially prolong the moment of death; does not include procedures to sustain patient cleanliness and comfort. Agent may withdraw up to time of principal's incapacity. Principal may revoke (1) in any manner by which s/he is able to communicate to health care provider or attorney-in-fact intent to revoke; (2) by execution of subsequent durable power of attorney; (3) upon divorce if spouse is agent. Out-of-state document is valid upon execution in compliance with formalities of that state where principal is resident or is located or with state of Oregon. Health care

provider acting on a durable power of attorney or health care agent in good faith is not liable for criminal, civil, or professional disciplinary actions. State-specific form is part of Advance Health Care Directive. See Chapters 7 and 9 for instructions for form on CD. (Section 127.531). Follow signature, witness, and notary requirements as noted on form.

Durable Financial Power of Attorney: No state-specific form provided by legislature. See Chapter 5 for legally-valid power of attorney forms to use. (Section 127.005). Follow signature, witness, and notary requirements as noted on form.

Pennsylvania

State Website: http://members.aol.com/StatutesPA/Index.html
State Law Reference: Pennsylvania Code.
Living Will Form: Declaration serves as Living Will. (Section 20-5404). This form is provided on the CD.
Other Directives: An organ donation form is provided on the CD under the Anatomical Gift Act (Section 20-8613).
Living Will Effective: The Declaration becomes effective when your physician receives a copy of it and determines that you are incompetent and in a terminal condition or a state of permanent unconsciousness. Not valid if pregnant. (Section 20-5405).
Living Will/Advance Health Care Directive Witness Requirements: Sign in the presence of two (2) adult witnesses. If you have someone sign the Declaration on your behalf, that person cannot serve as a witness. (Section 20-5404).
Advance Health Care Directive: State-specific form is provided by legislature and is included on CD. Referred to as Declaration. (Section 20-5404).
Durable Health Care Power of Attorney: Agent may authorize admission to medical facility and enter into agreements for principal's care and to consent, arrange, and authorize medical and surgical procedures including administration of drugs. Durable health care power of attorney is not affected by subsequent disability or incapacity. Agent must have actual notice of revocation for it to be effective. Divorce revokes power of attorney for spouse. Person acting in good faith reliance on power of attorney shall incur no liability as a result. State-specific form is part of Advance Health Care Directive. See Chapters 7 and 9 for instructions for form on CD. (Section 20-5404). Follow signature, witness, and notary requirements as noted on form.
Durable Financial Power of Attorney: State-specific form is provided by legislature and is included on enclosed CD. See Chapter 6 for sample form. You may also use a generic durable financial power of attorney form in Chapter 5. (Section 20-5601). Follow signature, witness, and notary requirements as noted on form.

Rhode Island

State Website: http://www.rilin.state.ri.us/Statutes/Statutes.html
State Law Reference: Rhode Island General Laws.
Living Will Form: Declaration serves as Living Will (Section 23-4.11-3). This form is provided on the CD.
Other Directives: An organ donation form is provided on the CD under the Anatomical Gift Act (Section 23-18.6+).
Living Will Effective: Your doctor must determine that your death would occur without use of life- sustaining medical care. Not valid if pregnant, unless pregnancy will not develop live birth. (Section 23-4.11-3).
Living Will/Advance Health Care Directive Witness Requirements: Sign in the presence of two (2) adult witnesses. Witnesses cannot be related to you by blood, marriage, or adoption. (Section 23-4.11-3).
Advance Health Care Directive: State-specific form is provided by legislature and is included on CD. Referred to as Declaration. (Section 23-4.11-3).
Durable Health Care Power of Attorney: Agent may consent to or refuse any medical procedure or intervention that will only prolong the dying process; this does not include refusal of intervention necessary to alleviate pain or provide comfort. Revocable at any time in any manner declarant is able to communicate intent to revoke, without regard to physical or mental condition. Effective upon communication to physician. Controls over living will executed by same person for any inconsistent provisions. Durable power of attorney executed in another state in compliance with laws of that state is valid. No civil, criminal, or professional liability when acting in accordance with the statute and in accordance with reasonable medical standards.. State-specific form is part of Advance Health Care Directive. See Chapters 7 and 9 for instructions for form on CD. (Sections 23-4.10+). Follow signature, witness, and notary requirements as noted on form.
Durable Financial Power of Attorney: State-specific form is provided by legislature and is included on enclosed CD. See Chapter 6 for sample form. You may also use a generic durable financial power of attorney form in Chapter 5. (Sections 18-16-1+). Follow signature, witness, and notary requirements as noted on form.

South Carolina

State Website: http://www.scstatehouse.net/
State Law Reference: Code of Laws of South Carolina Annotated.
Living Will Form: Declaration of a Desire for a Natural Death serves as Living Will (Section 44-77-50). This form is provided on the CD.
Other Directives: An organ donation form is provided on the CD under the Anatomical Gift Act (Sections 44-43-310+).
Living Will Effective: Two (2) physicians must determine you are in a terminal condition and

your death will result without using life-sustaining procedures. (Section 44-77-30).

Living Will/Advance Health Care Directive Witness Requirements: Sign in the presence of two (2) adult witnesses and a notary public. A witness cannot be a beneficiary of your life insurance policy, your health care provider, or an employee of your health care provider. Witnesses cannot be related to you by blood, marriage, or adoption, entitled to any part of your estate, or directly financially responsible for your health care. In addition, at least one (1) witness must not be an employee of a health facility in which you are a patient. If you are a resident in a hospital or nursing facility, one of the witnesses must also be an ombudsman designated by the State Ombudsman, Office of the Governor. (Section 44-77-40).

Advance Health Care Directive: State-specific form is provided by legislature and is included on CD. Referred to as a Declaration of a Desire for a Natural Death. (Section 44-77-50).

Durable Health Care Power of Attorney: Agent may make decisions regarding any medical procedure or intervention serving only to prolong the dying process, not including medication or treatment for pain alleviation or comfort care. Principal should indicate whether provision of nutrition and hydration through surgically implanted tubes is desired. Revocable by (1) written or oral statement or other act constituting notification to agent or health care provider of specific intent to revoke; (2) principal's execution of subsequent health care power of attorney. Out-of-state document is effective if executed in compliance with South Carolina law or laws of another state and recorded as required by Code of South Carolina, Section 62-5-501 (c) if the document relates to any powers other than powers of the agent to make health care decisions. No civil, criminal, or professional liability for relying in good faith on agent's health care decision. State-specific form is part of Advance Health Care Directive. See Chapters 7 and 9 for instructions for form on CD. (Section 62-5-504). Follow signature, witness, and notary requirements as noted on form.

Durable Financial Power of Attorney: No state-specific form provided by legislature. See Chapter 5 for legally-valid power of attorney forms to use. (Section 62-5-501). Follow signature, witness, and notary requirements as noted on form. Note that any financial power of attorney must be recorded in the same manner as a deed in the county office where the principal resides at the time the instrument is recorded.

South Dakota

State Website: http://legis.state.sd.us/statutes/

State Law Reference: South Dakota Codified Laws Annotated.

Living Will Form: Living Will Declaration (Section 34-12D-3). This form is provided on the CD.

Other Directives: An organ donation form is provided on the CD under the Anatomical Gift Act (Sections 34-26-20 through 34-26-47).

Living Will Effective: Declaration is effective when your death will result without using life-sustaining procedures, including the determination that there is no reasonable possibility that you will regain the ability to make your own health care decisions. Not valid if pregnant. (Section 34-12D-5).

Living Will/Advance Health Care Directive Witness Requirements: Sign in the presence of two (2) witnesses eighteen (18) years or older or a notary public. Although South Dakota does not have any restrictions on who can be a witness, we suggest that you not use your appointed attorney-in-fact or your health care provider. (Section 34-12D-2).

Advance Health Care Directive: State-specific form is provided by legislature and is included on CD. Referred to as Living Will Declaration. (Section 34-12D-3).

Durable Health Care Power of Attorney: Agent may make any health care decisions for principal which principal could have made if s/he had decisional capacity including rejection or withdrawal of consent for medical procedures, treatment, or intervention. Agent may not authorize withholding artificial nutrition and hydration for comfort care or pain relief. Artificial nutrition or hydration may be withheld under certain circumstances or if specifically authorized. Revocation must be recorded with register of deeds. No civil, criminal, or professional liability for physician acting in good faith on a health care decision by agent or attorney-in-fact. No state-specific form provided by legislature. See Chapter 7 for legally-valid for to use; form also provided on CD. Also may use Advance Health Care Directive. See Chapter 9 for instructions for this form on CD. (Sections 34-12C and 59-7-2.1). Follow signature, witness, and notary requirements as noted on form.

Durable Financial Power of Attorney: No state-specific form provided by legislature. See Chapter 5 for legally-valid power of attorney forms to use. (Section 59-7-9). Follow signature, witness, and notary requirements as noted on form.

Tennessee

State Website: http://www.michie.com

State Law Reference: Tennessee Code Annotated.

Living Will Form: Living Will (Section 32-11-105). This form is provided on the CD.

Other Directives: An organ donation form is provided on the CD under the Anatomical Gift Act (Section 68-30-101+).

Living Will Effective: The Living Will becomes effective when your death will result without using life-sustaining procedures. (Section 32-11-105).

Living Will/Advance Health Care Directive Witness Requirements: Sign in the presence of two (2) adult witnesses and a notary public. A witness cannot be a person who has claim against your estate upon your death, stands to inherit from your estate, be your doctor or an employee of your doctor, or be an owner, operator, or employee of a health care institution in which you are a patient. Witnesses also cannot be related by blood or marriage. (Section 32-11-104 and 32-11-105).

Advance Health Care Directive: State-specific form is provided by legislature and is included on CD. Referred to as Living Will. (Section 32-11-105).

Durable Health Care Power of Attorney: Agent may authorize any procedure, treatment to diagnose, assess, or treat a disease, illness, or injury, including surgery, drugs, transfusions, mechanical ventilation, dialysis, CPR, artificial nourishment, hydration or other nutrients, radiation. Death by starvation or dehydration allowed only if specifically directed with statutory phrase. Revocable by (1) notifying the attorney-in-fact orally or in writing; (2) notifying health care giver orally or in writing; (3) executing subsequent durable power of attorney; (4) divorce if former spouse was designated; (5) principal's current wishes supersede durable power of attorney. Out-of-state document is effective if document complies with laws of Tennessee or laws of the state of principal's residence. No criminal, civil, or professional liability for physician acting in good faith. No state-specific form provided by legislature. See Chapter 7 for legally-valid for to use; form also provided on CD. Also may use Advance Health Care Directive. See Chapter 9 for instruction for this form on CD. (Section 34-6-201). Follow signature, witness, and notary requirements as noted on form.

Durable Financial Power of Attorney: No state-specific form provided by legislature. See Chapter 5 for legally-valid power of attorney forms to use. (Section 34-6-101+). Follow signature, witness, and notary requirements as noted on form.

Texas

State Website: www.capitol.state.tx.us

State Law Reference: Texas Statutes and Code Annotated.

Living Will Form: Directive to Physicians and Family or Surrogate serves as Living Will (Health and Safety Code, Section 166.033). This form is provided on the CD.

Other Directives: An organ donation form is provided on the CD under the Anatomical Gift Act Texas (Health and Safety Code, Section 692).

Living Will Effective: This Directive becomes effective when your attending physician certifies in writing that you are in a terminal or irreversible condition. Not valid if pregnant. (Health and Safety Code, Section 166.031).

Living Will/Advance Health Care Directive Witness Requirements: At least one (1) witness cannot be related to you by blood, marriage, or adoption, designated to make treatment decisions for you, entitled to any part of your estate, or be your doctor or an employee of your doctor. A witness cannot be an employee of a health care facility in which you are a patient, an officer, director, partner, or a business office employee of the health care facility or any part of any parent organization of the health care facility, or have a claim against your estate after you die. (Health and Safety Code, Section 166.003).

Advance Health Care Directive: State-specific form is provided by legislature and is included on CD. Referred to as Directive to Physicians and Family or Surrogate. (Health and Safety Code, Section 166.033).

Durable Health Care Power of Attorney: Agent may make decisions regarding consent to health care, treatment, service, or procedure to maintain, diagnose, or treat individual's physical or mental condition. Agent may not consent to voluntary in-patient mental health services, convulsive treatment, psychosurgery, abortion, or neglect of principal through omission of care primarily intended to provide for comfort of principal. Effective indefinitely upon execution and delivery of document unless revoked. Revocable orally or in writing with specific intent to revoke or execution of subsequent power of attorney; divorce if spouse is agent. Effective upon receipt and notice to agent and health care provider. Durable power of attorney executed in another state valid if it complies with the law of that state or jurisdiction. Agent not liable for health care decision made in good faith. Physician not liable for acts or decisions made under durable power of attorney if done in good faith and does not constitute a failure to exercise due care in the provision of health care services. State-specific form is part of Advance Health Care Directive. See Chapters 7 and 9 for instructions for form on CD. (Health and Safety Code, Section 166.033). Follow signature, witness, and notary requirements as noted on form.

Durable Financial Power of Attorney: State-specific form is provided by legislature and is included on enclosed CD. See Chapter 6 for sample form. You may also use a generic durable financial power of attorney form in Chapter 5. (Probate Code, Sections 481+). Follow signature, witness, and notary requirements as noted on form.

Utah

State Website: http://www.le.state.ut.us/

State Law Reference: Utah Code Annotated.

Living Will Form: Advance Health Care Directive serves as Living Will, (Section 75-2a-117). This form is provided on the CD.

Other Directives: An organ donation form is provided on the CD under the Anatomical Gift Act (Section 26-28-101+).

Living Will Effective: Two (2) physicians must physically examine you and certify in writing you are in a terminal condition or persistent vegetative state. Not valid if pregnant. (Sections 75-2a-103 and 75-2a-109).

Living Will/Advance Health Care Directive Witness Requirements: Sign in the presence of two (2) witnesses eighteen (18) years or older. A witness cannot be entitled to any part of your estate, be financially responsible for your medical care, be related to you by blood or marriage, be the person who signed the Declaration on your behalf, or be an employee of your health care facility. (Section 75-2a-117).

Advance Health Care Directive: State-specific form is provided by legislature and is included on CD. (Section 75-2a-117).

Durable Health Care Power of Attorney: Agent may make any decisions regarding, including refusal of, any medical procedure or intervention that would serve only to prolong the dying process including artificial nutrition and hydration unless declaration specifically excludes; does not include medication, sustenance, or any procedure to alleviate pain; separate procedure for "do not resuscitate" directive. Current wishes of declarant take precedent over any directive. Revocable at any time by (1) signed revocation; (2) destruction of document; (3) oral expression of intent to revoke in presence of witness. Effective on receipt by physician. A similar instrument executed in another state is presumed to comply with Utah law and may be relied upon in good faith. No civil, criminal, or professional liability for good faith compliance with directive. State-specific form is part of Advance Health Care Directive. See Chapters 7 and 9 for instructions for form on CD. (Section 75-2a-117). Follow signature, witness, and notary requirements as noted on form.

Durable Financial Power of Attorney: No state-specific form provided by legislature. See Chapter 5 for legally-valid power of attorney forms to use. (Section 75-5-501). Follow signature, witness, and notary requirements as noted on form.

Vermont

State Website: http://www.leg.state.vt.us/statutes/statutes2.htm

State Law Reference: Vermont Statutes Annotated.

Living Will Form: Advance Health Care Directive serves as Living Will (Section 18-231-9700+). This form is provided on the CD. Vermont maintains a Living Will/Advance Directive Registry at www.healthvermont.gov/vadr

Other Directives: An organ donation form is provided on the CD under the Anatomical Gift Act (Section 18-109-5238+).

Living Will Effective: Document becomes effective if death would occur regardless of the use of life- sustaining procedures. (Section 18-231-9703).

Living Will/Advance Health Care Directive Witness Requirements: Sign in the presence of two (2) witnesses eighteen (18) years or older. A witness cannot be entitled to any part of your estate, be your spouse, attending physician or any person acting under the direction or control of your attending physician, or any person who has a claim against your estate. (Section 18-231-9703).

Advance Health Care Directive: State-specific form is provided by legislature and is included on CD. (Section 18-231).

Durable Health Care Power of Attorney: Agent is authorized to make health care decisions for principal during periods of incapacity as certified in writing by principal's attending physician including withdrawal of consent to any care, treatment, service, or procedure or to maintain, diagnose, or treat an individual's physical or mental condition; does not include consent to sterilization or admission to state institution. Principal's current wishes supersede directives at all times. Revocable by (1) notifying agent or health care provider orally or in writing or any other act evidencing specific intent to revoke; (2) executing a subsequent durable power of attorney; (3) divorce, if former spouse was principal's agent. Out-of-state document is effective if in compliance with the law of the state in which it was executed. No civil, criminal, or professional liability if physician acts in good faith; no immunity for failure to exercise due care in provision of services. No state-specific form provided by legislature. See Chapter 7 for legally-valid for to use; form also provided on CD. Also may use Advance Health Care Directive. See Chapter 9 for instructions for this form on CD. Follow signature, witness, and notary requirements as noted on form.

Durable Financial Power of Attorney: No state-specific form is provided by legislature and is included on enclosed CD. See Chapter 5 for legally-valid power of attorney forms to use. (Section 14-123-3508). Follow signature, witness, and notary requirements as noted on form.

Virginia

State Website: http://leg1.state.va.us/

State Law Reference: Virginia Code Annotated.

Living Will Form: Advance Medical Directive serves as Living Will (Section 54.1-2984). This form is provided on the CD.

Other Directives: An organ donation form is provided on the CD under the Anatomical Gift Act (Section 32.1-8-290).

Living Will Effective: This directive becomes effective in the event that you develop a terminal condition or are in a permanent vegetative state and can no longer make your own medical decisions. (Section 54.1-2984).

Living Will/Advance Health Care Directive Witness Requirements: Sign in the presence of two (2) witnesses eighteen (18) years or older. Witnesses cannot be related by blood or marriage. (Section 54.1-2982 and 54.1-2983).

Advance Health Care Directive: State-specific form is provided by legislature and is included on CD. Referred to as Advance Medical Directive. (Section 54.1-2984).

Durable Health Care Power of Attorney: Agent may make decisions regarding any medical procedure, treatment, intervention, utilizing mechanical or other artificial means to sustain, restore, or supplant a vital function, or is of a nature to afford patient no reasonable expectation of recovery from a terminal condition and when applied to a patient in terminal condition, would serve only to prolong the dying process. Includes artificially administered hydration and nutrition and CPR by emergency medical services personnel, but does not include any medication or procedure to alleviate pain or provide comfort care. Revocable at any time by (1) signed, dated writing; (2) physical cancellation or destruction; (3) oral expression of intent to revoke. Effective upon communication to attending physician. Directive executed in another state valid if in compliance with Virginia law or law of state where executed. No civil, criminal, or professional liability if acting in good faith. State-specific form is part of Advance Health Care Directive. See Chapters 7 and 9 for instructions for form on CD. (Section 54.1-2984). Follow signature, witness, and notary requirements as noted on form.

Durable Financial Power of Attorney: No state-specific form provided by legislature. See Chapter 5 for legally-valid power of attorney forms to use. (Section 54.1-3900+). Follow signature, witness, and notary requirements as noted on form.

Washington

State Website: http://www.leg.wa.gov/

State Law Reference: Washington Revised Code Annotated.

Living Will Form: Health Care Directive serves as Living Will (Section 70.122.030). This form is provided on the CD. Washington maintains a Living Will/Advance Directive Registry at www.doh.wa.gov/livingwill/

Other Directives: An organ donation form is provided on the CD under the Anatomical Gift Act (Section 68.50.520+).

Living Will Effective: Declaration applies when two (2) physicians diagnose you to have a incurable or irreversible condition that will cause death in a relatively short time and you can no longer make your own medical decisions. Not valid if pregnant. (Section 70.122.020).

Living Will/Advance Health Care Directive Witness Requirements: Sign in the presence of two (2) witnesses eighteen (18) years or older. A witness cannot be entitled to any part of your estate, related by blood or marriage, be your attending physician or any person acting under the direction or control of your attending physician, or be any person who has a claim against your estate. (Section 70.122.030).

Advance Health Care Directive: State-specific form is provided by legislature and is included on CD. (Section 70.122.030).

Health Care Power of Attorney: Appointed attorney-in-fact may make health care decisions on principal's behalf or provide informed consent. Continues until revoked or terminated by principal, court-appointed guardian or court order. Anyone acting in good faith and without negligence shall incur no liability. No state-specific form provided by legislature. See Chapter 7 for legally-valid for to use; form also provided on CD. Also may use Advance Health Care Directive. See Chapter 9 for instructions for this form on CD. (Section 11.94.010+). Follow signature, witness, and notary requirements as noted on form.

Durable Financial Power of Attorney: No state-specific form provided by legislature. See Chapter 5 for legally-valid power of attorney forms to use. (Section 11.94.010+). Follow signature, witness, and notary requirements as noted on form.

West Virginia

State Website: http://www.legis.state.wv.us/

State Law Reference: West Virginia Code Annotated.

Living Will Form: Living Will, (Section 16-30-4). This form is provided on the CD.

Other Directives: An organ donation form is provided on the CD under the Anatomical Gift Act (Section 16-19-1+).

Living Will Effective: Your physician must certify in writing that you are in a terminal condition and your death would occur within a short period of time without the use of life-sustaining medical care. (Section 16-30-4).

Living Will/Advance Health Care Directive Witness Requirements: Sign in the presence of two (2) adult witnesses and a notary public. A witness cannot be a person who stands to inherit from your estate, be directly financially responsible for your health care, be your attending physician, or be your health care representative or successor if you have a medical power of attorney. A witness cannot be related by blood or marriage or be the person who signed the document on your behalf. (Section 16-30-4).

Advance Health Care Directive: State-specific form is provided by legislature and is included on CD. Referred to as Living Will. (Section 16-30-4).

Health Care Power of Attorney: Agent may make any decision to accept or reject medical or surgical treatments which prolong the dying process artificially. Desires of principal at all times supersede effect of medical power of attorney. Revocable at any time by (1) destruction of document; (2) written revocation signed and dated; (3) verbal expression with witness present; (4) divorce if former spouse was designated. Out-of-state document is valid if in compliance with laws of West Virginia or state where executed and expressly delegates health care decisions. No criminal civil liability for good faith compliance with directions of medical power of attorney or representative. State-specific form is part of Advance Health Care Directive. See Chapters 7 and 9 for instructions for form on CD. (Section 16-30-4). Follow signature, witness, and notary requirements as noted on form.

Durable Financial Power of Attorney: No state-specific form provided by legislature. See Chapter 5 for legally-valid power of attorney forms to use. (Sections 39-4-1 through 39-4-7). Follow signature, witness, and notary requirements as noted on form.

Wisconsin

State Website: http://www.legis.state.wi.us/

State Law Reference: Wisconsin Statutes Annotated.

Living Will Form: Declaration to Physicians serves as Living Will (Section 154-03). This form is provided on the CD.

Other Directives: An organ donation form is provided on the CD under the Anatomical Gift Act (Section 157.06).

Living Will Effective: This directive becomes effective in the event that your attending physician and one (1) other physician certifies you have developed a terminal condition or are in a permanent vegetative state and can no longer make your own medical decisions. Not valid if pregnant. (Section 154.03).

Living Will/Advance Health Care Directive Witness Requirements: Sign in the presence of two (2) adult witnesses. A witness cannot be a person who stands to inherit from your estate, be directly financially responsible for your health care, be your attending physician, or be an employee of your health care provider or an inpatient health care facility in which you are a patient, unless the employee is a chaplain or social worker. A witness also cannot be related by blood or marriage. (Section 154.03).

Advance Health Care Directive: State-specific form is provided by legislature and is included on CD. Referred to as Declaration to Physicians. (Section 154.03).

Health Care Power of Attorney: Agent may make decisions in the exercise of the right to accept, maintain, discontinue, or refuse any care, treatment, service or procedure to diagnose, maintain, or treat physical or mental condition. Feeding tube may be withheld or withdrawn unless it would cause pain. Agent may not consent to withholding or withdrawing of orally ingested nutrition or hydration unless provision is medically contraindicated. Revocable at any time by (1) canceling or destroying document; (2) revocation in writing signed and dated; (3) verbal revocation in presence of 2 witnesses; (4) executing a subsequent power of attorney; (5) divorce if former spouse was attorney-in-fact. No civil, criminal, or professional liability for any physician if acting in good faith. No state-specific form provided by legislature. See Chapter 7 for legally-valid for to use; form also provided on CD. Also may use Advance

316

Health Care Directive. See Chapter 9 for instructions for this form on CD. (Section 155.05). Follow signature, witness, and notary requirements as noted on form.

Durable Financial Power of Attorney: State-specific form provided by legislature provides the principal with a choice as to whether the Power of Attorney will be durable or non-durable. See Chapter 6 for sample of form to use. May also use basic forms in Chapter 5 which are legally valid. (Section 243.07). Follow signature, witness, and notary requirements as noted on form.

Wyoming

State Website: http://legisweb.state.wy.us/

State Law Reference: Wyoming Statutes.

Living Will Form: Living Will Declaration (Section 35-22-403). This form is provided on the CD.

Other Directives: An organ donation form is provided on the CD under the Anatomical Gift Act (Section 35-5-102).

Living Will Effective: This Declaration becomes effective when two (2) physicians agree that you have a terminal condition from which there can be no recovery and your death is imminent. Not valid if pregnant. (Section 35-22-403).

Living Will/Advance Health Care Directive Witness Requirements: Sign in the presence of two (2) witnesses eighteen (18) years or older or a notary public. Witnesses cannot be entitled to any part of your estate or financially responsible for your medical care. A witness cannot be related to you by blood or marriage or be the person who signed the Declaration on your behalf. (Section 35-22-403).

Advance Health Care Directive: State-specific form is provided by legislature and is included on CD. (Section 35-22-403).

Health Care Power of Attorney: Agent may consent, refuse of consent, or withdraw of consent to any medical procedure, care, treatment, intervention, or nourishment by artificial means in the event of a terminal condition except for alleviation of pain and comfort care and consent to convulsive treatment, psychosurgery, or commitment to mental facility; does not affect health care treatment in an emergency. Principal's wishes if able to give informed consent take precedent over durable power of attorney. Revocable by (1) notifying attorney-in-fact in writing; (2) notifying health care provider in writing; (3) divorce if former spouse was attorney-in-fact; (4) a subsequent valid durable power of attorney for health care. No criminal, civil, or professional liability for any physician if acting in good faith. No state-specific form provided by legislature. See Chapter 7 for legally-valid for to use; form also provided on CD. Also may use Advance Health Care Directive. See Chapter 9 for instructions for form on CD. (Section 35-22-406). Follow signature, witness, and notary requirements as noted on form.

Durable Financial Power of Attorney: No state-specific form provided by legislature. See Chapter 5 for legally-valid power of attorney forms to use. (Section 3-5-101). Follow signature, witness, and notary requirements as noted on form.

Index

Nova Publishing Company
Small Business and Consumer Legal Books and Software

Legal Toolkit Series

Business Start-Up Toolkit	ISBN 13: 978-1-892949-43-1	Book w/CD	$39.95
Estate Planning Toolkit	ISBN 13: 978-1-892949-44-8	Book w/CD	$39.95
Legal Forms Toolkit	ISBN 13: 978-1-892949-48-6	Book w/CD	$39.95
No-Fault Divorce Toolkit	ISBN 13: 978-1-892949-35-6	Book w/CD	$39.95
Personal Bankruptcy Toolkit	ISBN 13: 978-1-892949-42-4	Book w/CD	$29.95
Will and Living Will Toolkit	ISBN 13: 978-1-892949-47-9	Book w/CD	$29.95

Law Made Simple Series

Personal Legal Forms Simplified (3rd Edition)	ISBN 0-935755-97-7	Book w/CD	$28.95
Powers of Attorney Simplified (2nd Edition)	ISBN 13: 978-1-892949-56-1	Book w/CD	$29.95

Small Business Made Simple Series

Limited Liability Company: Start-up Kit (4th Edition)	ISBN 13: 978-1-892949-54-7	Book w/CD	$29.95
Real Estate Forms Simplified (2nd Edition)	ISBN 13: 978-1-892949-49-3	Book w/CD	$29.95
S-Corporation: Small Business Start-up Kit (4th Edition)	ISBN 13: 978-1-892949-53-0	Book w/CD	$29.95
Small Business Accounting Simplified (5th Edition)	ISBN 13: 978-1-892949-50-9	Book w/CD	$29.95
Small Business Bookkeeping System Simplified	ISBN 0-935755-74-8	Book only	$14.95
Small Business Legal Forms Simplified (4th Edition)	ISBN 0-935755-98-5	Book w/CD	$29.95
Small Business Payroll System Simplified	ISBN 0-935755-55-1	Book only	$14.95
Sole Proprietorship: Start-up Kit (3rd Edition)	ISBN 13: 978-1-892949-59-2	Book w/CD	$29.95

Legal Self-Help Series

Divorce Yourself: The National Divorce Kit (6th Edition)	ISBN 1-892949-12-1	Book w/CD	$39.95
Prepare Your Own Will: The National Will Kit (6th Edition)	ISBN 1-892949-15-6	Book w/CD	$29.95

National Legal Kits

Simplified Divorce Kit (3rd Edition)	ISBN 13: 978-1-892949-39-4	Book w/CD	$19.95
Simplified Family Legal Forms Kit (2nd Edition)	ISBN 13: 978-1-892949-41-7	Book w/CD	$19.95
Simplified Incorporation Kit	ISBN 1-892949-33-4	Book w/CD	$19.95
Simplified Limited Liability Company Kit	ISBN 1-892949-32-6	Book w/CD	$19.95
Simplified Living Will Kit (2nd Edition)	ISBN 13: 978-1-892949-45-5	Book w/CD	$19.95
Simplified S-Corporation Kit	ISBN 1-892949-31-8	Book w/CD	$19.95
Simplified Will Kit (3rd Edition)	ISBN 1-892949-38-5	Book w/CD	$19.95

Ordering Information

Distributed by:
National Book Network
4501 Forbes Blvd. Suite 200
Lanham MD 20706

Phone orders with Visa/MC: (800) 462-6420
Fax orders with Visa/MC: (800) 338-4550
Internet with PayPal: www.novapublishing.com
Free shipping on all internet orders (within in the U.S.)